The Ten Cents War

The Ten Cents War

Chile, Peru, and Bolivia in the War of the Pacific, 1879–1884

Bruce W. Farcau

Westport, Connecticut
London

Library of Congress Cataloging-in-Publication Data

Farcau, Bruce W., 1951–
    The Ten Cents War : Chile, Peru, and Bolivia in the War of the Pacific, 1879–1884 /
Bruce W. Farcau.
        p.   cm.
    Includes bibliographical references and index.
    ISBN 0–275–96925–8 (alk. paper)
    1. War of the Pacific, 1879–1884—Campaigns. I. Title.
    F3097.F37   2000
    983.06'16—dc21   00–036709

British Library Cataloguing in Publication Data is available.

Library of Congress Catalog Card Number: 00–036709
ISBN: 0–275–96925–8

First published in 2000

Praeger Publishers, 88 Post Road West, Westport, CT 06881
An imprint of Greenwood Publishing Group, Inc.
www.praeger.com

Printed in the United States of America

The paper used in this book complies with the
Permanent Paper Standard issued by the National
Information Standards Organization (Z39.48–1984).

10 9 8 7 6 5 4 3 2 1

Contents

Introduction

Every year for more than a century, on the 23rd of March, a crowd of varying size, depending on the weather, gathers in the Plaza Murillo in the Bolivian capital of La Paz. Waving Bolivian flags and possibly carrying a homemade banner or two, the procession forms up and straggles through the center of downtown, tying up traffic along the Prado. The marchers shout unintelligible slogans, punctuated by choruses of "Viva!" or "Muera!" depending upon the subject, and listen to impassioned speeches by minor politicians and the labored efforts of a tinny municipal band at Plaza Abaroa, beneath the statue of one of Bolivia's many martyrs, while vendors hawk everything from soft drinks and meat pies to batteries and disposable razor blades. If there happens to be a crew present from a local television station, youngsters might mug for the camera. If not, the crowd soon disperses as everyone hunts for an available taxi or space on a passing microbus for the ride home.

This is the annual "march to the sea," Bolivia's *cri de coeur* for her coastal provinces lost in the late 1800s to Chile in the War of the Pacific. Since it is always easier in La Paz, a city of steep inclines and very thin air (at twelve thousand feet above sea level), to conduct marches that head downhill, the procession actually heads *away* from the sea, but it's the symbolism that counts. This misdirection is perhaps more symbolic of Bolivia's ill-fated struggle to hang onto her outlet to the sea than the organizers of the march might have intended. After countless demonstrations, petitions to virtually every international authority, and a plethora of conferences, bilateral ones, trilateral ones, and multilateral ones, Bolivia is no closer to regaining her lost territory than she was the day the last of her troops abandoned the field of battle to the victorious Chileans.

Bolivian school children may do a bittersweet dance, linked arm in arm, singing:

Ferrocarril, carril, carril (three large steps forward)
Arica – La Paz, La Paz, La Paz (three steps backward)
Un paso atras, atras, atras (three more steps backward)

making fun of the decision of a Bolivian government years ago to accept Chilean construction of a railway up from the coast as compensation for the lost territories, but there is no evidence of any enthusiasm for doing anything about it in a practical sense.

In Peru, Bolivia's unfortunate ally in the War of the Pacific, the wounds run less deep. The defeat was certainly humiliating, and Peru also lost a substantial chunk of potentially valuable real estate, but nothing so traumatic as being converted overnight into a landlocked nation. There are certain similarities with the Franco-Prussian War of that same decade in that, like Paris, Lima was captured by the invader, and the Peruvians also fought a kind of broken-backed, guerrilla war until the weary victors were obliged to offer terms, although keeping the territorial spoils as did the Prussians. But there the similarity ends. One does not hear of the same kind of *revanchism* in Peru over Tarapacá and Arica as in France over Alsace and Lorraine. In fact, the Peruvians have been satisfied with the belated return of the province of Tacna and the flexing of their military muscles with a more promising opponent, the much smaller and weaker Ecuador to the north, in a border dispute over remote jungle lands which sparked a minor war in 1940 and renewed skirmishing right up to the time of this writing, more than a half century later. In neither Bolivia nor Peru has there ever emerged a demagogue preaching a doctrine of economic austerity, massive rearmament and ultimate reconquest, among the many generals who have waltzed in and out of the revolving doors of the respective presidential palaces.

In Chile one senses an understandable pride in the fullness of their victory in the war and a perhaps more debatable pride in the modesty of their appropriations of neighboring lands. This was the last war against an armed foreign enemy in which the Chilean military took part, and this lack of a more "constructive" outlet for aggressive tendencies might have something to do with the ferocity with which the armed forces turned on their fellow citizens during the repressive regime of General Augusto Pinochet in the 1970s and 1980s; but that would be the subject of another sort of book.

As with most conflicts in what would later become the Third World, the War of the Pacific (1879-1884) was of great moment to the peoples directly involved, but it has largely been ignored outside the region as neither the United States nor any major European power had a stake in the game. It is the purpose of this book to rectify this oversight to some degree. This study is designed to bring to light the drama of the military campaign itself and the human tragedy of the conflict for the soldiers on both sides, in the hope of making the period more readily accessible to the average reader. As in the case of an earlier work on the Chaco War between Bolivia and Paraguay in the 1930s, it has always seemed to the author that it is the ultimate tragedy for the soldiers involved to have fought and died and then to suffer the final humiliation of having their struggle and sacrifice ignored by the world.

There is no concerted effort here to break new historiographic ground, but to make use of the plentiful published sources already existing on the war in the form of memoirs and contemporary histories produced by actual participants in the conflict or other citizens of the belligerent countries. Where the trick lies is to take this material, virtually all of which is the product of the pens of less-than-objective writers, and attempt to construct an accurate and comprehensible picture of a highly complex tapestry of conflicting personalities in thoroughly unstructured political systems centering on a theme of life and death for thousands of men. After years of suffering through the bitterness and acrimony of America's revisionist historians in dealing with their own nation's past record, it is somewhat refreshing to find that historians of other nations are not at all embarrassed to take up the cudgels and defend their own homeland's actions, no matter how debatable. But this does not make the historian's job any easier in sorting through the material in a search for something approaching the truth. Since there are virtually no books on the war available in English, at least none that are not primarily focused on the more general histories of one or another of the participant nations, it is also hoped that this study will attract some attention from an American (i.e., the United States) readership.

Since those few books that do exist in English that deal with this period of history tend to focus on the political or diplomatic aspects of the conflict, it is hoped that this book's emphasis on the course of the military campaign will also provide something of a fresh approach. Although the War of the Pacific has not received much attention from military historians, barely getting passing mention in Scheina's excellent history of Latin American naval history, there is some worthwhile ground to be tilled here.[1] The role of Chile's navy in supporting the land offensive was a superb example of Alfred Thayer Mahan's theory on the importance of naval power, and the clash of modern ironclads was much more significant than that of the primitive models used in the American Civil War.[2] Many others of the latest innovations in weaponry were also employed in the war to greater or lesser effect: torpedoes, naval mines, "dynamite guns," the repeating rifle, rapid-fire artillery, and even early machine guns, further refining the lessons of the Austro-Prussian and the Franco-Prussian Wars. The relatively small sizes of the armies involved also makes for cleaner examples when studying the tactics and strategy of the war.

The title, *The Ten Cents War*, derives from a contemporary nickname for the conflict based on Bolivia's unfortunate effort to exercise her sovereignty in the disputed territory and to impose a modest export duty on its products, an action that sparked over hostilities. Since the war was ultimately fought over the actual and potential revenues to be derived from exploiting the commercial value of the millions of tons of bird droppings to be found along the desert coast of Bolivia and southern Peru, another title suggested itself, but it was thought that this might give the impression of an overall lack of seriousness in the effort. While some aspects of the war certainly had an *opera bouffe* air to them, the war was quite serious enough for the thousands of men who lost their lives and limbs in it. Jean Paul Sartre once suggested, more or less seriously, that one solution to the Arab-Israeli conflict would be to establish an extensive industrial complex in the Sinai, on the Golan Heights, and along the West Bank of the Jordan, the theory being that the land would then be too economically valuable for the rivals to risk disrupting its commercial activities by their incessant wars. The case of the War of the Pacific demonstrates that suddenly discovered economic value in a disputed border region is not unlike a bone tossed between two street dogs. It does not necessarily produce neighborly cooperation.

As a Foreign Service officer having served in Bolivia, having traveled extensively in both Peru and Chile, and having discussed the war and its lessons with numerous military officers of all three countries, the author hopes to bring something of a personal perspective to this work without being overly tainted by any prejudice. At least, it is hoped, a natural affinity for the underdogs (Bolivia and Peru) will be counterbalanced by a respect for the business-like way in which the Chileans went about their expansion, not unlike the expansion to the Pacific of the United States against her weaker neighbors, another historical event which hardly seems likely to be undone in the foreseeable future.

NOTES

1. Robert L. Scheina. *Latin America: A Naval History 1810-1987*, Annapolis, MD: Naval Institute Press, 1987.

2. Alfred Thayer Mahan. *The Influence of Sea Power upon History 1660-1783*, New York: Hill and Wang, 1957.

Chapter One

The Stage

On first glance the territory stretching along the Pacific coast of South America from about latitude 19° South to 25° South would hardly impress one as being worth fighting over. Farther to the north, one finds emerald green jungles running right down to the palm-lined beaches around the equator, and to the south the coast is gouged into spectacular fjords flanked by thick stands of evergreen forest and snow-capped mountains. But this stretch of what is today the coast of northern Chile is subject to a unique meteorological and geographical phenomenon that make this terrain some of the least hospitable on earth.

There is something about the cold waters of the Humboldt Current, that sweep up the coast from Antarctica and the arrangement of the ranks of coastal hills hard up against the shore that causes the clouds that form over the water to cluster there, jealously holding onto their loads of moisture, and just sit, neither moving inland nor dropping rain. And so it is that, the skies in this narrow coastal strip are frequently overcast with a dull leaden sky above and the sun blocked from view for weeks on end, while the long plain, which lies behind the mountains that rise right up from the sea to three or four thousand feet, in a wall stretching for nearly one thousand miles from north to south and about a hundred miles wide, is the driest place on the face of the earth. Compared to the Desert of Atacama, the Sahara or the Mojave are virtual tropical rain forests. In the Atacama the *average* rainfall is less than half an inch per year, and that is only because an occasional freak storm, perhaps once in a lifetime, might dump several inches at one go.[1] For decades at a time, it never rains there at all, not a drop.

Even the runoff from the melting snows of the Andes to the east, most of which tends to flow to the east to feed the mighty river systems of the Amazon and the River Plate, passes through such cracked and dehydrated land that the little rivers are either simply lost in the thirsty sands or are so salty as to be worthless for plant or animal. For over six hundred miles from Arequipa in Peru down to Copiapó in Chile, only the brackish River Loa along the original Bolivian-Peruvian border maintains enough volume to find a way through the enclosing range of hills to the sea the year round.   These conditions are ameliorated somewhat as one climbs into the foothills of the Andes and more regular rain occurs, providing nourishment for a thin covering of scrub and *puna* grass. On the fringes of the desert basin of Atacama, where the ground water level rises to within a few feet of the surface, there are also growths of drought-resistant plants such as cactus and thorny, twisted algarrobo trees. And farther south, around Valparaíso, Chile, the average annual rainfall rises to some twenty-two inches, supporting Chile's rich agriculture and the cultivation of wheat, fruit, and wine. But in the Atacama itself one finds a moonscape of parched brown gravel, undulating sand dunes, and cracked lava flows like rivers in flood that have been suddenly turned to stone, in which for tens of miles at a time one cannot discover any trace of vegetable life. Compare this to the relatively lush Mojave Desert with its covering of tumbleweed and dozens of varieties of cactus and one can readily capture the bleakness of this landscape.

In pre-colonial times, the coastal strip and the desert behind it was virtually uninhabited, with only a few miniscule communities of natives deriving their living exclusively from the rich bounty of the sea. At one location near Paposo, the typical coastal fogs (not actual precipitation) were thick enough to support a meager collection of plant life, giving rise to some primitive agriculture at the southern fringe of the Atacama. One is put in mind of the fictional desert land in John Updike's *The Coup* in which the only plants were a thin rank of weeds along the highway that derived their moisture from the steam expelled by the overheated radiators of passing trucks. It's *that* kind of dry. Even as late as the mid-1800s, the tiny port town of Cobija had only a couple of brackish wells to supply the population and a special *juez de aguas* (water judge) to allocate a ration to each newly registered resident on the basis of family size and the nature of his business. A visiting American naval officer commented that when one was invited to dine by a local, rather than bringing a bottle of wine, "the present of a barrel of sweet water from Southern Chile or Peru was highly esteemed."[2]

As if this were not enough to make the entire region a nightmare for anyone attempting to recruit colonists, the west coast of South America is also subject to frequent, violent earthquakes, often accompanied by tremendous tidal waves which would send the terrified populations of the little port cities scrambling up the hills for their lives. The offshore earthquake of 13 August 1868 sent a tidal wave ravaging the entire coast from Ecuador to Chile, but it was the Atacama ports, trapped between the sea and the surrounding hills that were virtually swept out of existence with boats from the roadstead found up to half a mile inland afterward. After a serious tremor, residents of the area are well advised to watch the sea for telltale signs of its sudden retreat over hundreds of yards as the waters gather themselves for a tremendous rush shoreward.[3] And this is not to mention the visitations of disease that also scoured the coast. Yellow fever was common in the summer months, and cholera, always a threat where the lack of water made proper sanitation problematic, was more or less a permanent fixture throughout the region.

The coastal hills that gave rise to the rainless climate also served to discourage human settlement by crowding down to the sea, making it an "ironbound" coast, with virtually no viable harbors for hundreds of miles. This was, in part, due to the lack of rivers opening onto the sea, which might have provided some break in the solid line of cliffs rising from the surf, but even headlands like that at Mejillones that provides some protection to shipping in the roads, are rare. It is hard even to find adequate flat ground along the shore for a settlement of any size, and those that cling precariously to the edge of the land are sited, like Antofogasta, for their proximity to usable passes through the hills behind them rather than for the spaciousness of the area available for building.

Communications would also be a perennial problem for the region. The tiny port of Cobija, founded in 1587 as an alternative outlet for the rich silver mines of what would later be Bolivia, was a full 170 leagues (over five hundred miles) from Potosí, the nearest large city on the Altiplano. This translated into nearly a month's travel for pack trains of mules or porters, there being no road in existence for any kind of wheeled transport. This situation pertained all along the coast, with travelers to and from the inland cities having to find their way across the coastal mountains and then the waterless deserts before even attempting the passage of the towering Andes themselves. While the coastal mountains are not overly imposing in themselves, they are steep enough that, in later years, some of the minor ship loading facilities would construct funicular railroads directly from the beach and up the hillside behind it to the nearest pass at which cargo could be loaded and unloaded for transfer to mule trains.

As difficult as communication from the coast inland might be, it was even more problematic along the coast heading north and south. Until well into the twentieth century, there was no road at all worth the name paralleling the coast. It was one thing to oasis-hop for the hundred or so miles across the Atacama or Tarapacá Deserts along their narrow east-west axes. It was quite another to struggle through hundreds of waterless miles, across barren ground often cut by deep, dry arroyos from anywhere in the Atacama region to the population centers of either Peru or Chile. Consequently, all communication was by sea, which was facilitated greatly by the advent of the steamship, diminishing the impact of the often-contrary winds and the strong northbound current. This was to have a tremendous influence on the course of the war, dominance in which would go to the side that was able to establish control of the sea lanes.

As unattractive as this kind of climatic and geographical arrangement might appear, it was precisely the unique combination of characteristics in the Atacama that was the root cause of its commercial value in the mid-nineteenth century. The chill waters of the Humboldt Current that push up the west coast of South America provide ideal living conditions for an immensely rich concentration of marine life, starting with the humble plankton, which in turn attracts shoals of anchovies and progressively larger and larger fish right on up the food chain, and the waters teem with dozens of varieties in huge numbers. The fish, in turn, have attracted tens of thousands, hundreds of thousands of sea birds, pelicans, cormorants, gulls, and others, who have hunted these waters for thousands and tens of thousands of years. Naturally, while the birds take their sustenance from the sea, they spend much of their time on the adjacent land, nesting, mating, and squabbling, and, of course, depositing their droppings in a cavalier and promiscuous manner.

Now, such a mass of aquatic fowl is not unheard of where food is so readily available, and particularly where the geography has made the area unattractive to bothersome humankind. What was different about the Atacama coast was that, instead of being periodically washed away by rainfall, here the droppings, or guano as they are called, simply accumulated, year after year, generation after generation, and century upon century on the rocky headlands along the coast and on the numerous small islands nearby. Anyone who has changed the paper on the bottom of the parakeet cage knows how productive even a single small bird can be, but imagine a million much larger ones at work in a relatively restricted area since long before recorded time, and it will be easier to visualize actual cliffs of guano, thirty, forty, or even fifty yards high, glistening white in the sun at the edge of the waves. This was what one found in the mid-1800s for miles along this stretch of the Pacific coast of central South America.

The presence of millions of tons of bird droppings would ordinarily not be considered an added attraction for most people, and such was the case for centuries. It had been reported by the Spanish colonists that the Incas had used bird guano as a natural fertilizer to a limited extent prior to the European "discovery," and in 1808 the noted explorer and naturalist Alexander von Humboldt visited the region and took a sample of the nitrate-rich guano back to Europe for study, although he had no success in interesting either the European scientific or commercial communities in his discovery. In the succeeding years, occasional shipments of guano were sent to England, but these found such a negative reception that they were ultimately dumped in the River Thames.

The second characteristic of the Atacama also derived from this lack of rainfall. As the snows along the western face of the Andes melted each spring, the runoff flowed down into the long narrow basin formed by the coastal hills, carving narrow arroyos and forming broad, shallow lakes until the water evaporated in the unrelenting sun or soaked down into the sands. All of the minerals picked up by the waters in their brief trek across lands that had also once been the bed of an ancient sea, accumulated in vast salt pans along the floor of the valley. With no outlet to the sea through which these minerals, most notably sodium nitrate, could be washed away and no rainfall to leach them down into the earth, they built up millennium after millennium, often being covered by layers of blowing sand, but lying there awaiting discovery.

It was not until 1840 that Alexandre Cochet, a French scientist resident in Peru, retrieved samples of both guano and *caliche*, as the nitrates were called, and conducted experiments in the small laboratory that he had set up in the Peruvian desert province of Tarapacá, determining that valuable quantities of nitrate of soda could be extracted from both substances. Nitrates had been used as a fertilizer for centuries in some form, but when Cochet published his findings in 1841, both on the extraction of nitrates from guano and for their effects on plant growth, there was a sudden run on the government in Lima by speculators vying with each other to bid on contracts for the exploitation of the guano deposits, bringing in as much as $600,000, a massive sum at the time, in one fell swoop.[4] The market for the product was certainly present, since the Industrial Revolution had created an urgent need for vastly expanded agricultural production on a decreasing land base in Europe, and the market for American cotton made necessary a reliable means of renewing the exhausted soil of the southern plantations.

It was understandable that, although the sought-after nitrates could be found both in guano and in the *caliche* of the desert salt pans, the guano would be developed first, being conveniently located both on the surface, ready for extraction without processing on the site, and right at the edge of the ocean, eliminating the need for any transportation before being loaded directly onto ships for the trip to Europe or North America. The extraction of the guano was relatively uncomplicated, involving merely of hewing out piles of the grayish-white substance and shoveling it into bags for loading onto lighters and thence to the cargo ships that waited in the roadstead. But the working conditions were far from ideal, and there was always a shortage of willing labor for the task.

The guano workers would live in tents or crude shacks constructed directly *on* the guano deposits, which formed the "ground" to a depth of many meters, either on barren islands offshore or on the rocky headlands. The digging and hauling activities raised permanent clouds of acrid dust that penetrated the eyes, the nose, the mouth, contaminated the water (all of which had to be brought in from Chile or Peru), and liberally garnished the poor food the men ate. And everything was overlaid with an appalling stench that could be detected miles out to sea, an odor not just of hundreds of sweating bodies that would not be washed for weeks on end, but of rotting fish, salt, and excrement from which there was no escape.

It is hardly surprising that there was little response to the call for workers to load guano at the miserly wages that were being offered, and the contractors had to content themselves with the sweepings of the prisons of Lima, La Paz, and Valparaíso to fill their ranks. As the industry developed, however, more laborers were desperately needed, and Peru, during one of its more liberal administrations, had abolished slavery in 1854 (with compensation for the owners but nothing for the former slaves themselves). Consequently, thousands of Chinese coolies were contracted for in Macao and Hong Kong, just as they were later to work on the American transcontinental railway, with some eighty thousand of them working in Peru by 1875 (over four times the total number of slaves in existence at the time of the emancipation.)[5] Little more than slaves, these indentured workers were brought across the Pacific under conditions that would have made any survivor of the "middle passage" from Africa feel right at home, apart from the lack of leg irons. They were then confined to isolated work camps on the islands or at the edge of the desert for months on end, breathing the fetid air, drinking brackish water, and eating putrid food until the end of their contracts or until a fever or a pulmonary disease, made worse by the squalid living conditions, mercifully took them off. The suicide rate among the demoralized Chinese workers became a cause for concern for the guano speculators, who had, after all, invested good money in their transport to South

America and in a small advance payment. At one point in 1872, the governments of both Macao and Hong Kong, appalled by stories of mistreatment of the Chinese in the guano fields and by a bloody mutiny on one of the "slave ships," temporarily outlawed the contracting of laborers for Peru and Bolivia, forcing the guano shippers to go directly to Shanghai for their labor force.[6]

It was not until the 1850s that the mining of nitrates in the Atacama and Tarapacá Deserts got underway to a significant degree, over a decade behind the guano boom. This was due largely to the fact that this enterprise required a substantial capital investment including the construction of railways and even the building of whole towns, not unlike the mining boom towns that sprang up across the American West during the various gold and silver rushes of this same period. Everything from tools and equipment to food, firewood, and water would have to be imported to these "roaring camps," and it was only when the supposedly inexhaustible supplies of guano began to run thin, with the quality of the product quickly decreasing as the more promising deposits were played out, that prospectors began combing the arid wastes in search of viable sites. Also, unlike guano, which was generally plainly visible on the surface, locating the desert nitrate deposits involved some old-fashioned prospecting, since the concentrations could be mere inches or many feet under the drifting sands, their presence hinted at only by a slight upswelling of the floor of the salt pan and a lesser density in the soil of the area.

Once located, the nitrate-rich soil would be collected in large copper vats and "cooked" in a kind of soup from which the sodium nitrate would be skimmed and crystallized in nearly pure form. It was only in 1853 that the process was perfected, and as the demand for nitrates grew, not just for fertilizer but for the production of recently invented TNT and other explosives, heavy machinery excavation with dynamite rapidly replaced hand work with picks and shovels at the sites. Production first began in Peru in Tarapacá, and even richer deposits were later discovered in Bolivian Atacama in 1857. From nominal production of a few thousand quintals of *caliche* exported by Peru in 1830, the industry grew to 720,000 quintals (at four pesos each, loaded onboard a ship) in 1854, and the addition of Bolivia as an exporter soon doubled, then tripled this amount.[7]

While some Chinese laborers were employed in the nitrate fields as they were in loading guano, most of the workers in both Peruvian and Bolivian territory were recruited from among the thousands of Chilean *rotos*, landless, unemployed peasants who swarmed in their thousands the whole length of the Pacific coast of South America in search of work. They were prized for their industriousness and built most of the railroads then sprouting all over the western half of the continent. It was largely Chilean capital, along with large influxes of funds from Great Britain, France, other European nations and the United States that supported this development, and it was this lack of involvement by either Peru or Bolivia in the region that would strengthen Chile's hand when the border dispute gained force in the second half of the century.

One of the reasons why the nitrate regions of Atacama and Tarapacá were populated largely with foreigners, be they Chileans, Chinese, or others, rather than Bolivians and Peruvians was a traditional reluctance of residents of the highland plateau, the Altiplano, to move to lower altitudes. The highlanders feared all sorts of tropical diseases that they believed, with some justification, permeated the lowlands, either along the coast or eastward in the Amazon Basin, and this fear far outstripped the land hunger of even the poorest peasants.

More significantly, however, it should be remembered that both Bolivia and Peru at this stage lived with an essentially colonial land tenure system in which the Indian peasants were virtually tied to the land, if not in the legal sense as slaves, then through the complimentary ties of tradition and debt bondage. This was in contrast to Chile, which had had a relatively thin native population at the time of the European conquest, and whose Indians, like those of the American Plains, had fought on over the centuries, being pushed gradually southward, while the country was colonized by waves of European immigrants.

Peru and Bolivia had a different background. Here the Inca Empire had presented a highly organized and densely concentrated population that had, after initial resistance and the standard decimation by European diseases, been simply incorporated into the Spanish Empire *en masse*, and included along with the land they tilled as part of the *encomienda* system of rewards to the *conquistadores*. Independence may have brought an end to the existence of the *encomienda* system as such, but the peasants remained bound to the land to a great extent and were not free to seek their fortunes elsewhere, even though the limited arable land of the Altiplano was already overpopulated even in the nineteenth century. The Chilean *hacendado* may have groused at the emigration of large numbers of laborers, but he had no legal hold on them in most cases in that even the poorest *inquilino* had a certain status born of his European racial antecedents that the Aymara and Quechua speaking Indians, who made up the majority of the populations of both Peru and Bolivia, lacked.

Thus, even though the several hundred kilometers of arid coastline that had been granted to Bolivia upon its independence were of the utmost importance to the highland nation as its only outlet to the sea, the region would come to be inhabited to a large extent by citizens of her more dynamic and aggressive neighbor. Tarapacá province may not have had the same significance to Peru, but the discovery and development of the nitrate fields there would eventually provide the largest single share of the revenues of the Peruvian government. Yet this area, too, would be colonized and worked primarily by immigrant Chileans. Like the influx of American settlers into largely unpopulated Texas in the early 1800s, this demographic development gave impetus to Chile's later claims to the area.

It is probably worthwhile at this point to delve a little deeper into the nature of the three countries that would become involved in one of the very few major international conflicts that South America would see in the nineteenth century. An understanding of the backgrounds and problems of each country will go far toward explaining both the slide toward war and define the parameters within which the war was fought.

NOTES

1. Isaiah Bowman, *Desert Trails of Atacama*, New York: American Geographical Society, 1924, p. 40.

2. Ibid., p. 75.

3. Roberto Querejazu Calvo, *Guano, Salitre, Sangre: Historia de la Guerra del Pacífico*, La Paz: Editorial Los Amigos del Libro, 1979, p. 72.

4. William Jefferson Dennis. *Tacna and Arica: An Account of the Chile-Peru Boundary Dispute and of the Arbitrations by the United States*, New York: Archon Books, 1967, pp. 29-30.

5. Fredrick B. Pike, *The History of Modern Peru*, New York: Praeger Publishers, 1982, p. 112.

6. Ronald Bruce St. John, *The Foreign Policy of Peru*, Boulder, CO: Lynne Rienner Publisher, 1992, p. 94.

7. Querejazu, op. cit., p. 127.

Chapter Two

The Contenders

PERU

Peru had emerged from the maelstrom of the wars of independence as potentially the most powerful nation on the Pacific coast of South America. With her substantial population and extensive landmass, Peru bestrode the Andes with access not only to a number of good seaports but also to the Amazon Basin. Peru was rich in natural resources, silver, copper, and sugar, in addition to guano and nitrates later on, and there was a large and docile native population available to do the hard manual labor of converting these resources into the wealth required to support the Creole upper classes. There was also the on-again, off-again possibility of a confederation with Bolivia along the lines of the old viceroyalty of Alto Peru, which would have created a country rivaling Brazil in size. The concept was dear to the heart of the Liberator, Simón Bolívar, but the last serious effort at making this a reality had been extinguished in a war with Chile in 1832. However, the middle of the nineteenth century brought with it a steady decline in Peru's fortunes from when she had been the jewel in the Spanish imperial crown.

By the mid-1800s Peru faced problems on numerous fronts. While the country was large in size, it was broken into unconnected chunks by the arms of the Andes. Some of the land was rich and arable, but more of it was inaccessible mountains or equally inaccessible rain forest. The population was large in Latin American terms, nearly three million by the end of the 1870s; but the majority was composed of descendants of the Incas, many of whom spoke Quechua as their native tongue and little or no Spanish at all. The cultural gulf between the Indian masses and the European and Creole upper class was exacerbated by an economic and social one in that the Indians were considered little more than property and were totally segregated in terms of living conditions from their rulers.   None of these characteristics tended to give Peru a strong national identity or helped to mold the disparate elements of the state into a smoothly functioning machine.

Initially, the first term of office of President Ramón Castilla seemed to bode well for the development of stable and even progressive political institutions in Peru, the laying of the foundation of future greatness for the nation.   Lasting from 1845 to 1851, it would be the longest administration for a single president in Peru during the entire century, and the last uninterrupted one for decades. Castilla instituted a number of modernizing programs, reopening the military academy at Bellavista and creating a general accounting office, a first for a nation that had, until that time, never even had a formal budget.   He championed a vision of continental solidarity, prompted in part by a fear of the United States in light of its war of conquest against Mexico, and hosted a regional conference in Lima in 1847 which aimed at a regime of collective security for South America and a codification of international law, although, in the event, the results were more theoretical than practical.   But Castilla's first love was undoubtedly the iron horse, an innovation that he imagined would tie together Peru's diverse population centers, open up new lands for cultivation and mining, and bring the nation's produce to market.   He engaged in an ambitious program of railroad construction, including the continent's first working line, from the port of Callao to Lima in 1851.

It was the fortuitous discovery of the guano deposits of the southern coast, or of their commercial value, that, like the Midas touch, proved to be a curse disguised as a blessing.   Rather than giving rise to a new class of native entrepreneurs, the government found it more convenient to contract with foreign firms that had the capital with which to provide large cash advances and a steady income with no risk involved.   In 1842, the government signed a contract which brought in thirty pesos per ton of guano, but this could be paid off in credits on the country's foreign debt, which speculators bought up at a 40 percent discount in Europe, thus earning huge profits for them but relatively little for Peru.[1]   By 1849 the firm of Gibbs and Sons of London had the franchise for the sale of Peru's guano throughout Europe, with the exception of France, which was the preserve of Montane and Company of Paris.   The massive influx of unearned revenue covered most of the government's expenses and fomented a cult of conspicuous consumption in the Peruvian upper class, including those government officials responsible for the granting of guano franchises.[2]   To make matters worse, the money was no longer made as a direct payment to the government in Lima or even as a retirement of the foreign debt but in the form of a loan itself, paid up front, but at interest.   The requirement for the concessionaires to come up with this substantial cash outlay before actually entering into operation was what eliminated any chance for local entrepreneurs to participate and drove the business into the hands of large foreign financial institutions.[3]

With the Peruvian government receiving less than one-third of the sale price of the guano, most of the profits from the industry remained in Europe, between the earnings of Gibbs and Sons and Montane and Company and the lavish spending on luxuries and manufactured goods by wealthy Peruvians. No native industry was developed, and only that infrastructure existed which tended to facilitate the exploitation of the guano, such as minimal docking facilities along the southern coast. Consequently, the only significant job market created in Peru was in the ranks of the bureaucracy, and corruption became rampant. More importantly, with this ready source of seemingly inexhaustible wealth, there was no incentive for the government to develop a coherent economic policy, to establish an internal tax structure, or to diversify the economy in any meaningful way. While it would be some time yet before the full impact of this shortsighted policy would be felt, the seeds were clearly sown for an ultimate reckoning.

José Rufino Echenique succeeded Castilla and immediately put into practice an even more ambitious economic program than his predecessor, albeit one that was totally unconnected to the realities of the country. To settle a long-standing dispute, Echenique chose to recognize the internal debt generated in Peru during the war of independence. Although undertaken with the best of intentions, the government was suddenly saddled with an immense debt, and claims were recognized on the flimsiest or most fraudulent of evidence, spreading corruption even further throughout the upper ranks of the government.

Castilla had come to look upon the presidency as something like his personal property, and, impatient with what he perceived as Echenique's bumbling (even though Castilla had hand-picked him for the job), in 1854 Castilla raised the banner of rebellion in Arequipa, supported by a youthful army commander, Mariano Ignacio Prado, of whom more will be heard anon. During the course of his nearly year-long struggle with Echenique's forces, Castilla found it expedient to issue proclamations summarily ending the colonial relic of payment of tribute to the government by the Indian communities (either in the form of compulsory labor on public works, in cash, or in kind) and another emancipating the 20,000 African slaves still held in the nation with a compensation of 300 *soles* each for their owners. While this astute political move undoubtedly gained him the enthusiastic support of both the Blacks and the Indians in the civil war, it burdened the stumbling economy even further. Indian tribute, a holdover from *conquistador* days, made up nearly 10 percent of the central government's budget and an even higher amount of that of the municipalities in which the Indian populations were concentrated. Apart from the immediate outflow of six million *soles* as compensation for the former slave owners, emancipation further undermined the economy in that the freed slaves now often refused to perform the menial labor of former times, and agricultural production dropped significantly, thus producing another drain on the balance of payments as food was now often imported along with the eighty thousand Chinese laborers brought in to work the guano deposits and thousands of Chileans recruited for agricultural work and to build the railroads.[4]

However, the economic storm clouds gathering on the horizon were still invisible to Castilla upon his ultimate resumption of the presidency in 1855. He now engaged in an ambitious program of military modernization, issuing the oft-quoted dictum that, "If Chile buys one warship, Peru must buy two."[5] In the new constitutions of 1856 and 1860, he also ended the state collection of tithes on behalf of the Church, but these tithes were replaced with a stipend to the Church of an even higher amount than that of the tithes without any compensating taxes being levied to cover the additional expense. The economy had deteriorated to such an extent that, whereas the cost of imports more or less equaled the country's exports in 1845, by 1859 the former outstripped the latter by a ratio of more than four-to-one. But even now the problem was disguised as the revenues from guano, and increasingly from advances on expected revenues, continued to make up the difference.[6]

In 1859 Castilla ordered the invasion of Ecuador in the hope of forcing a resolution of a long-standing border dispute over large tracts of land in the Amazon Basin and possibly even of gaining control of the port of Guayaquil. When the government in Quito collapsed in the face of Peru's overwhelming military superiority, in a move that would come back to haunt his successors in Lima in coming years, Castilla set up a puppet government in the occupied territory that was willing to agree to virtually all of his demands. But the bitter opposition of the Ecuadorean people to the treaty eventually convinced Castilla that only a lengthy, and costly, military occupation of Ecuador could enforce the treaty conditions. He was obliged to bring his army home leaving the situation unchanged.

Since Peru's most recent constitution, that of 1860, prohibited the president from serving consecutive terms, Castilla was obliged to content himself with manipulating the 1862 elections, obtaining a victory for his protégé San Román, who was replaced upon his sudden death the next year by Juan Antonio Pezet.

In August of 1863 an apparently minor incident occurred that was to have far-reaching ramifications for all three of the belligerents in the coming War of the Pacific. A number of Basque agricultural workers, who had been recruited by the Talambo estate in southern Peru, began to agitate for better terms of employment, which resulted in a violent confrontation with the local authorities and at the death of at least one of the Spaniards. The Spanish government, which was just then going through an aggressive phase of relations with its former colonies, having sent an expeditionary force to join the French in occupying Veracruz in Mexico and having engineered the brief return of Santo Domingo to the Spanish Empire, found the actions of the Peruvian courts to be unacceptable and sent a naval squadron to the Pacific to give its protests some weight. The squadron commander, Rear Admiral Pinzón, grossly exceeding his instructions from Madrid, opted to occupy the Chincha Islands, one of Peru's richest guano-producing areas, and threatened to retain the islands until Spain should receive satisfaction.[7]

Since the Spanish squadron easily out-gunned the combined fleets of all of the South American Pacific Coast republics at the time, and since Peru had become so totally dependent upon a regular flow of revenue from the guano fields, President Pezet saw no alternative to signing a humiliating peace with Spain in January 1865. The treaty identified Spain as the aggrieved party and allowed for payment of a three million-peso indemnity in exchange for the return of the islands.

Public outrage at the treaty was quick in coming and was widespread throughout Peru. Arequipa rebelled under Colonel Mariano Ignacio Prado, and Pezet resigned in favor of his vice president, General Pedro Diez Canseco, in November 1865, but Prado ousted him as well and was declared provisional president at the end of the month. At the same time the new Spanish naval commander, José Manuel Pareja, complicated the situation by taking umbrage at pro-Peruvian comments in the Chilean press and bombarding the undefended port of Valparaíso. Chilean diplomats quickly mobilized and formed a quadruple alliance with Peru, Bolivia, and Ecuador, while the Chilean navy scored a minor but exciting victory at sea with the capture of the corvette *Covadonga* in an action that was tremendously embarrassing for the Spanish. When the Peruvian port of Callao managed to beat off an attack by the Spanish fleet and with all of the ports for hundreds of miles closed to him, the frustrated Admiral Pareja simply committed suicide, and his fleet eventually turned and sailed for home.

Apart from playing a role in the border negotiations between Bolivia and Chile, which will be discussed later, the brief war with Spain convinced both Peru and Chile of the overriding importance of sea power in any conflict fought along the guano coast. Under Castilla's rearmament policy, Peru had ordered two powerful new ironclads, the *Huascar* and the *Independencia* from British shipyards, both of which were delivered in 1866. These ships enjoyed the same invulnerability to virtually anything any of the wooden warships then possessed by the other Latin American navies that *CSS Virginia* had enjoyed over the Union fleet in the American Civil War a few years earlier. They gave Peru a brief period of total naval domination of the Pacific coast. Chile, however, had placed orders for two even newer and more powerful ironclads, and much of the diplomacy of the subsequent decade would revolve around their final delivery.

The Prado administration would be dominated by liberals, who soon drafted yet another constitution, enacted in 1867, which greatly reduced the power of the executive and curtailed the influence of the Church in the field of education. While Prado attempted manfully to bring about economic reform, cut back the bloated bureaucracy, reduce expenditures, and relieve the country's dependence on guano, his actions only alienated large sections of the political community, and he was ousted in his turn in early 1868. General Pedro Diez Canseco again assumed the role of provisional president until elections could be organized and held that August.

José Balta's administration is chiefly noteworthy for its particular richness in presidential timber. Future president Francisco García Calderon, an honest lawyer with modestly liberal tendencies, was named Minister of the Treasury, but he was soon replaced after a vote of censure by the legislature with Nicolas Pierola, a man around whom Peruvian politics would revolve for years to come. Pierola was a former newspaper editor from Arequipa, a devout Catholic not yet thirty years of age who had seriously considered a career in the priesthood, and who firmly believed that the Peruvian people needed a strong hand at the helm in order to prosper.

The other significant aspect of the Balta administration was the contract signed with the firm of Auguste Dreyfus of Paris for the exploitation of the guano deposits, a contract engineered by Pierola's ministry.[8] At a stroke, previous franchises were invalidated, and Dreyfus was granted a concession for the export of two million tons of guano at a rate of sixty *soles* per ton, a marked improvement over the price paid previously to the government. Even more attractive to Lima was the provision for a 2.4 million *sol* advance with an additional 700,000 *soles* to be paid each month for one year and an assumption by Dreyfus for servicing Peru's foreign debt in exchange for the title of exclusive agent for Peruvian guano in Europe and as Peru's financial representative in France. For the first time the government was not only presented with a substantial lump sum to clear up old accounts, but was guaranteed a steady income. Unfortunately, instead of taking advantage of this safety net to put the country's financial house in order, establish a reasonable source of internal revenue, and gear expenditures to income, Pierola simply used the Dreyfus contract as collateral for even larger loans at ever-increasing rates of interest. This policy was continued at an even greater pace by Balta after Pierola's resignation in 1871, and by 1872 the national debt had grown to £49 million sterling, an increase of 1,000 percent over its level at Balta's inauguration.[9]

Little of this borrowed money went toward revenue-creating ventures such as irrigation projects or infrastructure-building in the form of desperately needed schools. Balta had the railroad bug even worse than his predecessors, and the swashbuckling American entrepreneur, Henry Meiggs, after going broke speculating on California lands and industries, turned up in Peru and became the creator of a railroad empire. Under his leadership, lines were undertaken connecting Mollendo to Arequipa, thence to Puno and on to Cuzco and another from the port of Callao to La Oroya, a mining area beyond the Andes. While breath-taking in scope and impressive as engineering feats for their day, these projects were in no way related to traffic patterns of Peruvian trade or the needs of the population in general. The state-dominated railroad industry consistently lost money while soaking up every spare penny of investment capital in the country.

1871 saw the creation of the first proper political party in Peru, as opposed to loose congregations of politicians around a charismatic leader. Manuel Pardo was the presidential candidate for the *civilista* party and, as the name suggests, would be the country's first civilian chief executive since independence. A self-made millionaire and former minister of the treasury under Prado in 1866, he had sought a means of freeing the country from the clutches of the siren guano and rationalizing the economy, hoping to create a basis for future wealth rather than relying on a non-renewable and increasingly finite source of income.

In the May 1872 elections, Pardo was an easy winner, but, just prior to his inauguration, General Tomás Gutierrez launched a military coup d'état, arresting President Balta and declaring himself dictator. Pardo fled to Callao and was taken under the protection of Admiral Manuel Grau. Meanwhile, Pardo's enlightened tenure as mayor of Lima had made him extremely popular with the working classes, and a violent popular uprising ensued in which Gutierrez and his two brothers were not only brutally murdered by the mob but their bodies horribly mutilated as well, due at least in part to the blame the populace placed on them for the assassination of President Balta while in a military prison.

Pardo inherited a nation on the verge of bankruptcy. By 1873 *all* income from the exportation of guano was going to the servicing of the national debt run up by the Balta administration; and in 1874, for the first time since independence, Peru was forced to issue unsupported paper money as a stopgap measure. Both the quality and the accessibility of the guano deposits had by this time seriously declined, lowering the price and increasing extraction costs. In 1869 guano sales had brought in £4 million of which £1 million went to debt service. By 1875 the state was receiving only £2.6 million from guano sales of which fully £2.57 million went for interest payments.[10] The one ray of hope was that nitrates, specifically nitrate of soda, from desert deposits in Tarapacá Province, had recently superceded guano as the fertilizer of choice in Europe and also commanded a strong market for the manufacture of explosives.

Pardo frantically sought means of cutting government expenses, reducing the size of the army by three quarters to twenty-five hundred men and canceling contracts for the construction of two new ironclad warships in British shipyards (both of which would be ultimately purchased and used by the Chileans). He was confident that the secret alliance of Peru with Bolivia (of which more later) with the possible inclusion of Argentina in the near future, would be more than sufficient to provide for defense against an increasingly aggressive and powerful Chile to the south.

Rather than focusing on the urgent problems of the nation, however, the *civilista* legislators chose to spend their time getting even with their political opponents of the Balta administration. In October of 1872, no less that sixteen Balta-era ministers were interpolated on a variety of charges in an effort to fix the blame for the country's economic straits on a few individuals, with Pierola figuring prominently among the accused. Although all were ultimately acquitted, or at least had their charges dropped for lack of any evidence that would not have equally implicated virtually every politician and member of the oligarchy, Pierola took the affront very much to heart and fled to Chile in self-imposed exile, now a sworn enemy of the *civilistas*. From his foreign sanctuary, Pierola became the intellectual author of numerous uprisings, especially in chronically discontented Arequipa; each was suppressed in its turn.

Because of the constant threat posed by Pierola, Pardo chose his long-time ally and former mentor, the soldier Manuel Ignacio Prado as his heir apparent for the 1876 elections, thus discarding the central tenet of the *civilista* program. Although in the largely "arranged" elections of the time, Prado won easily, notwithstanding considerable violence at the polls, he subsequently found ruling far from easy. As a military man, Prado received no support from the *civilistas*, and as a colleague of Pardo, he got even less from the followers of Pierola, thus falling neatly between two stools.

Hardly recognizing defeat, Pierola mounted another insurrection in October 1876. This one met with somewhat greater success in that his minions managed to seize control of the ironclad *Huascar,* possibly with the connivance of naval officers upset at the defeat of Admiral Lizardo Montero, Prado's opponent in the presidential campaign. There followed a brief episode of piracy, thinly veiled as political protest, during which the *Huascar* ravaged shipping along the coast and even dueled with the British cruiser *Shah*. In this encounter, *Huascar's* 4½-inch iron plate proved impervious to the best the obsolescent wooden *Shah* could do with smoothbore 10-inch guns and escaped - although Peruvian gunnery was bad enough that the British ship's lack of armor was not a factor. A historic milestone was reached when the *Shah* launched the first self-propelled "Whitehead" torpedo in the battle, although *Huascar* had little difficulty in evading the slow, short-range missile.[11] The crew finally surrendered to the authorities at Callao in exchange for amnesty.

Pierola at least temporarily gave up the struggle and traveled to Europe. Pardo, who had moved to Chile in the hope that his absence from the Lima scene would remove one element of conflict, returned to Peru in mid-1878 after Pierola's departure from South America only to find an assassin's bullet awaiting him. Pierola was blamed for the crime, not surprisingly, although no substantial evidence surfaced then or later directly implicating him as having directed the attack.

Thus, on the eve of the War of the Pacific, Peru found herself in a state of virtual bankruptcy with a political landscape littered with real corpses. Her army of twenty-five hundred men was inadequate even for simple police duties in a huge nation of nearly three million people. Even her formerly dominant navy had already been qualitatively outclassed by the Chileans. Her president, while experienced in both military and political affairs, had no identifiable power base of his own, and the nation had been in a state of virtually constant civil war for years with the corresponding disruption in economic life.

BOLIVIA

If the situation of Peru was dismal at the start of the final quarter of the nineteenth century, that of Bolivia was little short of disastrous. Bolivians have developed a certain black sense of humor about their country's fortunes, referring to the nation as "the beggar on the throne of gold," or "the land of the future today, just as it was three centuries ago." Even the name of the country is a little pitiful, chosen in a vain effort to lure "the Liberator," Simón Bolívar to assume the presidency of the new republic in 1825.

Bolivia covers a huge area, currently the size of Texas and California combined (even after the territorial losses of the wars against Chile, Brazil, and Paraguay) with a population in the 1870s of approximately two million, not including unincorporated natives living in the Amazon Basin. Virtually all of this population was concentrated in the western third of the nation, the Andean highlands ranging from nine to thirteen thousand feet above sea level, the

Altiplano, with the jungles to the northeast, and the barren scrubland to the southeast, are largely uninhabited. The highlands provided a relatively stable source of food ranging from potatoes on the Altiplano to tropical fruits and rice in the deep valleys on the eastern slopes of the Andes. It was also a rich source of minerals, notably the fabled Cerro Rico of Potosí, a veritable mountain of silver that provided the basis for much of the wealth of the Spanish Empire in the sixteenth and seventeenth centuries.

Unlike the other Southern Cone republics like Argentina and Chile, where the native population had been largely eliminated by war and disease during the colonial period, Bolivia's population, even more so than Peru's, remained overwhelmingly Indian, with a thin crust of *mestizos* and Europeans at the top. In the mid-1800s, as little as 20 percent of Bolivians spoke Spanish *at all*, even as a second language, leaving the tongue of all political and commercial affairs running a poor third to Quechua and Aymara in popular usage. The rugged spine of the Andes, which ran through the most densely populated part of the country, prevented easy communications among the nation's few, meager cities (La Paz being the largest at only forty-three thousand inhabitants) and between Bolivia and the outside world - even when Bolivia possessed a sovereign outlet to the sea.[12]

Bolivia's economy was among the most primitive in the hemisphere at this time. *"Ni producen, ni consumen,"** was a common complaint of the Spanish *hacendados* of the Indian communities during colonial times, and little had changed. The vast majority of the population essentially took no part in the economy, producing enough food to survive but little surplus and being only casually interested in any manufactured goods the outside world might have to offer in exchange for any surplus they did accumulate. Since agricultural land and the Indian masses to work it did not comprise the basis for wealth in Bolivia, the natives had been left largely to their own devices, mostly living in small, self-contained communities in the windswept Altiplano, although some large haciendas did exist in the richer, lower valleys. While manufacturing industry was not well-developed anywhere in Latin America at this time, it was wholly non-existent in Bolivia, and every item of use to society beyond basic foodstuffs had to be imported over a tortuous and expensive route from Europe or North America.

Bolivia's wealth was derived, as it had been since colonial times, from mining activities, starting with the fabled silver mines of *el Cerro Rico de San Luis de Potosi*. Although many of these mines had been played out by the second half of the nineteenth century, and while tin mining had not yet taken on the importance it would in the early twentieth, the exploitation of deposits of gold and silver still formed the basis of many local fortunes. One of the complicating factors for Bolivia, as the crisis related to the discovery and early exploitation of nitrate deposits in the coastal region loomed, was that, despite the expertise of the most powerful elements of the Bolivian oligarchy in the mineral extraction business, both their attention and capital were largely tied up with existing

---

* "They neither produce, nor consume."

projects, and it would be Chilean money, engineers, and even mine laborers who would lead the way in bringing the Atacama nitrates to market.

But, as unimpressive as the level of evolution of the Bolivian economy might be, it was Bolivian politics that was the real plague of the nation. A common saying in Bolivia (even in the late twentieth century), is that Bolivia is the land where any boy can grow up to become president, and most of them do.

After the turmoil of the wars of independence of the continent, in which Bolivia was the last country to secure the withdrawal of Spanish troops in 1825, Bolivia's last stable government, that of José Ballívian, was ousted in 1847 by General Manuel Isidoro Belzu. Although Belzu hung onto power until 1855, he faced no less than forty more-or-less serious armed uprisings during that period. He was strongly supported by the populists, favoring the Indians and working classes and attacking the oligarchy composed of the landed elite, wealthy merchants, and the entrepreneurs of the mining industry. Belzu finally retired voluntarily, the first Bolivian president to do so since Mariscal Santa Cruz, and passed power on to his son-in-law, General Jorge Córdova, through an election arranged by a "tame" legislature, although this regime only lasted two years until 1857.

His successor, José María Linares, was Bolivia's first civilian president, although he was a long-time coup plotter against Belzu. Linares established a formal dictatorship in 1858, something his military predecessors had, for some reason, never bothered to do.[13] Since Linares had come to power through the support of the landed and industrial elite, he naturally supported a policy of *laissez faire* economy, and it was during this period that some of Bolivia's great mining dynasties, like the Aramayos and the Pachecos came into their own.[14]

Linares was replaced in January 1861 in a coup led by his own minister of war, General José María Achá. While Achá continued most of Linares' free trade policies, he brought Bolivian politics to new lows of barbarism with the Massacre of Loreto in which some seventy opposition political leaders, including ex-President Córdova were summarily executed for allegedly plotting to return Belzu to power. Heretofore, opposition leaders might only be jailed or, more commonly, exiled, and this level of blatant violence was unheard of. Despite this incident, however, it briefly appeared that Bolivian politics might be entering the early stages of evolution as elections were planned for 1865 and something like political parties were forming around Linares for the constitutionalists and Belzu for the populists.[15]

Whatever this process might have become was immediately put in abeyance by the seizure of power in December 1864 by an even more brutal dictator, General Mariano Melgarejo. If the dedication of many of Bolivia's leaders before and since to the national welfare has been debatable, Melgarejo never even made a pretense to such motives. An illegitimate son of *mestizo* background, he became infamous as a drunken, womanizing despot who readily sold out the interests of his country for simple personal gain. Surrounded by a clique of ignorant military officers just as immoral as himself, he raped the country for five full years. Apart from simply looting the national treasury, issuing devalued coinage, and the shameful sale of over forty thousand square miles of valuable Amazon lands to Brazil, with the proceeds of these adventures going directly into Melgarejo's own pocket, his venality and vanity were ultimately contributing factors to the War of the Pacific and still greater misfortune for Bolivia. [16]

Besides being brutal and corrupt, Melgarejo was an easy mark for flattery and any token of respect from foreign dignitaries, probably because he was so insecure in his position as head of state. A clever diplomat will normally be able to detect such foibles in his interlocutors and will also be able to exploit them to his advantage, and Aniceto Vergara Albano, the head of the Chilean delegation to Bolivia in early 1866 was a very clever diplomat indeed. The diplomatic maneuvering of this period will be discussed in greater detail in the next chapter, but suffice it to say that, by playing on Melgarejo's vanity and including an honorary commission for Melgarejo as a general in the Chilean Army, Vergara was able to get virtually anything he wanted out of the dictator. Vergara's original mission was to ensure Bolivian support for Chile in the conflict with Spain, at least to deny the Spanish flotilla the use of Bolivia's ports, and he obtained that. Then, instead of compensating Bolivia for this solidarity, as he fully expected to be obliged to do, Vergara was able to obtain Bolivian cession of all territory in the Atacama south of the 24th parallel, while entering into a condominium with Chile to share in the proceeds of the minerals extracted between the 23rd and 25th parallels. Not bothering with the formality of dealing with ministers in his little kingdom, Melgarejo sought no advice from his counselors on this subject, and the deal was done. [17]

Besides giving away huge chunks of the Bolivian national patrimony and disgracing the office of the presidency with his boorish, hedonistic behavior, Melgarejo also earned the violent opposition of growing numbers of Bolivians by seizing the lands of the Indian communes, and declaring it state property to which titles must be purchased. Since the Indian population conducted bare subsistence agriculture, the only people with cash available for such purposes were the white upper class; bloody protests resulted throughout the nation. Melgarejo and his ragtag army had put down one rebellion after another since assuming power, but in January of 1871 he was finally bested by General Agustín Morales and forced into exile.

Although Morales was nearly illiterate, he was a vast improvement over Melgarejo. With the support of Linares' constitutionalists, he restored the Indian lands and eliminated some of the more corrupt monopolies and contracts granted by his predecessor. He also attempted to undo some of the confusion sewn by Melgarejo in his dealings with Chile and approved the Lindsey-Corral Agreement of 1872, of which more later. The agreement was well meant, but carried within it the seeds of the ultimate conflict with Chile. This period of responsible government was too good to last in Bolivia, and Morales was killed by an assassin's bullet in 1872.

Surprisingly enough, after a brief interregnum, Adolfo Ballivián was selected as president the following year in the first free and popular elections Bolivia had held. He signed the new treaty with Chile that replaced Lindsay-Corral, but Ballivián lasted barely one year in office, dying of natural causes and being replaced by Vice President Tomás Frías. With extensive experience in foreign affairs, it is conceivable that Frías might have been able to steer Bolivia through the dangerous shoals of her relationship with Chile in the coming years, but he, too, was ousted, this time by a coup led by the commander of the "Colorados" infantry regiment, Colonel Hilarion Daza. As an opening act of his administration, Daza plundered the national treasury to repay the army officers who supported his bid for power. He would vie with Melgarejo for the title of most abhorred of Bolivia's presidents, and it was this man who would lead Bolivia into her war with Chile.

CHILE

At least one historian has taken exception to the common appellation of Chile as "the Prussia of South America," the frequent insistence that Chile possessed an ethnically homogeneous, politically mature, and economically advantaged population which enabled her to victimize her less fortunate neighbors.[18] There is certainly a natural tendency to ascribe to the victorious side in any conflict powers that make the outcome of the conflict, in hindsight, seem predestined. It is true that Chile in the mid-nineteenth century clearly had some problems to overcome, but the important factor in discussing any war is the *relative* power of the belligerents. The pike is the great white shark of the millpond, and, compared to the political and economic basket cases to her north, Chile, with all her shortcomings, did present a formidable image.

Like all of the New World republics, Chile was something of a melting pot, with substantial numbers of Italian, German, and English immigrants along with the original influx of Spanish colonists. What Chile lacked in relation to Peru and Bolivia was a vast majority of indigenous peoples, segregated from the rulers of society by language, culture, and customs, in addition to economic and social divisions. It may be true that the majority of Chilean *rotos*, the landless peasant tenant farmers who made up the bulk of the rural population, may have had only a limited sense of national identity, hardly being able to recognize any social unit beyond their own province or even the hacienda of their master, but regionalism was hardly rare in that era.[19] The United States, after all, had just come through a horrific civil war due largely to the regional loyalties of many of its citizens. The Araucan Indians of Chile had never formed part of the Incan Empire and proved to be one of the few indigenous people to offer an effective resistance to the Spanish invasion, by withdrawing into their thick forests and developing viable tactics against Spanish cavalry based on infantry units armed with pikes. They would gradually be pushed southward, as the American Indian would be pushed west, but the Araucan Indians were never incorporated into (and enslaved by) the Spanish colonial society as were the Quechua and Aymara speakers to the north.

Geographically, Chile was also a much more cohesive whole than either of her opponents, with relatively smooth transportation links, even before the railroad in the nineteenth century, along her densely populated central valley and along the coast, with no point in the long, narrow nation being more than a week's travel from the sea. This contrasted sharply with the vast territories of both Peru and Bolivia, with little, if any, benefit from sea or riverine transportation lines, and with land communications interrupted by massive arms of the Andes.

Chile was rather less oriented toward an extractive economy than were either Peru or Bolivia, devoted as they had been during colonial times primarily to the mining of silver for the Empire. Chile did have an extensive mining industry, producing silver, coal, and copper, but wheat and cattle for export also represented a substantial part of the nation's wealth. Mining, particularly in silver, took on more importance in the 1870s with the large silver strike at Caracoles in the Atacama (developed by Chilean capital and engineering skill although on Bolivian territory), but there was a marked downturn in this field with the growing shift to the gold standard throughout the world, driving down the price of other precious metals.

Chilean agriculture enjoyed boom times during the 1840s due to the insatiable demands of the California gold fields for wheat and cattle products, and just about the time that California was transformed from a gold mine into a bread basket, the gold rush sprang forth in Australia, and Chile was in a handy location to meet that need. Also, at about this time Chilean wines were beginning to earn the reputation that has continued to this day, making them still another viable export.[20]

Largely because of the lack of a substantial Indian population to use as a source of cheap labor, Chile was a pioneer in Latin America in the mechanization of agriculture, with over five hundred threshing machines, both horse and steam-driven, in use by the end of the 1860s. The economic boom of the middle of the century also funded over one thousand miles of rail lines by the 1870s, and Chile possessed over sixteen hundred miles of telegraph lines with links to Buenos Aires and even to Europe once the Brazilian submarine cable had been laid in 1874. The Chilean industrial sector was certainly miniscule in comparison to the United States or any of the major European nations, but neither Peru nor Bolivia had any identifiable manufacturing capability at all. The Carlos Klein and the Levis and Murphy foundries could produce steam engines, rolling stock, as well as a variety of military stores for which the Peruvians and Bolivians would be totally dependent upon imports.[21]

Although, like Peru and Bolivia, Chile was still predominantly rural, Santiago and Valparaíso each had three to four times the population of La Paz, Bolivia's largest city while the overall population of both countries was close to two million. Furthermore, Chile's cities were undeniably more modern, with Santiago enjoying gas lighting from 1857, horse-drawn trams, and a steady expansion of paved streets and imposing public buildings and private homes throughout the middle of the century.

Of course, Chile was subject to just as many natural disasters as other developing nations during this period. A constant flow of workers from the countryside to the cities resulted in the growth of belts of slums surrounding an opulent central core (in the typical Latin American inversion of the North American housing pattern), and the poor sanitation and lack of medical attention in these areas gave rise to devastating epidemics. Tuberculosis and syphilis were more or less regular features of life, particularly for the working classes, and typhoid swept through the country in the mid-1860s and again in the 1870s. A particularly virulent form of small pox caused thousands of deaths in the winter of 1862-1863 and returned in 1868 and 1872, having the further effect of terrorizing the population, driving people away from the markets, and practically paralyzing the country for weeks at a time. A series of droughts and floods also crippled the wheat crop in the late 1870s with overall exports down one-third in 1878 from the 1873 total and leaving over 300,000 agricultural workers unemployed.[22]

It was in the area of political development, however, that Chile stood head and shoulders above her neighbors on the continent. Starting with the administration of Bulnes in 1841, there followed an unbroken series of regularly held and respected elections, with a typically nineteenth century level of manipulation and restrictions on suffrage, in which the president would be chosen for a five-year term followed by a more or less guaranteed second term. Thus Bulnes served until 1851, followed by Manuel Montt and José Joaquín Pérez, each with a ten-year mandate. After this date, a modification of the Chilean constitution prevented immediate reelection of a president, but the subsequent presidents served out their full five-year terms without hindrance. To be sure, there were more or less serious rebellions in 1851 and 1859, virtual small civil wars, but both were ultimately put down by the legitimate government, and there was literally nothing to compare with the revolving door situations, or even multiple rival presidents that were more the rule than the exception in Peru and Bolivia. Even after the switch to the single-term presidency, there was a considerable continuity in policy from one administration to the next, yet there was an opportunity for something very like democratic change as the power of the incumbent to choose his successor was not absolute. This would lead President Montt to declare in 1858 that "We have the honor to have proved to the world that the Spanish American people can govern themselves by their own unaided efforts and can continue to prosper,"[23] an issue that the performance of most of the Latin American republics had evidently put into question over the preceding half century and one which would continue to hold true for Chile for the remainder of that century.

This is not to say that the Chilean political scene was placid, or even cordially adversarial. True political parties arose in Chile around long-term issues, primarily the role of the Church in society and the question of free enterprise versus mercantilism. There were also splinter groups centered around particular politicians, but Chile went into the War of the Pacific with five major parties ranging from the Conservatives on the right through the Nationalists (or Montt-Varistas), Liberals, and Liberal Democrats, to the Radicals on the left.

If a sense of inviolability surrounded the office of the president, unlike in other Latin American republics, his cabinet was not so protected, and the Chilean legislature devoted much of its time to the interpolation of cabinet members, particularly the minister of government (something of a combination of the American Secretary of Interior and the Attorney General, but with substantially more authority still, almost like a prime minister), giving the political scene a kind of parliamentary flavor. There was little evidence that rival politicians ever put the broader interests of the nation ahead of their own immediate goals, and this bitter combativeness and selfishness continued on right through the war. It is important to note, however, that, while Chilean politicians were not reluctant to paralyze the workings of the government in pursuit of temporary tactical advantage domestically, even if it meant putting their nation's fighting men at risk, they did consistently draw the line at the armed overthrow of the regime, something that did not occur in Peru or Bolivia. This gave the Chilean political system what twentieth century political scientists would label as the invaluable commodity of "legitimacy," something which not only further reinforced the authority of the government, but enhanced the credibility of the regime in the eyes of foreign investors, making available considerably more resources to Chile than the grasping, corrupt regimes in Lima or La Paz could possibly tap.

After a very strong showing in the 1860s and into the 1870s, Chile entered a period of economic decline in the mid-1870s that would continue up through the start of the war. As noted above, the shift by most countries to the gold standard hurt the mining industry, while the especially lucrative markets for Chilean wheat and beef - California and Australia - soon became self-sufficient or even competitors on the world market. As exports declined, the foreign debt rose, more than doubling from 1860 to 1870.[24] This occurred at the same time as the widespread droughts and recurrent epidemics throughout the country. Bank failures began in 1877; by the following year, only one bank in the country was in a position to cover deposits with its assets. Consequently, over fifty thousand Chileans were obliged to emigrate in search of work, most of them to Peru to work on railroad construction, and many to begin work on the Panama Canal, in addition to thousands moving north to the nitrate fields in the Atacama.

The government cut back sharply on spending and raised import duties, the government's traditional primary source of revenue, on all but those items destined to support domestic industrial development. So desperate was the Pinto administration that it was obliged to experiment with a number of rather egalitarian tax systems including inheritance tax and a tax on the sale of property, which struck at the wealth of the entrenched upper class. Even a modest income tax (3 percent of income over $300 per year) was passed in 1878 and had produced over $600,000 in revenue by 1880 despite widespread tax evasion.[25] It is hardly surprising, therefore, that the apparently unlimited wealth to be derived from nitrates suddenly loomed very large in the eyes of the *Casa de la Moneda*, the Chilean equivalent of the White House.

So it can be seen that Chile certainly had problems to deal with in the second half of the nineteenth century and was far from the glowering monolith of unlimited political, military, and economic power that she has sometimes been depicted to be. However, in comparison to the chaos that reigned in her two neighbors to the north, Chile enjoyed considerable advantages, an edge that would prove to be more than sufficient to ensure victory in the war, just as Chile's problems tended to drive her to policies that would lead to the conflict.

One view of this situation is that, far from making the Chilean government reluctant to enter into an international conflict at this time, the veritable penury in which the Chileans found themselves in the late 1870s actually served as a spur for war. It was not the simple formula of an administration seeking a foreign adventure to distract the populace from unpleasant news on the domestic front. It was more that, having felt themselves virtual masters of their corner of the world only a few years before, the Chilean people felt themselves falling into an abyss from which only an aggressive foreign policy might rescue them. Having lost much of their self-esteem, the Chileans were all the more likely to bridle at any perceived slight from abroad and to answer it violently. In fact, the popular view had become that only through a policy of confrontation could the imminent disappearance of the Chilean nation be avoided. It was thus that, while peaceful solutions to the crisis that developed between Chile, Bolivia, and Peru in 1879 might have existed, such solutions were simply not wanted by the politically influential portion of the Chilean population.[26]

NOTES

1. Luis Pasara, "El Guano y la Penetracion Inglesa" in Jorge Basadre, *Reflexiones en Torno a la Guerra de 79,* Lima: F. Campodonico, 1979, p. 18.

2. Emilio Romero, *Historia Económica del Peru,* Lima: s.n., 1949, p. 148.

3. Pasara, op. cit., p. 20.

4. Fredrick B. Pike, *The History of Modern Peru,* New York: Praeger, 1982, p. 113.

5. Jacinto Lopez, *Historia de la Guerra del Guano y el Salitre,* Lima: Editorial Universo, 1980, p. 46.

6. A. J. Duffield, *Peru in the Guano Age,* London: s.n., 1877, p. 88.

7. Ronald Bruce St. John, *The Diplomatic History of Peru,* Boulder, CO: Lynne Rienner, 1992, p. 70.

8. Pasara, op. cit., p. 24.

9. Alberto Ulloa y Sotomayor, *Don Nicolas Pierola: Una Epoca de la Historia del Peru,* Lima: Imprenta Editorial Minerva, 1981, p. 73.

10. Pedro Dávalos y Lissón, *La Primera Centenia: Causas Ggeográficas, Políticas, y Económicas que Han Detenido el Progreso Moral y Material del Peru en el Primer Siglo de su Vida Independiente,* vol. 4, Lima: s.n., 1926, p. 369.

11. Donald Macintyre and Basil W. Bathe, *Man-of-War: A History of the Combat Vessel,* New York: McGraw-Hill Book Company, 1969, p. 147.

12. Herbert S. Klein, *Bolivia: The Evolution of a Multi-Ethnic Society,* New York: Oxford University Press, 1982, p. 123.

13. Ibid., p. 131.

14. Waltraud Queiser Morales, *Bolivia: Land of Struggle,* Boulder, CO: Westview Press, 1992, p. 43.

15. Klein, op. cit., p. 135.

16. Alcides Arguedas, *Los Caudillos Barbaros,* La Paz: Gisbert & Cia., S.A., 1975, p. 142.

17. Roberto Querejazu Calvo, *Guano, Salitre, Sangre: Historia de la Guerra del Pacífico,* La Paz: Editorial Los Amigos del Libro, 1979, p. 64.

18. William F. Sater, *Chile and the War of the Pacific,* Lincoln, NB: University of Nebraska Press, 1986, p. 2.

19. Ibid., p. 76. Sater apparently draws his conclusion based on a single "Atropos" editorial which appeared in 1861, nearly a generation before the War of the Pacific.

20. Thomas McLeod Bader, *A Willingness to War: A Portrait of the Republic of Chile during the Years Preceding the War of the Pacific,* Ann Arbor, MI: Xerox University Microfilm, 1967, pp. 22-23.

21. Sater, p. 116.

22. Simon Collier and William F. Sater, *A History of Chile 1808-1994,* New York: Cambridge University Press, 1997, p. 125.

23. Bader, p. 25.

24. Chile, Ministerio de Hacienda, Oficina de Estadisticas Comerciales, "A Compartive Summary of Commercial Statistics of Chile, 1874," Valparaíso, 1975, p. 1.

25. Sater, p. 133.

26. Bader, p. 366.

Chapter Three

The Issue

Like most of the border conflicts that have bedeviled Latin America since independence, the War of the Pacific traces its roots back to the administrative divisions of the continent under Spanish rule. The Spanish Empire in the Americas spanned a continent and a half, running hundreds of miles from east to west and thousands from north to south over impassable mountains and jungles at a time when all communication moved at the speed of a horse or a sailing ship. Naturally, a realm of that extent had to be carved up into more manageable units. Viceroyalties were created for New Spain (Mexico, Central America, and much of the Western United States), New Granada (Colombia, Venezuela, Ecuador, and Panama), La Plata (Argentina, Uruguay, and Paraguay), and Peru (Peru and Bolivia). There was also an *Audiencia* (council) *de Charcas* that administered present-day Bolivia, and a captaincy-general for Chile. While these units broke up into a larger number of independent states after independence, once the unifying efforts of Simón Bolívar had failed, where the original administrative units touched on one another, this was where the boundaries of the new states were considered to lie.

The principle involved was called *uti possidetis*, the rule that colonial boundaries would become international boundaries, and it was accepted as the basis of boundary determination by all of the new republics, giving them a ready-made body of documentary evidence to support their eventual territorial claims. This concept was readily accepted by all parties, despite the many other differences they may have had, for two good reasons. First, as the post-colonial states of Latin America combined and divided like petrie dish amoebae, it would have been difficult for anyone to predict with any certainty which states would ultimately be the more powerful ones and which the weaker. In this kind of Rawlsian "veil of ignorance," it seemed best to lay down a set of rules that would protect all states in later years, regardless of relative power ratios.*

---

* Without going into great detail, the political philosopher John Rawls described a system of determining the justice of a political system. He imagined a state in which the social

Secondly, such a division of territory was relatively easy to accept because the states of Latin America in the early 1800s were geographically isolated. The colonial and post-colonial societies tended to cluster around a handful of widely separated urban centers, each surrounded by agricultural hinterlands of varying size, but even these were divided from the nearest neighbors by vast tracts of inhospitable, unproductive, and often impassable land, jungles, mountains, and deserts. It was hardly worthwhile, then, at the moment of independence, to squabble about just where the actual boundary line might be drawn. By the second half of the 1800s, however, the growth of population and the extension of the developed area of the continent meant that these scattered societies were starting to rub together in various spots, and border disputes began to arise.

The trouble with *uti possidetis* was that the borders between the various administrative units of the Spanish Empire were never meant to be international boundaries. The descriptions of the limits of each province, and sometimes only verbal descriptions existed since the actual ground remained largely unexplored and unmapped, were often vague and contradictory, based on the area a given explorer claimed to have covered, measured in such imprecise terms as days of travel or leagues (which might range from two to four or more miles in length, depending on the author's preference) and all done at a time when the accurate location of parallels of latitude was an inexact art and that of finding longitude was an unfathomable mystery. In itself, this was not an insurmountable problem in colonial times, since there always existed a higher authority, the Spanish crown, to which the provincial governments could appeal when the location of boundary lines came into question. With the collapse of the colonial empire, however, this court of appeals disappeared, and the disputants were left to confront each other face to face.

A number of cases cropped up throughout the continent, therefore, during the course of the nineteenth century in which the new republics bickered and squabbled over disputed territories. Generally, each side would attempt to amass an impressive array of documentation from the colonial period supporting its claim to the land and would sometimes submit the issue to arbitration by a third party. However, where the disputed territory was particularly valuable or of strategic importance, neither side, and particularly the side with the weaker juridical claim, would be likely to accept a contrary decision, and the case must be decided by an appeal to the force of arms, either by threat or open warfare. The issue of the Atacama fit this latter description most closely.

For the first couple of decades after the withdrawal of the Spanish from the region, there was no dispute over the location of the Bolivian-Chilean border running inland from the coast. Chile had more serious disputes with Argentina over control of the Straits of Magellan and Patagonia, and Bolivia had on-going disputes with all of her neighbors over thinly settled lands along the fringes of the old *Audiencia de Charcas*, but there seemed little reason to quarrel over

---

and political structure was established by all parties without any knowledge of what position they would hold in the society, whether rich or poor, weak or powerful, thus ensuring that all would opt for overall equality in order to avoid landing in a disadvantageous position later on. He dubbed this process the "veil of ignorance."

which nation controlled how many miles of the absolutely barren, rainless, and uninhabited region of the Atacama.

The original grant by Emperor Carlos V of Spain after the conquest of the region in the sixteenth century to Pedro de Mendoza for the area that would become Chile ran from approximately 25°31'36" South down to Cape Horn, while Diego de Almagro and Francisco Pizarro shared the bulk of the Inca Empire north of that line. After a bitter civil war between the conquistadores, Father La Gasca, the mediator sent out to the New World by Madrid made the new dividing line at 27° South, near the present town of Copiapó, although the southern boundary of the of the *Audiencia de Charcas*, Bolivia's ancestor, was kept at 25°31'36", leaving a sizeable gap which was presumably designed to prevent future conflicts, something apparently considered viable in this area given the total worthlessness of the land involved. This award was reinforced by Spanish titles issued in 1681.[1]

From this point of view, the province had rights over some 170 leagues (about five hundred miles) of coastline more or less opposite the city of Potosí with its silver mines. The port of Cobija was founded in 1587 and administered from Potosí, although most of the silver from the mines continued to be packed out to the larger ports at Arica and Callao to the north.[2] It was a difficult trek from the highlands down to Cobija, some twenty-five to thirty days for a mule train or company of porters.

Little changed immediately following independence. Antonio José de Sucre, Bolivia's first president and sometime president of Peru as well, hoped to transfer ownership of Arica to Bolivia but failed to do so. His successor, General Andrés Santa Cruz tried to build up the tiny port of Cobija instead to serve as Bolivia's outlet to the sea, but it is significant that he had to recruit some sixty-two Chileans to live there in 1828, and by 1831 the population had only grown to some four hundred souls and to 550 by 1840, including some three hundred Bolivians, with most of the town's water, meat, and vegetables being brought in by barge from Valparaíso.[3] This pattern of disinclination of the highlanders to populate the lowland regions was to continue as most of Bolivia's export-import traffic continued to move via Arica and while there was little in the arid desert to attract colonists in any case.

The Chilean Declaration of Independence in 1818 did not specifically mention national boundaries, implying acceptance of the colonial ones, while that of Bolivia in 1825 mentioned the inclusion of the province of Potosí, whose southern boundary was still on the books as the Rio Salado at 27° South and included the Atacama Desert.[4] The Chilean Constitutions of 1822, 1823, 1828, and 1833 all mentioned the nation's northern border but only with the vague term "from" (*desde*) the Atacama Desert or "up to" (*hasta*) and it was on this semantic difference that the initial differences of opinion arose.[5] Did this mean that Chilean territory stopped where the deserted started, that it included the entire desert, or that, as in a situation where a river or mountain chain marks a boundary, that the dividing line ran somewhere down the middle of this barren, uninhabited land? The question remained hardly worth the effort to discuss until the advent of the guano/nitrate boom that began in the 1840s.

As discussed previously, it was at this time that the economic value of guano and nitrates was discovered - both as chemical fertilizers and in the manufacture of munitions - and the deposits of both in the Peruvian province of Tarapacá began to be exploited. Naturally, since the geological make-up of the Atacama was identical to that of Tarapacá, hopeful prospectors began to explore farther and farther to the south. In July of 1842, President Bulnes of Chile authorized an expedition into the Atacama in search of worthwhile nitrate and guano mining sites. The results were disappointing, with nothing economically viable found to the south of 24° South, well beyond the tacitly accepted northern border of Chile, and it is hardly coincidental that Bulnes chose this moment, in October of that year, to declare unilaterally that the Chilean border now lay at the 23rd parallel. Actually, he also included the bay and port of Mejillones in Chilean territory, which lay just north of 23° South, but since this was the only significant port in the Atacama south of Cobija at the time, it seemed worthwhile to appropriate it as long as he was taking this step forward.[6] The Chilean argument was that their territorial rights had always extended this far north, although there was no documentary or traditional evidence to support this, and that the carelessness of previous administrations in pressing those rights in no way surrendered them to Bolivia, whose flag currently flew over the small port of Mejillones and had for years. The Chilean congress unanimously approved this declaration.

In taking this line, the Chileans were apparently going with the interpretation of using the Atacama as their northern border more or less as if it were a river that should be divided in the middle. Since, geographically, the Atacama is considered to extend from the River Loa in the north at 21°28' South to Copiapó at about 27° in the south, the middle would have fallen somewhere around 24°, and, even taking the Chilean border accepted by Bolivia of the Rio Salado at 25°39' South, the line would have fallen around 23°30', but President Bulnes clearly wanted to include Mejillones to facilitate the extraction of guano and arbitrarily did so. It is perhaps significant that the government in Santiago had never found it necessary to create a province of Atacama until 1844, well after Bulnes' unilateral declaration.

Naturally, Bolivia protested the Chilean encroachment immediately, but the objections were generally ignored in Santiago. During the course of the 1840s and 1850s, Chilean prospectors set up guano extraction stations along the coast in the neighborhood of Mejillones, usually under the protecting guns of Chilean warships, whose sailors would regularly set free any errant Chilean prospectors arrested by the Bolivians. Bolivian authorities in Cobija duly reported the incursions, and the Bolivian Foreign Ministry duly issued formal protests that Santiago continued to ignore. Periodic Bolivian diplomatic missions to Santiago, such as that of José María Santivañez in 1860, proposed various face-saving solutions, all of which began with the assumption that Bolivia would abandon at least part of the territory granted to it under *uti possidetis*, but each successive Chilean administration stuck to Bulnes' setting of the border at Mejillones, which the Bolivians just as stubbornly continued to consider a strictly "internal" declaration by Chile.[7]

It was only in 1863 that the Bolivian government was finally shocked into more concrete action by the actual occupation of Mejillones by a detachment of troops landed from the Chilean frigate *Esmeralda* under the command of Captain Juan Williams Rebolledo. Its patience spent and spurred on by popular demonstrations against Chile in the streets of Bolivia's cities, on 5 June 1863 the Bolivian legislature formally authorized the president to "declare war on the government of the Republic of Chile, in the event that, all conciliatory and diplomatic means being exhausted, no return of the usurped territory or a peaceful solution compatible with national dignity can be achieved."[8]

At this point it seemed highly unlikely that any solution was about to be reached, but the conflict over the boundary was overtaken by the larger conflict brought about by the encroachment of the Spanish flotilla on the Peruvian Chincha Islands and their rich product of guano. Bolivia initially remained neutral in the dispute, even after the adhesion of Chile to the Peruvian cause, and Spanish ships were able to obtain provisions at Cobija, the only port open to them for hundreds of miles in either direction. This fact was not lost on the Chileans, and it was primarily to deal with this situation that the Chilean envoy Aniceto Vergara Albano was sent to La Paz in March of 1866.

As it happened, the obsequiously pro-Chilean Bolivian President Melgarejo had already cancelled Bolivia's neutrality the previous month, at least to the point of closing her ports to the Spanish, since Bolivia, without a navy, had nothing else to contribute to the struggle. Allegedly, Vergara was armed with instructions from Chilean President Joaquin Pérez to grant the Bolivians virtual *carte blanche* in drawing the borderline wherever they chose. The potential future income from guano exploitation, much of which would flow into Chile in any event since Chilean capital and talent were developing the region almost exclusively, seemed a small price to pay for essentially guaranteeing that the powerful Spanish fleet would be obliged to withdraw in short order, as in fact occurred. Melgarejo, however, completely enchanted by the Chilean diplomat's compliments and attentions, refused to lower himself to haggle over such mundane issues while the war was on (although he chose not to take any part in it), and it was not until after the last Spanish masthead had disappeared over the southern horizon that he finally sat down to discuss the boundary dispute.[9]

Needless to say, the Chileans were substantially less motivated to make concessions now that the immediate threat had disappeared and were even buoyed by the valiant performance of their own tiny navy in confronting superior Spanish forces. What resulted was the Treaty of 1866 that at least had the merit of obliging both sides to recognize a common basis for division of the territory, however flawed the agreement and however unpopular, particularly in Bolivia. Heretofore, there had been simply widely divergent claims supported on the Chilean side by the use or threat of armed force.

The provisions of the treaty called for setting a formal frontier at 24° South with the condition that Bolivia and Chile would share equally in the duties on the guano and minerals extracted from the area between 23° and 25°, with a slight addition of a triangle of territory made by running a line north from the point where the 25th parallel intersected the crest of the Andes, Chile's normal inland limit, up to the 23rd parallel, thus giving Chile some hundreds of square miles extra (since the Andes shifted slightly westward toward the coast in this area). Thus, Bolivia formally gave up all claim to any territory south of the 25th parallel, while Chile retained at least some interest in all the territory of her most extravagant claims, even adding some east of the Andes. Furthermore, since the Chilean study of the region made back in 1842 showed no significant nitrate or guano deposits south of 24° South, only Chile benefited from this strange condominium. Mejillones would be the main clearinghouse for guano exports, and both countries would station customs officials there, although the port was located north of the 23rd parallel. All other exports from the region would be duty-free as would imports of Chilean products brought in through Mejillones, thus giving the budding Chilean manufacturing industry a substantial advantage in the Bolivian marketplace.[10] The treaty was quickly ratified in Santiago, and, since Melgarejo paid no attention to popular protests in Bolivia, it was formalized there as well. The treaty was quickly ratified in Santiago, and, since Melgarejo paid no attention to popular protests in Bolivia, it was formalized there as well.

One of the main flaws with the 1866 treaty was that it failed to specify what other "minerals" besides guano were meant to be included in the 50-50 split in duties between the two countries. Since it was the territory north of the 24th parallel that proved to be rich in a variety of natural resources, it was naturally Bolivia that attempted to restrict this definition and Chile that tried to expand it. This dispute came to a head in 1871 with the discovery of a massive silver vein at Caracoles. While the town of Caracoles was just south of the 23rd parallel, Bolivia claimed that the mines themselves, notably the "La Deseada" mine, were east of the territory covered by the treaty, thus making all proceeds Bolivian property, and Chilean engineers insisted that the mines did lie within the treaty territory, with the Chilean claims being supported by the fact that virtually all the capital and ten thousand miners involved in the operations were Chilean.[11]

The pro-Chilean Melgarejo might have agreed to some kind of solution that would have been acceptable to Chile, but he had been ousted by the much less malleable General Morales who dedicated much of his short administration to undoing as much of Melgarejo's work as possible. With this in mind, Morales dispatched Rafael Bustillo, former Minister of Foreign Affairs, to Santiago to renegotiate the 1866 treaty. Bustillo was received graciously enough by President Perez, but serious discussions were put off for one month until October 1871 when the newly elected Federico Errazuriz Zañarte would assume the presidency. However, seeing the current arrangement as highly favorable to Chile, Errazuriz simply ignored the Bolivian envoy, leaving his irascible Foreign Minister, Adolfo Ibañez to deal with Bustillo, offering one unacceptable proposal after another, such as the ending of the condominium in exchange for *all* the revenue of the guano exported from Mejillones or the outright purchase of the land south of 23° South by Chile.

It was about this time that the first suggestions were floated by the *Casa de la Moneda* (Chile's White House) that Bolivia cede the whole of the province of

Atacama to Chile in exchange for which Chile would support Bolivia in a war to take a large slice of Peruvian territory, including the port of Arica. This scheme proved of lasting attraction to Chile in that it would not only give Chile the Atacama's valuable guano, nitrates, and silver deposits, but it would still leave a buffer of Bolivian territory between Chile and Peru, while weakening the only other Pacific coast nation capable of posing a serious military threat to Chile. At the same time, such an action would permanently estrange Bolivia from Peru, preventing any future alliance while making Bolivia just as permanently dependent upon Chilean support to prevent Peruvian revanchism. Morales flatly rejected the proposal, but it made such logical sense to Santiago that it would be raised anew again and again throughout the rest of the decade and right through the War of the Pacific itself.[12]

To complicate things further, the ex-dictator Melgarejo was smoldering in exile in Santiago at the time. With the support of General Quintin Quevedo and a handful of other expatriate rebels, Melgarejo was busily plotting a return to power. In July of 1872 Bustillo discovered, since diplomats in those days performed many of the services now reserved for professional intelligence officers, that Quevedo and a handful of émigrés planned to take ship in Valparaíso for the new Bolivian nitrate port of Antofogasta and begin a march on La Paz from there, gathering support as they went. Bustillo launched a formal demarche to the Chilean government, and the authorities apparently did detain some Bolivian revolutionaries, although no arms were discovered. Quevedo, however, evaded pursuit aboard the ship *Paquete de los Vilos*, and stormed ashore at Antofogasta, taking prisoner the few Bolivian gendarmes present at the port. Regular Bolivian troops soon marched on the town, and Quevedo quickly abandoned the project, taking refuge aboard the Chilean frigate *Esmeralda*, then at anchor in the harbor.[13]

In a rage, Bustillo accused the Chilean government of complicity in the Quevedo affair and was declared *persona non grata* for his trouble and bundled off back to La Paz. The Chileans denied any involvement, although it is possible that Chilean speculators may have provided funding for the uprising, in the hopes of obtaining favorable mining concessions from a grateful Melgarejo upon his return to power. Melgarejo would soon find a bloody end in Lima in a mundane family dispute, and the imminent threat from Bolivian political exiles seemed to have receded, the fact that the ill-fated expedition had originated in a Chilean port and that the culprits had taken refuge on a Chilean ship gave La Paz cause to believe that Chile intended to resolve the outstanding disputes in the Atacama through some kind of force. It was also increasingly evident that Bolivia lacked the military strength to resist any serious encroachment in its coastal province.[14]

It was thus that the regimes of Morales in Bolivia and that of José Balta in Peru began talks regarding a formal alliance between the two nations directed against Chile. Such an alliance was a natural development, especially after Chile had placed an order for two new ironclads with a British shipyard, both of which would be superior to anything in the Peruvian Navy. As tensions rose between La Paz and Santiago over the Quevedo affair, Peruvian Foreign

Minister José de la Riva Aguero commented in August 1872 that "Peru cannot be indifferent to the occupation of Bolivian territory by foreign forces," as a clear warning to Chile.[15]   The assassination of Morales in December 1872 caused a delay in the negotiations, but the treaty was finally signed in February 1873.[16]

As a treaty of defensive alliance, the 1873 treaty was really rather thin. It called for each party to oppose the loss of territory by the other or a forcible change of government imposed by a third power. In such an instance, the signatory not under attack promised to break diplomatic relations with the aggressor, but beyond that it left it to each party to determine the proper measure of force to commit in support of its ally. The only other consideration was that each party promised not to make a separate peace with the aggressor. But the key provision was that the existence of the treaty was to be kept a strict secret.

Much has been made, particularly by Chilean government officials during the war years of the secret nature of this document and the righteous indignation they felt at this obviously anti-Chilean posture by their partner in the Atacama condominium and the nature to whose aid Chile had rallied in the war with Spain. Given the fact that Bolivia went through no less than five administrations and Peru three from the start of the talks until the outbreak of the war, it seems unlikely that the Chileans were taken much by surprise. This is all the more unlikely given the frantic efforts by Peruvian diplomats to enlist the membership of Argentina in the alliance, spreading the knowledge even further afield. In fact, it is likely that *La Moneda* learned of the existence of the "secret" treaty as early as October 1873 but intentionally chose to keep this fact a secret in its turn in the hope of luring Bolivia and Peru into some ill-conceived action based on the supposition of Chilean ignorance which might ultimately work to Chile's benefit.[17]

At the time, the risk of discovery seemed acceptable in the hope of gaining the support of Argentina, with her substantial army and navy, for the alliance. It should be remembered that Chile and Argentina were involved in a long-standing dispute over both control of the Straits of Magellan, which Chile felt it necessary to dominate for their entire length or face a possible blockade by Argentina, and huge stretches of Patagonia on the east side of the Andes. Despite the best efforts of both Bolivia and Peru, and a generally favorable hearing their arguments received in Buenos Aires, nothing finally came of the campaign, even though adherence to the alliance was actually approved by the Argentine lower house in September 1873 before being rejected by the Senate. The majority of Argentine leaders feared that Chile would simply turn to Argentina's primary rival for supremacy on the eastern side of the continent, even more powerful Brazil, and form its own alliance, leaving Argentina dependent upon her two weak and unstable allies in the face of a superior force.[18]

Although the alliance with Peru, secret or not, greatly enhanced Bolivia's position vis-à-vis the Chileans, La Paz and Santiago also made a serious effort during this period to work out the kinks in the 1866 treaty in such a way as to avoid future conflicts altogether. The first attempt was made even while the secret alliance was being hammered out. Chilean envoy Santiago Lindsay met frequently with Bolivian Foreign Minister Casimiro Corral in La Paz in late 1872 to deal with the two primary points of confusion in the 1866 treaty, the exact nature of the Atacama minerals in whose export duties Bolivia and Chile were to share and the eastern limit of the zone of condominium. While the Chilean legislature approved the agreement quickly, the Bolivian congress of 1873 put off any decision until after the 1874 elections, and the new delegates then rejected the measure.[19]

Undeterred by this setback, Bolivian and Chilean diplomats continued to work on the problem and, in August of 1874, a new treaty was signed and ratified by both countries. The crest of the Andes would be the new eastern boundary of the condominium zone, and only the export of nitrates would result in shared duties, although Bolivia agreed to pay a certain fixed sum (to be determined by international arbitration) to Chile in exchange. The clause of the treaty that would prove most significant in coming years, however, was added almost as an afterthought. Since most of the companies working in the Atacama were wholly or largely Chilean, it was agreed that Chilean firms would not have to pay any additional taxes of any kind for a period of twenty-five years.[20] Chilean customs officials would still be posted to Mejillones, a sore point on the issue of Bolivian sovereignty, but the much clearer division of the territory eased tensions considerably. This modification of the treaty was decidedly to Bolivia's benefit, and it is possible that a recent heating up of the tension between Argentina and Chile over their disputed borders, coupled with the fact that Chile's new ironclads had not yet been delivered, may have motivated Santiago to be more amenable.

It would be worthwhile at this point to discuss the formation and development of the Antofagasta Nitrate and Railroad Company (ANRC), a firm that would figure prominently in the slide toward open war. One of the first things that Morales had done after the overthrow of Melgarejo was to cancel the unprofitable contracts the dictator had granted to a number of foreign companies to mine nitrates in the Atacama. Two of the largest former contractors, the Chilean firm of Ossa and Puelma and the British-Chilean Melbourne, Clark & Company, combined to form the ANRC in 1872 with a number of senior Chilean politicians among the stockholders, including Foreign Minister Alejandro Fierro.[21] The ANRC was granted a virtual monopoly over nitrate extraction in the Bolivian Atacama with a heavy subsidy from the Bolivian government in both lands and in funding for the establishment of the physical plant necessary for processing the nitrates. The firm was also involved in railroad construction, with plans to link both Antofagasta and Mejillones with the silver mines of Caracoles, tying in the largest nitrate mining sites along the way, and ultimately to the Altiplano, although this latter phase was never actually undertaken.[22]

With most of the points of dispute cleared away, relations between Bolivia and Chile improved somewhat over the next few years, but pressures were nevertheless building toward war. In early 1975 Chile received delivery of two new ironclads, the *Valparaíso* (later renamed the *Blanco Encalada*) and the

Cochrane, giving Chile theoretical control over, not just the coastal area itself, but also Peru's and Bolivia's transportation lines to Europe, whence any significant new arms deliveries must come. At the same time, all three nations entered into a period of gradual but accelerating economic decline as was discussed in the preceding chapter. For Bolivia and Chile, therefore, the revenues derived from the Atacama nitrate operations assumed ever greater importance and motivated each government to seek out means of increasing its share of those revenues by one means or another. Chilean relations with Peru also suffered during this period for the simple reason that Peruvian nitrates were apparently of substantially superior quality to those obtained by Chilean firms in the Atacama, and the Peruvian nationalization of the nitrate industry in her own territory effectively denied this field of investment to Chilean firms. Although Peru had every right to conduct business within her own borders by her own lights, resentment grew in Chile which was fed by a jingoistic press and unscrupulous opposition politicians who were willing to use any issue as a club with which to attack Chilean President Aníbal Pinto for lack of decisive action.[23]

In May of 1877 a devastating tidal wave struck the Pacific coast of South America, causing extensive damage to Arica, Pisagua, and Callao, but the hardest hit was the port of Antofagasta, with most of the buildings in town being swept away. The municipal council of the port, which interestingly was composed almost entirely of Chilean nationals, voted a municipal tax of ten *centavos* per quintal (about 100 pounds) of nitrates exported through the port in place of some lesser municipal fees then in place and, presumably to provide a larger revenue base, in order to finance the reconstruction of the town. The council also proposed collecting a small fee from each property owner to cover the expense of providing street lighting. Since the ANRC owned approximately half of the real estate in Antofagasta, the company was expected to contribute to this as well. In February 1878, the Bolivian legislature validated the new municipal tax.

The directors of the ANRC protested immediately, and their local manager, John Hicks, a British citizen, simply refused to pay, citing a clear violation of the provisions of the 1874 treaty that had promised no new taxes for twenty-five years for Chilean businesses. The Bolivian government countered by referring to a little-known statute passed in November 1873 which prohibited any decree by the central government that invalidated *municipal* taxes and had Mr. Hicks arrested for his fervent defense of company interests.[24]

The Chilean ambassador in La Paz, Pedro Nolasco Videla, protested immediately and vociferously, threatening that Chile might find it necessary to "reclaim" the territory "ceded" to Bolivia under the 1874 treaty - that from 23° to 24° South - if the treaty were being abrogated. ANRC officials, however, had no real desire for a permanent disruption of the nitrate trade and suggested paying a *voluntary* contribution of a flat 1,600 pesos per year, which would cover the street lighting fees and a certain amount toward the municipal reconstruction costs. Bolivian Foreign Minister Manuel Ignacio Salvatierra, while refusing to nullify the municipal council's action formally, promised simply that the tax would not be collected, and Santiago grudgingly accepted, possibly because tensions with Argentina over Patagonia were running particularly high at the moment, and *La Moneda* did not want to face two foreign opponents at the same time.[25]

For the moment, it seemed that cooler heads had prevailed, but this was merely the calm before the storm as, in December of that year, an event that seemed to defuse one international crisis merely served to fuel another. The Fierro-Sarratea Treaty between Chile and Argentina seemed to put an end to the dispute over Patagonia and the Straits of Magellan (although this latter issue would still be percolating for another century and more). The treaty was roundly attacked by the political opponents of the Pinto administration in Santiago as a sell-out of the Chilean patrimony, even though Chilean claims to the vast, unpopulated tract of land on the other side of the virtually impassible Andes was always thin at best.

Pinto weathered this domestic storm, but it seems that the virulence of the press attacks, accusing Pinto of cowardice and buckling under foreign pressure, had an unfortunate impact on Bolivian President Hilarion Daza. Far from recognizing that Chile had eliminated a major foreign threat through the treaty, freeing her to devote all of her attention to the north, Daza apparently believed that the Fierro-Sarratea Treaty really was a sell-out, indicative of a lack of backbone in *La Moneda* that he might well exploit to his advantage. Consequently, barely a week after the signing of the Chilean-Argentine treaty, Daza announced that the suspension of the Antofagasta ten-centavo tax was at an end and that it must now be paid *retroactively* from the date of its original passage.[26]

Clearly, there was something more at work here than the simple desire to bring in a minimal amount of additional revenue. Daza, a tempestuous soldier of limited education who had led a palace revolution against President Ballivian, the signer of the 1874 treaty, apparently saw the no-tax clause as one of the last insults to Bolivian sovereignty imposed by Melgarejo's despised 1866 treaty, denying as it did the Bolivian government's right to perform its duties on its own soil as it saw fit. The very fact that the legislature in La Paz found it necessary to vote on what they claimed was a strictly municipal issue when the tax was first levied implied that the conflict with the 1874 treaty was clearly seen and that a conscious precedent was being set. In fact, all parties, including the ANRC and the Chilean government, recognized this fact as well, thus the strong protests and the clever maneuver by the ANRC to provide funds without formally acknowledging the authority of the Bolivian government to collect them.[27]

If Daza had expected a quick capitulation or tacit acceptance of his move, he made a serious miscalculation. The indomitable Mr. Hicks again refused to pay a cent, and the Chilean ironclad *Blanco Encalada* was sent to anchor in Antofagasta harbor while the rest of the Chilean fleet was being mobilized. Not to be cowed, Daza declared that the contract for nitrate extraction of the ANRC was thenceforth cancelled and ordered all company property to be impounded by the state until it could be sold at auction, setting 14 February 1879 as the date for the sale.[28] Daza was apparently working on the theory that, if no contract existed, the party subject to the tax would also cease to exist, thus technically removing the basis for the conflict.

Popular demonstrations swept the capitals of both countries, with gangs of youths waving the national flag, stoning the odd business owned by "enemy" citizens, and loudly calling for even stronger action by their government. The directors of the ANRC, in order to spare their faithful servant another stint in a Bolivian jail, ordered Mr. Hicks to take refuge aboard a Chilean warship in the harbor, of which there were plenty as *Cochrane and O'Higgins* had now joined *Blanco Encalada* off the port.

Meanwhile, on 10 February, Ambassador Videla in La Paz delivered an ultimatum, originally dated 20 January but just arrived by messenger from Santiago, that demanded Bolivia accept international arbitration of the dispute within forty-eight hours, or the government of Chile would consider the 1874 treaty null and void and would order the "reoccupation" of "Chilean" territory "ceded" by the treaty, that is, everything up to and including Mejillones. President Daza waited until the deadline had come and gone and replied on the 12th simply that the tone of the Chilean ultimatum, "could induce my government to judge that your excellency is not disposed to continue a policy of peace, conciliation, and fraternity such as should reign between the states of this continent."[29]   Videla consequently asked for his passports and informed Santiago that diplomatic relations had been severed.

On the morning of the 14th, two hundred Chilean soldiers and sailors landed at Antofagasta, and the commander informed Colonel Severino Zapata, the prefect of the port, of their intention to "reoccupy" the territory. Since Zapata had only a few dozen gendarmes on hand, he saw no point in resisting and withdrew to Cobija, his passage and that of the other Bolivian officials present being facilitated by the Chileans. It should be noted that, of a population of nearly six thousand at this point, Antofagasta was home to over five thousand Chileans, two hundred Argentines, a handful of Europeans, and less than six hundred Bolivians, and the Chileans were able to raise a substantial militia from among their own countrymen in the "reoccupied" territory.[30]

News of the landings reached La Paz within a few days, but, for reasons never quite made clear, Daza withheld any proclamations for another week, allegedly to avoid putting a damper on the Carnival celebrations then underway, but, on 27 February, the Bolivian legislature issued the authorization for a declaration of war, although the formal declaration would not be forthcoming until 14 March. Now the diplomatic confrontation shifted into high gear. Only one piece remained to fall into place to determine whether a real war would now occur or whether some sort of deal might yet be struck. This was the question of whether or not Peru would honor the 1873 "secret" treaty and come to Bolivia's aid.

There was a strong pacifist sentiment in Peru when word first arrived in Lima of the Chilean incursion. After all, no blood had yet been shed, and there would still be a substantial swath of Bolivian territory separating Peru from Chile. It was also widely discussed in the fashionable coffee shops of Miraflores that the war would turn on control of the sea, since land transportation up and down the coast was virtually impossible for large armies, and the newly augmented

Chilean navy was feared to be markedly superior to that of Peru. So, why get involved in a war over the territory of another country when the chances of success were so slim? And, was it not likely that, without Peru's support, Bolivia would simply see the wisdom in acceding to Chilean demands and avoiding the war altogether?

President Mariano Ignacio Prado, however, like a player in a complex game of chess, had to think several moves ahead. It was not simply a question of Peru's honor in abiding by her word in the treaty, since a strong argument could be made that Bolivia had stumbled into this crisis of her own choosing without consulting with her ostensible ally and had even declared war without previously informing Lima. His concern was that, if Peru should deny support to Bolivia, the latter would be forced to seek an accommodation with Chile that would probably include a new Bolivian-Chilean alliance aimed at seizing Arica for Bolivia. While Peru and Bolivia, with a combined population double that of Chile, would stand a fair chance of defeating Chile, and even Peru alone might be able to defend herself against Chile alone, there was no chance that Peru could resist a combination of Chile and Bolivia. And, once Peru had been stripped of her lucrative nitrate provinces, to say nothing of the loss of territory and population, who could say when the arrogant Chileans might be satisfied when no country along the Pacific coast could stand against them?

Consequently, Prado sent José Antonio Lavalle to Santiago to see if the conflict could be avoided at the last moment, while José Arnoldo Márquez was sent to Buenos Aires in a last, desperate effort to secure an alliance with the other major power of the Southern Cone.[31] The Márquez mission was doomed from the outset, with Argentina just having signed the Fierro-Sarratea Treaty and with the fear of possible Brazilian intervention just as potent as it had been several years before when Argentina had chosen not to join in the original Bolivian-Peruvian pact. In hindsight, Lavalle's mission stood no better chance, but it took substantially longer to play out.

Lavalle departed Lima on 22 February, well before the Bolivian declaration of war, but nothing irreversible was to occur for some time, so he did have some freedom of maneuver in Santiago. As minister plenipotentiary, Lavalle had instructions to seek a return to the status quo of 1 November 1878, with the suspension of the ten *centavo* tax still in place, the property of the ANRC unencumbered, the ANRC contract with the Bolivian government still in effect, and with Chilean troops to be withdrawn from Antofagasta. The entire issue was then to be submitted for arbitration with Peru offering its good offices for the purpose. It should be noted that Lavalle had the verbal consent of the Bolivian government for this approach, as even Daza had apparently realized that, with Peru's reluctance to war at this point, a peaceful solution had better be sought. Lavalle was not received by President Pinto and Foreign Minister Fierro until 11 March, however, a full ten days after his arrival, which did not bode well for the Chilean attitude, and he was immediately questioned about the existence of the 1873 "secret" treaty between Peru and Bolivia. This placed Lavalle in an extremely uncomfortable position for a diplomat. Even though the treaty was essentially an open secret by this time, it was not officially acknowledged, and its clandestine character gave Peru's offer of mediation a highly insincere ring.[32]

After what must have been considerable hemming and hawing and pleas for the necessity of consulting with Lima, Lavalle met again with Pinto on 21 March only to receive a formal demand from the president that Peru specifically declare its neutrality in the conflict between Chile and Bolivia. Pinto added that the return of the Atacama to Bolivia was now quite out of the question, claiming that outrage on the part of the Chilean public at such an action would bring his government down, even if he had been personally inclined to such an action. In response to this pressure, Pinto had already ordered additional troops to Antofagasta and was preparing columns to occupy the rest of the Bolivian coastal province, up to the Peruvian border in order better to protect the nitrate region from a Bolivian counterstroke. As a sweetener, Pinto suggested that Chile could impose a unilateral restriction on nitrate exports from this newly acquired territory, which would certainly be a financial benefit for Peru's nationalized nitrate industry if Peru would acquiesce in the Chilean occupation of the territory.[33]

Lavalle replied unofficially that he did not believe that President Prado would be able to accede to such demands or to accept such a blatant bribe precisely because opposition political pressure would oust him just as Pinto feared would be the case in Chile. Chilean Ambassador Godoy in Lima had received a similar response directly from President Prado and had requested his passports. Word had now reached Santiago of the Bolivian declaration of war, and, on 4 April the Chilean legislature authorized the severance of diplomatic relations with both Bolivia and Peru, and on 5 April, Chile formally declared war on the allies.[34]

So, what then was the actual cause of the war? The issue of the ten-*centavo* tax, which gave the war its popular name in the press, is far too simplistic. Neither Bolivia, Chile, nor the ANRC could possibly have considered the revenue to be gained or lost by this law even remotely to validate the immense expenditures that even a brief conflict would inevitably entail. Lest the economic determinists assume that this is a classic case of one of the early forms of multi-national corporations leading a Third World government about by the nose, it is worth noting that one of the first acts of the Chilean government after the start of the war was to impose a *forty centavo* tax on nitrate exports, and this was only the start as war costs rose and the war stretched on month after month.[35]

The official Chilean argument was that Bolivian provocation threatened the Chilean communities who had created "cities in the desert" and that the combination of Bolivia and Peru in a hostile alliance threatened Chile's sovereignty and territorial integrity, with the decision to war being taken in Santiago only after "much agonizing."[36] This view would ignore the steady progress of the Chilean border from 27° South, up through the effective border thirty-five years before at 25°30', to 24° with the treaty of 1866, to 23° on 14 February 1879 and on to the River Loa almost immediately thereafter. The most extreme Chilean territorial claims, unsupported by tradition or law, had transformed themselves into historical necessity. The advance beyond even these limits would be justified by the dictates of national security, as would be the case in the further advance into Peruvian territory, prompted by the intransigence of the allies and the justifiable right of the conqueror to exact reparations in money or in kind from the vanquished.

On the other hand, the sorry state of the Chilean armed forces at the outbreak of the war, as will be discussed in the following chapter, hardly supports a theory of conscious, premeditated aggression. Looking at the situation with the attitude of the late twentieth century, we can see that Chile had it perfectly within her power to institute a naval blockade of the Bolivian coast which would have cut off all revenues to a government already on the verge of bankruptcy, and it is highly unlikely that Peru, with her inferior navy, would have challenged the action, particularly since such would not have invoked the "secret" treaty at all, with no territorial losses or imposed change of government involved. But this would be to ignore the mindset of the late nineteenth century, one that manifested itself in the European powers and the United States just as much as in the developing nations, a mindset that granted overwhelming importance to the maintenance of national honor and the rights of expatriate businessmen, providing the theoretical basis for "gunboat diplomacy" that would be practiced extensively, particularly in Latin America, well into the next century.

The argument that the attitude of the peoples of the region was just ripe for war seems best to fit the bill. The Chileans were suffering from a severe case of self-doubt rising from the economic decline of the past decade after a period of boom times, and the national sense of racial and social superiority to the "Indian" peoples to the north called for a cleansing contest in which they fully expected to emerge victorious. For similar reasons, the Bolivians were not about to be humiliated (again) by Chile, and Peru found herself dragged into the conflict for fear that neutrality would drive Bolivia into the arms of the Chileans.

Lastly, all three governments were to a considerable extent prisoner to the whims of the crowd. While only Chile had a functioning democracy at the moment even in the broadest definition of the term, all recognized freedom of the press, to a certain degree, and opposition political groups could make their wishes known. None of the regimes had a firm enough grasp on power to risk taking the wildly unpopular stand that conciliation would have entailed. Woodrow Wilson might have taken note of this phenomenon when constructing his own theory of international relations, relying on public opinion and the good will of the informed voter to prevent nations from going to war. When it comes right down to it, the public can be very foolish, vindictive, and shortsighted in any nation, at any time.

NOTES

1. Miguel Mercado M., *Historia Internacional de Bolivia*. La Paz: Editorial Don Bosco, 1972, p. 413.

2. Roberto Querejazu Calvo, *Guano, Salitre, Sangre*. La Paz: Editorial Los Amigos del Libro, 1979, p. 4.

3. Valentin Baldivieso Abecia, *Las Relaciones Internacionales en la Historia de Bolivia*, vol. 1, La Paz: Editorial Los Amigos del Libro, 1979, p. 518.

4. William Jefferson Dennis, *Tacna and Arica,* New York: Archon Books, 1967, p. 11.

5. Mercado, p. 415.

6. Gonzalo Bulnes, *Guerra del Pacífico,* vol. 1, Santiago de Chile: Editorial del Pacífico, 1955, p. 33.

7. Mercado, p. 422.

8. Ibid., p. 423.

9. Querejazu, op. cit., p. 55.

10. Dennis, p. 46.

11. Querejazu, op. cit., p. 74.

12. Abecia, vol. 1, p. 668.

13. Robert N. Burr, *By Reason or Force: Chile and the Balance of Power in South America.* Berkeley: University of California Press, 1975, p. 122.

14. Alcides Arguedas, *Los Caudillos Barbaros,* La Paz: Gisbert & Cía., S.A., 1975, p. 273.

15. Arturo Garcia Salazar, *Resumen de Historia Diplomatica del Peru, 1820-1884,* Lima: Editorial Los Andes, 1928, pp. 159-160.

16. Thomas McLeod Bader, *A Willingness to War: A Portrait of the Republic of Chile during the Years Preceding the War of the Pacific,* Ann Arbor, MI: Xerox University Microfilm, 1967, p. 152.

17. Bader, p. 292.

18. Burr, p. 126.

19. Abecia, vol. 1, p. 751.

20. Ibid., 768.

21. Abecia, vol. 2, p. 52.

22. Simon Collier and William F. Sater, *A History of Chile, 1808-1994,* New York: Cambridge University Press, 1997, p. 87.

23. Ronald Bruce St. John, *The Foreign Policy of Peru,* Boulder, CO: Lynne Reinner, 1992, p. 92.

24. Querejazu, op. cit., p. 182.

25. Ibid., p. 195.

26. St. John, p. 103.

27. William F. Sater, *Chile and the War of the Pacific.* Lincoln: University of Nebraska Press, 1986, p. 9.

28. St. John, p. 104.

29. Querejazu, op. cit., 233.

30. Ibid., p. 247.

31. Fredrick B. Pike, *The History of Modern Peru,* New York: Praeger, 1982, p. 142.

32. Abecia, vol. 2, p. 66.

33. Sater, p. 11.

34. St. John, p. 108.

35. Abecia, vol. 2, p. 32.

36. Sater, p. 3.

Chapter Four

Opening Moves

It is a natural tendency, when looking at a war in retrospect, to see the outcome as all but inevitable. The advantages of the victors assume overwhelming proportions and the flaws of the defeated seem irremediable. Such has been the case with the War of the Pacific. Chile's complete victory has earned the country the sobriquet of the "Prussia of South America," even though this was the only war in which Chile would be engaged in over more than a century and a half. Such a perception gives rise to the assumption that the war was one of out-and-out aggression by a regional super power against virtually defenseless neighbors, and this is one of the many points of coincidence between elements of the War of the Pacific and the war between the United States and Mexico a generation before. A closer look will demonstrate that the two sides were much more evenly matched than the results might indicate and, at a number of junctures during the conflict, the issue was much more of a "near run thing" than has generally been recognized.

At the outbreak of the war, the Chilean armed forces did not inspire much awe in either their size or organization. Due to the economic crisis through which the country passed in the 1870s, the regular army had been cut by some 20 percent to less than three thousand men. There were about five hundred cavalry, four hundred artillerymen, and the remainder infantry divided into five small regiments.[1] The National Guard, something comparable to the state militias of the United States prior to the Civil War, stood at barely 18,000 men, down from nearly 30,000 in 1873, and actual strength was consistently lower than that authorized by the legislature.

The only significant arms purchases for the army had been a shipment of sixteen modern Krupp field guns, six Gatling-type machineguns, and some consignments of Winchester and Spencer repeating rifles back in 1874, with many National Guard units still armed with venerable Springfield cap-and-ball muskets of American Civil War vintage.[2] By the standards of the region, however, the Chilean Army was fairly well equipped. The regular infantry was armed with the modern Belgian Comblain rifle of which Chile had a stock of some 13,000, with the Winchester and Spencer carbines going to the cavalry, thus allowing for a rapid expansion of the regular army and the call-up of large contingents of the National Guard without waiting for new arms shipments, unlike the situation for the allies. The uniformity of Chilean equipment also went far to simplify logistical arrangements in the supply of ammunition to the field. There were also several thousand older weapons on hand for the National Guard and several million rounds of ammunition as well as a rudimentary capability for manufacturing small arms cartridges that would relieve the country at least of the immediate need to import munitions in order to undertake the first moves of the conflict.[3]

In the preceding decades, much of the active duty army had been deployed along the southern frontier, engaged in small unit actions against the wily and resourceful Araucan Indians, an undertaking that gave small unit commanders some experience in fieldcraft and combat but did little to prepare the army or its commanders in large scale maneuver or logistics. In fact, after the brief war against the Bolivian-Peruvian confederation, the army had eliminated the quartermaster corps entirely in the 1840s and relied on civilian contractors and local requisitions to procure and deliver supplies for the troops, a system which may have worked adequately for skirmishes with the Indians but did not stand up to the strains of a major campaign hundreds of miles from the country's population centers and for an army that eventually swelled to some 40,000 men. It almost goes without saying that an army that saw no need for logistical support would see no need for an adequate medical corps, and this had also been disbanded as a cost-cutting measure in 1878.[4]

The initial army of invasion landed at Antofagasta consisted of a mixed force of five hundred men under Colonel Emilio Sotomayor. This was gradually built up during late February and March 1879 to some 2,000 men of all three arms plus an equal number provided by recruits from the Chilean workers resident in Antofagasta, Salinas, and Caracoles for whom a supply of Belgian Comblain rifles had been shipped to the occupied territory. The regulars included the 2nd and 3rd Line Regiments, a single cavalry company, a battery of field artillery, and another of naval artillery installed to protect the port of Antofagasta itself.[5] As small a force as this was, it represented virtually Chile's entire prewar military establishment.

The Pinto government counted on the National Guard to supply the manpower that would undoubtedly be necessary in a war against Chile's two northern neighbors. Legally, all able-bodied men nominally were supposed to belong to the Guard and to drill with their local unit on Sundays and holidays and to rally to the colors in times of national crisis. Such requirements were largely ignored by the upper classes and strongly resented by the workers who had no desire to spend their only day off marching about in the dust and heat. Because of this theoretical *levée en masse*, there was a specific prohibition in Chilean law against conscription, which presented the government with unusual problems in filling out the ranks of the regular battalions to make them regiments of twelve hundred men each, a fourfold increase in the size of the army without considering the National Guard.[6]

As in most every war since the dawn of time, there was an enthusiastic flood of young men to the recruiting stations at the first news of the outbreak of the war and the call for volunteers, men fearful of "missing" the glory. As in most Latin American countries, the military in Chile was not considered a favorable career for the sons of the upper crust of society and was used primarily as a means of social advancement for new immigrants and the lower middle class. However, but the sudden fervor for war encouraged hundreds of well-to-do youths to enlist, usually taking advantage of family connections to obtain genteel positions on the staff of a senior officer rather than as a common foot soldier. The ranks of the army were also swelled by the thousands of *rotos*, the common workers who had been employed in Peruvian mining operations, on farms, and on railroad construction and who were summarily expelled from the country at the declaration of war and now returned home with no place to go and no job prospects, to say nothing of a personal interest in gaining revenge.

However, this source of manpower quickly petered out. The Pinto administration offered a bounty for new recruits, since the common soldier's pay of eleven dollars per month plus a small stipend for family men, was hardly a living wage; but there was, in fact, no money in the treasury to make good such largess, and the government was faced with the unappealing proposition of hundreds of disgruntled young men, cheated out of their promised money and now, thanks to the army quartermaster, fully armed and organized in fighting units. Finally, the government was forced to resort to conscription on a large scale, but there was widespread corruption, with wealthy families paying for fraudulent medical exemptions or hiring proxies while press gangs roamed the countryside and the city streets, sweeping up the idle and the unwary, but this would only be seen later in the war.[7]

The Chilean navy, the vaunted force that struck terror into the hearts of the other nations of the continent, was hardly in any better condition in 1879. Since the vulnerability of the republic to hostile seapower had been clearly demonstrated during the conflict with Spain in the 1860s, culminating with the bombardment of defenseless Valparaíso, there had been a strong impulse to create a force that would dominate the waters from the Straits of Magellan up to Panama and beyond. President Errazuriz had therefore contracted with the British firm of Earle's Shipbuilders at Hull for the construction of two ironclads, the *Cochrane* and the *Blanco Encalada*, identical armored frigates that were delivered in 1874 and 1875 respectively. Each boasted six massive 9-inch guns, each weighing twelve tons and throwing a shell weighing 250 pounds plus a pair of smaller 70-pounders and another pair of 9-pounders for close-in work, all of which were muzzle-loaders. They were the latest thing in naval engineering with 2,960 horsepower engines capable of turning their twin propellers for up to thirteen knots with a displacement of just over two thousand tons and a protective layer of 9½ inches of steel armor plate amidships at the waterline, tapering to 4½" at bow and stern, with 6-8 inches of armor topside backed by 14 inches of solid teak.[8] They were thus faster than anything possessed by any nation along the Pacific coast of South America, threw a greater weight of metal, and were virtually invulnerable to the fire of any gun deployed in the region.[9]

These two behemoths were ably supported by four wooden steam corvettes, the O'Higgins Chacabuco, Esmeralda, and the Magallanes, all British-built as well. The first two were identical, at eleven hundred tons with three 115-pounders, two 70-pounders, four 40-pounders, and a pair of 6-pounders and rated at eleven knots (with clean bottoms, although neither could actually do much more than seven knots at the start of the war). The Esmeralda was older, smaller, at 850 tons, and slower at barely six knots, and was armed only with a dozen light 40-pounders. The Magallanes was slightly smaller than the Esmeralda but could cruise at nearly eleven knots and carried a single 115-pounder, plus a 64-pounder and a pair of 20-pounders. The gunboat Covadonga, captured from the Spanish in 1866, displaced about four hundred tons and could keep pace with Magallanes, but carried only a pair of 70-pounders and a single 40-pounder.[10] The navy also possessed a single steam transport, the Tolten, although the important sealift capability of the fleet would be augmented substantially by merchantmen chartered for the purpose during the course of the war.

None of the Chilean ships had been specifically prepared for war in early 1879, another key indication that the outbreak of fighting was not a premeditated action by an aggressor. Both of the new ironclads already needed careening and the repair of some plates, and the boilers of the wooden ships all needed work. Furthermore, a hurricane in 1875 had severely damaged most of the fleet, and this was only just being made good by the start of the war. In fact, only Magallanes and the small transport Tolten were unquestionably ready for sea when war was declared.[11]

Besides the small size of the regular armed forces, their lack of experience in large unit operations, and the total absence of any sort of logistical support structure, the greatest weakness of the Chilean army and navy was its leadership. The officer corps was a peculiar body, even for Latin America, in that individuals seemed able to drift into and out of the service at the highest ranks with very little effort. In addition, a substantial portion of the officer corps actually held positions in government, either as elected officials or in positions that would normally be reserved for civilian bureaucrats, and all were active members of the various political parties.[12]

Perhaps this could be viewed as an evolutionary step forward over the practice of military men in Peru and Bolivia, and much of the rest of Latin America, where politically motivated officers tended to use their control over armed troops to seize political power. As noted previously, there had not been a serious military intervention in Chilean politics for years, but in Chile politicians used assignments in the military to advance their political fortunes and military officers used political connections (and even ministerial positions) to further their military careers. Neither practice tended to give rise to a thoroughly professional officer cadre capable of handling large bodies of troops in the field or the logistical arrangements necessary to support them.

While this would have been bad enough, the political activity of individual officers also gave rise to suspicion and jealousy within the government itself and prevented any kind of smooth cooperation between the civilian administration and the military, even in time of war. President Pinto found himself in a position at the outbreak of the war similar to that of U.S. President James K. Polk during the war with Mexico earlier in the century. Both chief executives were obliged to fight a largely unplanned war with senior generals, all of whom were members of the opposition party and very likely candidates for the presidency in their own right in the coming elections, particularly if they should manage to secure noteworthy victories in the war. Each president was thus placed in a no-win situation in which a defeat in the war would redound to his own disgrace as author of the nation's war policy, while victory, under the guidance of a general who was a partisan of the opposition, would almost certainly lead to defeat for the president's party in the next general elections. Polk was simply obliged to agree to the appointment of, first, Zachary Taylor, and then Winfield Scott, as commanders of the American armies in the field and then stand by while Taylor did, indeed, go on to win the presidency after his stunning achievements on the battlefield. Chile's President Pinto, however, came up with a unique solution for his political dilemma, albeit one that seriously handicapped the armed forces in their struggle with the external enemy and might easily have led to defeat in the war.

General Justo Arteaga Cuevas, a seventy-four-year-old veteran of the War of Independence, had been selected to command the Field Army in the Atacama based solely on his indisputable seniority. Unfortunately, the florid, overweight, and largely senile Arteaga had almost no other qualities that might have recommended him for the position. The most recent military experience he had had was in Chile's last serious coup attempt when, as a supporter of the losing side, Arteaga narrowly escaped execution by firing squad in 1851.[13] Arteaga made up for his lack of martial qualifications by strong political backing, having been a Conservative deputy himself, and with the outspoken support of one son, Domingo, also a Conservative deputy and another son, Justo, the editor of the influential newspaper *Los Tiempos;* and President Pinto was desperate to keep the Conservatives pacified during the war. In the event, Arteaga's political qualifications were the only ones he brought to the job. He was quite incapable physically of conducting a vigorous campaign in the hostile and desolate theater of operations where the fighting would occur, and his languid mental state prevented him from contributing a single viable idea to the deployment and use of the growing armies that the government would place at his disposal.

Rear Admiral Juan Williams Rebolledo, commander of the Chilean fleet, also brought a certain amount of political baggage with him and inspired no more confidence in the government at La Moneda. The son of a British sailor, who had served with distinction in the War of Independence, Williams was now in his fifties and so not as handicapped by sheer age as Arteaga, but he was no more dynamic. He had been in the fleet since 1844 and his primary claim to fame was having captained the frigate *Esmeralda* during the capture of the Spanish corvette *Covadonga* during the war of 1866. Since this had been the one bright spot for Chile in the brief military conflict, he was immediately created a virtual legend and a much-feted war hero. In fact, however, the aged *Covadonga* had hardly been a match for the *Esmeralda*, being less than half as large and carrying barely a third of the weight of metal in firepower. The "battle" had lasted only a few moments, essentially consisting of the *Esmeralda* firing a few ranging shots in the direction of her opponent, before the Spanish surrendered, with no casualties on either side.[14] Be that as it may, Williams became, by default, the only conceivable commander of the Chilean fleet for the new war, although the obsessive fear of defeat which would lead him to adopt a strictly defensive strategy was totally at odds with the aggressive concepts of Pinto and his cabinet.

There was actually little risk that any major political party in Chile would openly oppose the war itself, but a hostile party could make its presence felt by criticizing every action of the government in the prosecution of the war. The balding, white-haired Pinto, with his carefully trimmed goatee, looked more like a college professor than head of state and was no more stolid a figure than his appearance might imply. He had been hand-selected for the post by his predecessor, Federico Errazuriz, who had technically been elected as a Conservative himself. Errazuriz's policies, however, had led him further and further away from the Conservative fold and into the arms of the Liberals, to the point of earning him excommunication by the Church for his progressive policies on education, among other things, and this process was only accelerated after Errazuriz's death in 1877 when Pinto began to attempt to create his own political identity substantially further to the left than his mentor had been. Pinto's government, therefore, included individuals of both philosophies, and he could not afford to alienate any of them, particularly by violating the military's strict rules of seniority and passing over either Arteaga or Williams for the command. At the same time, if Arteaga in particular were to win a signal victory on the battlefield, he would almost certainly be the Conservative candidate for the presidency in 1881, while Pinto would be held to account for any shortcomings in the government support for the war effort, which the economic crisis would inevitably cause to occur. While Williams did not have the kind of political clout that Arteaga enjoyed, his status as a national icon prevented his removal no matter how unsatisfactory his performance at sea.[15]

Pinto's solution to this conundrum was the appointment of Rafael Sotomayor, brother of the commander of the initial Chilean expeditionary forces in the Atacama, the president's close political confidant from the Nationalist Party, and former Minister of Finance, as General Secretary and Advisor to the Fleet and the Army. This position could most closely be compared to that of a kind of political commissar with broad, ill-defined duties and authority in relation to the military hierarchy but with the clear advantage of having a direct communication link with the president. Sotomayor's role was to be both informative, providing Pinto with an endless stream of communiqués that were often at variance with the reports filed by Arteaga and Williams, and consultative, with Sotomayor sitting in on all major councils of war and issuing decrees in the president's name as to what should be done.[16]

Ostensibly, Sotomayor's primary function was to have been to take charge of the logistical support for the army in the absence of an organized quartermaster corps. In this role his close connections with both La Moneda and the legislature would have been ideal for explaining the need for particular expenditures and forcing through procurements that might have not been so effective if coming from a line military officer. However, both Sotomayor and his successor in the post, José Francisco Vergara, got directly involved in discussions of military strategy, even to the point of countermanding orders to military units in the name of the President. Sotomayor did perform a valuable task in overseeing the establishment of regular supply lines for food, water, animals, and munitions, an aspect of warfare that Arteaga and his staff generally ignored, and showed initiative in bringing civilian experts in for running the railroads and water desalinization plants captured in the new territories, which proved vital to the support of the forces in the field. It could also be argued that he had a certain native talent for military strategy that few of his professional counterparts enjoyed. But his actual purpose at the front was less as a supply sergeant than as a figure who, through voluminous correspondence with Pinto, could be shown to have been the intellectual father of every successful maneuver and the thin, still voice of protest against every failed project. Since none of this correspondence was coordinated with Arteaga or Williams, it could be released to the press selectively by the president in support of whichever position subsequent events showed to be most productive.

Needless to say, there was considerable friction between the military commanders and this neophyte "advisor." That Sotomayor frequently had perfectly valid suggestions to offer made little difference, since this was a slight to the honor of the military institution itself and to the individual commanders in particular. While personal pride is often considered to be an exaggerated quality among the officer corps in Latin American countries, it is amazing that the Chilean high command accepted this situation, however resentfully, and it is hard to imagine that either Presidents Polk or Lincoln could have gotten away with a similar arrangement when dealing with recalcitrant generals or officers of questionable loyalty or competence in the supposedly much more professional and dispassionate U.S. military. Historically it has only been when the military has stood in a relatively weak position in relation to the civilian authority, as was the case in the Soviet Union from the time of the Revolution to the fall of communism, that the military has been obliged to tolerate such a system, yet Pinto managed to pull it off, for better or worse. Chile thus entered the war with the best-equipped force of the three belligerents but one which was deeply, perhaps fatally, divided from within.

Objectively it would have appeared that Bolivia and Peru had an insurmountable advantage over their opponent in terms of sheer numbers. With a combined population nearly double that of Chile, one would have assumed that the allies could have fielded an armed force of similar proportions, but this was simply not the case.

The Peruvian Army at the outset of the conflict was substantially larger than that of Chile, at least on paper. The regular army numbered well over five thousand men divided into eight infantry regiments of approximately 450 men each, three cavalry regiments of slightly smaller size, and two artillery regiments with a total of one thousand gunners, in addition to some hundreds of gendarmes, an armed and generally mounted paramilitary police force in the rural areas. These were armed with a hodge-podge of weapons including about twenty-four hundred Castañon rifles, a Peruvian copy of the French Chassepot, a few hundred original Chassepots, and some Comblains, Remingtons, and other small arms including a fair number of cap-and-ball muzzle loading muskets of considerable vintage. There even existed a stock of Peabody-Martini rifles whose bore sights were marked in Turkish characters.[17] The Peruvian National Guard numbered, theoretically, some sixty thousand men, but these had not been called to the colors for any reason for over four years, not even for routine drill, and they could be considered as little more than a pool of potential recruits for whom the government had nothing like an adequate supply of weapons. Peruvian arsenals also contained barely one million rounds of small arms ammunition, less than a third that held by the Chileans, and with none of the manufacturing capacity to produce more on short notice. The wide variety of weaponry further complicated the supply of munitions for a quartermaster service that was none too efficient in any case.[18]

Where the war had been greeted in Chile with wild jubilation tempered with righteous indignation and a strong sense of certain victory, the mood in Lima as the war clouds gathered was far more gloomy. The Chileans expected to "regain" territory, and a very rich territory that the work of their laborers and the money and wit of their entrepreneurs had developed, but the Peruvians' most positive scenario was a return to the *status quo ante bellum,* hardly something to cheer about. The Chileans felt a strong sense of racial and national superiority to their neighbors to the north, while the Peruvians, if anything, held a certain inferiority complex to the dynamic southerners. Most importantly, it was immediately recognized, from the president down to the man in the street, that Peru's only reason for involvement in the war at all was to avoid a worse fate if she should fail to honor the "secret" treaty with Bolivia and then subsequently have to face an alliance of both Bolivia and Chile. There was animosity toward Chile in plenty, but there was no real enthusiasm for the undertaking.

Consequently, there was a strong pacifist sentiment in Peru from the outset of the war. Although there was the traditional early rush of young men to the colors in search of glory, this was rather limited, and the government was obliged to resort to conscription (which was not illegal at least, as it was in Chile) from the outset, since the country was already in a virtual state of bankruptcy and no funds existed for paying bounties or increased salaries for soldiers. It was even difficult for President Prado to find sufficient numbers of notables to take key cabinet and other government positions.[19]

The deployment of the army, prior to the outbreak of the war, was indicative of the focus of military attention in Peru. While the Chilean Army had been posted in small detachments to the Araucan frontier, fending off Indian raids, the

Peruvian Army had stationed one infantry regiment at Cuzco, an artillery regiment in Ayacucho, and virtually all of the rest of the army in the vicinity of Lima, Chorillos, and Callao.[20] In light of the turbulent political history of Peru, it was thus clear that the primary role of the military was to intervene in the struggle for control of the government, not to defend the nation's frontiers against foreign enemies. While Peru's frequent military uprisings and coups had involved a certain amount of activity by army units, even open combat, they provided experience of only marginal utility in terms of preparing officers and men for conventional warfare. While the fighting during the palace revolutions or in putting down popular uprisings could occasionally turn bloody, it was almost always of short duration, very much a "come as you are" affair with little need for detailed logistical or operational planning, and it was seldom that a unit of more than regimental size would be involved.

What the Peruvian officer corps may have lacked in military experience they made up in numbers. The war found no less than twenty-six generals and over one thousand other officers on active and reserve duty in the Peruvian Army compared with only five generals and about four hundred officers in the Chilean army at this time. Naturally, the Peruvian Army, on paper, was at least 60 percent larger than the Chilean, but even the Chileans considered their own armed forces to be top heavy.[21]

The Peruvian coastline was virtually undefended, with only the port of Callao mounting some fifty-three guns, ranging from 32-pounders up to 500-pounders, the same armament that had successfully beaten off the Spanish squadron during the war of 1866.[22] However, the defenses had not been much improved since that time, and the nation's other ports, like those of Chile, had no defense whatsoever except that provided by the fleet. The Peruvian government would move quickly to rectify this situation, particularly in the case of Arica and Iquique, ports that would be vital to the support of their army in the south, but it was generally understood that the fleet would be the country's first, and only real line of defense from the sea.

For a brief time after the withdrawal of the Spanish squadron in the preceding decade, Peru enjoyed a period of virtually total dominance in the waters adjoining the Pacific coast of South America, but those times had passed with the arrival of the new Chilean ironclads shortly prior to the start of the war. At the time of the War of the Pacific, naval architecture and design was going through a period of unprecedented advance with the introduction of steam power, armor plating, more powerful and faster-firing guns, and torpedoes (of both the floating mine and self-propelled varieties, both of which were still referred to by the same term), and each advance made all ships not so equipped virtually worthless in combat. This situation would continue through the rest of the century until, with the introduction of the dreadnought, ship design would again plateau off into a period of much more modest progress and relative advantage. It was Peru's misfortune that its best ships were just one generation (albeit of less than a decade chronologically) behind those of her opponent.

The Peruvian fleet, like that of Chile, was built around the two newest ironclads, the *Huascar* and the *Independencia*, both built by Laird Brothers shipyards at Birkenhead, England in the 1860s. The *Huascar* measured 200 feet in length and displaced just over eleven hundred tons. Her 300 horsepower engine could produce up to 11 knots, and the ship was protected with armor plating 4½ inches thick down to 3½ inches below the waterline, and with 2-inch plate on the decks and 3 inches on the conning tower. The turret was protected by 5½ inches of steel backed by 13 inches of teak and another half inch of iron. She was armed with a pair of 250-pound Armstrong muzzle-loading guns in a rotating turret forward of her waist, normally masked by iron gunwales, but these could be dropped for combat, leaving only the turret and a relatively small superstructure exposed and presenting the enemy with a very small silhouette as a target, although this hardly improved her sailing capabilities.[23] The frigate *Independencia*, also from Laird Brothers and a year older than the *Huascar*, was larger, some 215 feet in length and over two thousand tons, although thus still somewhat smaller than either of the two Chilean ironclads. Her engines could also turn for 11 knots, and she was likewise protected by 4½ inches of armor. Her armament consisted of a pair of 150-pounders, twelve 70-pounders, four 32-pounders, and four 9-pounders, again, all muzzle-loaders.[24]

At a glance, it can be seen that the Peruvian and Chilean ironclads were evenly matched as to speed, but the Chilean batteries carried six 250s each, and they were protected by just over twice the armor. The Chileans thus enjoyed substantially greater range and hitting power while being essentially impervious to anything the Peruvians could throw at them, while neither side possessed a speed advantage that would allow it to either seek or avoid combat.

The Peruvians also possessed a pair of monitors, both built in the United States for the Mississippi River campaign of the American Civil War. Like the original "cheesebox on a raft" that gave its name to this class of ship, the *Manco Kapac* and the *Atahualpa,* formerly the *Catawba* and the *Oneota* respectively, were completely unseaworthy and had to be towed from port to port, their engines barely able, at the best of times, to make four knots. They did each carry a pair of huge 15-inch, 500-pounder Rodmans in a turret with 10" of armor plate, making them valuable at least in the role of floating batteries in the defense of a port, but they were incapable of taking to deep water to challenge the Chilean fleet at sea.

The Peruvians also possessed the French-built wooden corvette *Union* of 1,150 tons and capable of 11 knots with a battery of twelve 70-pounders and a single 9-pounder, and the British-built gunboat *Pilcomayo* of 600 tons and a speed of 12 knots with a pair of 70-pounder Parrott rifles, four 40s, and four 12-pounders.[25] These last two ships were useful auxiliaries and adept commerce raiders but could offer little help in a general fleet action which involved the more modern ironclads. The Peruvians also had a number of transports, the *Chalaco, Talisman,* and *Limeña.*

On paper then the Peruvian fleet looked reasonably formidable, if not quite the match of the Chileans' most modern craft. However, the reality of the situation was rather different. The *Independencia* had been in dry-dock since mid-1878 changing out her boilers, and the *Huascar*, while equipped with new boilers, was in dire need of other repairs to her engines. The boilers on the monitor

Atahualpa were in such a state that they could only withstand five pounds pressure, not enough even to maintain steerage way within the harbor, and those on the *Union* were hardly in better shape. Of the entire fleet, only the tiny *Pilcomayo* was really ready for sea. When war appeared inevitable between Bolivia and Chile in mid-February 1879, the naval high command immediately inspected the entire fleet and ordered all ships into dry-dock for quick repairs.[26]

To make matters worse, the status of personnel in the navy was no better than that of their hardware. To the great embarrassment of the Peruvian naval command, it was realized in April 1879 that a large percentage of the sailors on Peruvian ships, both naval combatants and merchantmen, were Chilean nationals. In a surge of patriotic fervor, the Peruvian government had ordered the expulsion of all Chileans with the declaration of war, and this left the fleet woefully short-handed, although the action was probably justifiable at least in the case of the navy. The places of the departing Chileans were filled with raw recruits and their lack of seamanship and gunnery experience would cost the Peruvians heavily in the battles that were to follow.[27]

Of the three belligerents, notwithstanding the shortcomings of the other two, Bolivia was far and away the least prepared to go to war in 1879. Of course, Bolivia did not possess a navy at all, which was why, on April 15 in Lima, Bolivian envoy Ignacio Reyes Ortiz was obliged to promise President Prado that his government would provide a contingent of no less than twelve thousand soldiers to the allied army, compared to eight thousand for Peru, the difference being made up by the contribution of the Peruvian fleet to the equation.[28] At the time, however, Bolivia was no more in a condition to put twelve thousand men into the field than she was to produce a modern battleship.

The Bolivian army at the outbreak of the war numbered no more than 2,175 men divided into three infantry regiments, two cavalry squadrons, and two sections of artillery. Like the Peruvian army, the Bolivians had only had actual recent experience in conducting frequent overthrows of the government, with or without attendant violence, but never involving serious combat between modern, well-equipped military forces. In fact, the army had been set up precisely to prevent just such a situation from occurring.

The premier unit of the army was the "*Colorados*" (the redcoats) Regiment, the palace guard that had been commanded by the current president, Hilarion Daza, when he had helped to install Tomas Frias in the presidency. Daza, a barely educated soldier in his early thirties, had been made Minister of War in gratitude for his support, but he had retained command of the "*Colorados*" himself, as he did when he seized the presidency for himself in 1876. The reason for this was that, with control over the "*Colorados*," no combination of forces within Bolivia, even the rest of the army combined, could pose a real threat to Daza. And Daza made a point of ensuring that he retained that control.

The "*Colorados*," with six hundred men a substantially larger unit than any other in the army, were equipped with new Remington repeating rifles, besides their own small artillery section, while the other infantry regiments, "*Sucre*" and "*Illimani*," had to make do with inferior Martini-Henrys or even cap-and-ball muskets, and the cavalry with lances and aging carbines. The pay of a private in the "*Colorados*" under Daza's tutelage was equivalent to that of a captain in any other regiment, and the president regularly attended reviews of the regiment and social occasions hosted by its officers, generously providing ample food and drink for all ranks. This attention might have done little to endear Daza to the rest of the army or to enhance the war fighting capabilities of its soldiers, but there would be no question that the "*Colorados*" would resist any attempt to oust him, while without their support, no conspiracy had a chance of success. Daza clearly had his priorities.[29]

The Chilean and Peruvian armies may have been somewhat top heavy in terms of officers, but the Bolivian was ridiculously lop-sided. For just over two thousand troops, there were sixteen general officers, twenty-one colonels, 215 majors, one hundred captains, and 256 lieutenants, most of whom, like Daza had earned their rank, not through experience in battle or professional training, but as a reward for political loyalty to the winning side in one or more of Bolivia's endemic coups. As it turned out, the rapid expansion of the armed forces for the war made this surplus of officers come in handy, although it is debatable whether their presence on the battlefield was an asset or a liability for the war effort as a whole.

The reaction to the war in Peru might have been lukewarm, but in Bolivia it was overwhelmingly enthusiastic. The sons of the *best* families of La Paz hastened to enlist, forming the "Murillo" Cavalry squadron of some three hundred members, lavishly equipped and supplied with elaborately tailored uniforms. Given their social standing, these patriots were allowed to elect their own officers rather than receiving them from the pool of underemployed brass then available to the army. Not to be outdone, the skilled worker guilds of the capital quickly formed three regiments of their own: "Victoria," "Illimani 2," and "Paucarpata." The upper classes of Cochabamba, Bolivia's second city, created the "Vanguardia" battalion of two hundred men under Colonel Eliodoro Camacho, while six hundred workers marched to war as the "Aroma" Regiment. The mining town of Oruro formed "Tapacani," "Viedma," "Tarata," and "Mizque," while miners from Potosi became the "Dalence" Infantry Regiment. In all, these volunteers added more than four thousand men to the army, and other contingents would continue to pour in as they wound their way from Bolivia's interior cities over the weeks to come, from April into May and beyond.[30]

Ladies of all classes spent their evenings embroidering banners for their men, and popular collections were taken up for supplies of all sorts. Politicians vied with each other in the fulsomeness of their praise for the courage of Bolivian youth and the justice of their cause. Every new regiment that arrived by rail or road was met with massed brass bands and blizzards of confetti as they set up camp in the parks around the city. There was no question in anyone's mind that the war would be brief, glorious, and victorious. It does not seem to have dampened anyone's spirits that the Peruvians, hard-pressed enough for arms with which to equip their own men, were obliged to lend the Bolivian army fifteen hundred obsolete rifles or that, even so, hundreds of young men swung off down the road to the coast with no weapons at all.

Still, the display must have presented a lively spectacle. The regular regiments each wore jackets in a distinct color, the "Colorados" red, "Sucre" yellow, and "Illimani" green, the colors of the Bolivian flag. With these they wore white trousers and cartridge pouches, belts and straps stiff with pipe clay. The volunteer regiments wore whatever color happened to appeal to them. The most popular headgear was the slouched kepi in the French style, the same cap favored by both sides in the American Civil War (and with the armies of both Peru and Chile).

By mid-April Daza considered his army ready, poorly equipped and virtually untrained in large part, but ready to march to the coast. With the president marched 5,421 men of all three arms, and they were seen off with one of the largest demonstrations that the capital had ever produced. The long columns of men, horses, and guns wound their way through the narrow, steep streets of La Paz under a deluge of confetti to the tinny sound of a dozen competing brass bands, then trudged up the switchback road that led up from the valley in which the city sheltered to the featureless Altiplano and the road to the coast, more than 250 miles away. But before the first man had set foot upon the road, Bolivians had already fought, and lost, the first battle of the war.

The town of Calama was a convenient way station on the trade road from the Altiplano down to the coast and it sat at the crossroads of trails connecting Cobija, Potosi, and San Pedro de Atacama. Located on the Rio Loa, it had sufficient water to support a modest harvest of alfalfa, fodder for the pack mules that made their way along the route. With a population of only 700 and perhaps 60 horses and a few dogs, it hardly seemed fated for a place in history. And, actually, it is only in the history of Bolivia that it does have a place. In any history of the war, the fight at Calama would not normally rate even a footnote, but it has become a national symbol for the highland nation and provided one of the nation's leading martyrs.

On 16 February word arrived in the town of the start of the war with Chile, and the bells of the small church were rung to summon the population, but there appeared little for them to do, and they went back home. The next day Lieutenant Colonel Emilio Delgadillo arrived with twenty-three bedraggled soldiers from one of the abandoned coastal garrisons and with him, news that Chilean troops had arrived at Caracoles, barely a dozen miles away. More likely, these were simply Chilean workers already living in Caracoles who had risen in favor of Chile.[31]

The stout citizens of the town, and those of the surrounding region who had come in for the emergency, immediately formed a committee of defense under Ladislas Cabrera Vargas, prefect of the region, and including Eduardo Abaroa, a petty official from San Pedro de Atacama, Fidel Carranza, a local landowner, and Andres Lizardo Taborga as secretary. They immediately rejected any idea of evacuation and conducted a quick inventory of their means of defense. They collected seventeen rifles in various states of repair, plus those brought in by Delgadillo's men and another twenty soldiers who had arrived from Chiuchiu.

Colonel Severino Zapata, former prefect of Antofagasta, now a fugitive moving up from the coast, sent another ten rifles from Cobija along with several junior officers and another eleven troops for the defense.[32]

By this time, the Chilean army of occupation had grown to approximately 4,000 men including local recruits, and the Chilean government had made the decision to occupy the whole of the Bolivian littoral, not just the portion south of the 23rd parallel, in order to provide security for the "Chilean" portion of the Atacama. Since there was virtually no Bolivian military presence in the area, a number of columns were sent out to take formal possession of the area. One of these was under the command of Colonel Eleuterio Ramirez, commander of the 2nd Line Infantry Regiment; his task was to occupy Calama, even though Colonel Emilio Sotomayor, still commander of the Chilean forces in the Atacama prior to Arteaga's arrival, had determined that the town had no strategic value in itself, being too far from the Altiplano and too small to support an overland advance by the Bolivian army along that axis. Ramirez's force consisted of three companies from his own 2nd Line, one from the 4th Line, two mountain guns, and a troop of cavalry for a total of 544 men. They set out on the two-day march to Calama on 21 March.[33]

By this time the little Bolivian garrison had grown to 135 men, including nine civilian volunteers, with the arrival of Colonel Zapata himself in the town. They were armed with a total of thirty-five Winchesters, eight Remingtons, thirty assorted muzzle-loading muskets, a dozen shotguns, fourteen revolvers, and thirty-two homemade lances. Among the defenders were found no less than five colonels, two lieutenant colonels, six majors, two captains, twenty-five lieutenants, three sergeants, two corporals, and a medical doctor. Yet, interestingly, it was Cabrera, the civilian lawyer-prefect, who took command, possibly having something to do with the fact that he was brother-in-law of Foreign Minister Reyes Ortiz, with the slender, affable Eduardo Abaroa, another civilian, as his deputy.[34]

The key to the defense of the town, as Cabrera saw it, would be control of the wooden bridge over the Rio Loa and the two fords, one up river and one down from the bridge, that the Chileans would have to cross to reach Calama. He had some of the men pull up planks from the bridge and dug his troops in, hidden by the brush near each crossing. Then he waited. On the afternoon of the 22nd, a two-man reconnaissance patrol that Cabrera had sent to scout out the Chilean advance failed to return, and, on the next morning, another patrol consisting of several Bolivian soldiers, a major, and a couple of spare lieutenant colonels were also captured, signaling at least by their absence the arrival of the main Chilean force.[35]

From his Bolivian prisoners, Lieutenant Colonel Ramirez knew that the defenders had dismantled the bridge, and he had taken the precaution of bringing several carpenters and a wagonload of planks along with his detachment. He anticipated, however, that the small defensive force would be concentrated within the town itself, and he failed to conduct any reconnaissance, simply splitting his command into three parts well short of the river. He would remain with the main body of two companies of the 2nd Line that would cover the carpenters as they repaired the bridge, while Captain San Martín took a company of the 4th Line, twenty-five cavalrymen, and one gun to the right hand ford and Captain Carvajal took the other company of the 2nd Line, sixty-five riders, and the other gun to the left hand ford. They would cross the river more or less simultaneously and hit the town from three sides, presumably putting a quick end to any resistance.[36]

As the Chilean cavalry cantered up and began to pick their way through the muddy waters of the Loa at each ford, however, a sudden volley blazed out from the underbrush at a distance of less than twenty meters. San Martín's men miraculously escaped unscathed, but Carvajal's column suffered a dozen casualties in a matter of seconds, and the Chileans hastily pulled back to reform. At this moment, overwhelmed by their own success, Abaroa, one Major Juan Patiño, and eight soldiers rushed forward from their hiding place near the bridge, tossed planks onto the bridge supports to cover the gaps and took off in pursuit of the enemy. Unfortunately for them, the more than five hundred Chileans had no intention of escaping, and the Bolivians were quickly cut off and hunted through the thick underbrush by Ramirez's infantrymen while the two flanking columns shot their way across both fords and scattered the other defenders and quickly took the town itself without further ado.

Mr. Abaroa, however, had a date with immortality. As his men fell about him, he holed up in a protected position, firing furiously with his own Winchester and another rifle taken from a wounded comrade. The Chileans surrounded him and, not wanting to take any more losses for an objective of little military importance, called on him to lay down his arms and surrender. Abaroa's reply, "Let your grandmother surrender, dammit!"* would be learned by generations of Bolivian school children, and a bronze statue of the wounded man, still in his frock coat, gesturing defiantly at the enemy, graces one of the nicest plazas in La Paz. The Chileans felt obliged to shoot him in response.[37]

Naturally, the Chileans hardly realized that they had helped to create a historical figure, and the rest of the occupation of the Bolivian coastal area went ahead without further incident. At this point Peru had not yet formally entered the war, and there was still some hope that she would not do so or that Bolivia would break her alliance and join with Chile, accepting the loss of her former territory in exchange for a slice of even more useful Peruvian coastline to the north. With Chile's formal declaration of war on Peru on 5 April, both of these hopes were abandoned, and the build-up of Chilean forces in Atacama continued apace. But the significance of the little skirmish at Calama was that, after months of diplomatic posturing and pompous formal notes flitting back and forth between Santiago, La Paz, and Lima, now shots had been fired and men were dead on both sides. Very few men, to be sure, and in a part of the world where violence was hardly unknown, but there was something about the blood

---

* It is difficult to translate accurately into English the expression, *"Que se rinda su abuela, carajo!"* *Carajo* is really somewhat stronger than "dammit" and has no precise meaning. The quote is highly popular among children for its sauciness in normally conservative Bolivian society, and anyone given to fits of swearing is often referred to as an "Abaroa."

shed on the fringes of this little oasis in the Atacama desert that implied that a
real war was about to take place and that there was no longer any turning back.

The Chilean strategy now focused on seizing the nitrate-rich province of
Tarapacá from Peru, both to deny the Peruvians this source of revenue to
support the war effort, and to use as a bargaining chip, either to force reparations
out of the defeated alliance, or simply to keep as compensation for having been
obliged to go to war in the first place. Further, President Pinto and his advisers
agreed that secure occupation of Tarapacá could not be ensured without the
simultaneous occupation of a buffer to the north in the form of the provinces of
Tacna and Arica, where the allied armies would soon be concentrating. The
plan then was to force a decisive battle on Peruvian territory, crush the allied
army, and then dictate terms that both Bolivia and Peru would be obliged to
accept, while the Chileans occupied and profited from all of the nitrate deposits
for as long as it might take to come to an agreement. Since it was not possible
to march a sizeable field army across the desolate desert territory from
Antofagasta to Tarapacá, a new landing would have to be made farther up the
coast, and, before this could be considered, the Peruvian squadron would have to
be dealt with.

NOTES

    1. Diego Barros Arana, *Historia de la Guerra del Pacífico 1879-1881*. Santiago:
Editorial Andres Bello, 1979, p. 73.

    2. Thomas McLeod Bader, *A Willingness to War: A Portrait of the Republic of
Chile during the Years Preceding the War of the Pacific*, Ann Arbor, MI: Xerox
University Microfilm, 1967, p. 352.

    3. Andres Avelino Caceres, *La Guerra del '79: Sus Campañas*, Lima: Editorial
Milla Batrea, 1973, p. 16.

    4. William F. Sater, *Chile and the War of the Pacific*, Lincoln: University of
Nebraska Press, 1986, p. 84.

    5. Gonzalo Bulnes, *Guerra del Pacífico*, vol. 1, Santiago: Editorial del Pacífico,
1955, p. 117.

    6. Sater, p. 76.

    7. Ibid., p. 78.

    8. Leland Herschel Jackson, *Naval Aspects of the War of the Pacific, 1897-1883*,
n.p., 1963, p. 36.

    9. Jacinto Lopez, *Historia de la Guerra del Guano y el Salitre*, Lima: Editorial
Universo, S.A., 1980, p. 100.

    10. Bulnes, vol. 1, p. 126. Please note that there is considerable difference of
opinion regarding the armament and capabilities of the ships involved in the War of the
Pacific, particularly in the Chilean fleet, although the relative strengths are generally
clear. See also Lopez, pp. 99-104.

    11. Sater, p. 18.

    12. Simon Collier and William F. Sater, *A History of Chile, 1808-1994*, New
York: Cambridge University Press, 1997, p. 137.

    13. Ignacio Santa Maria, *La Guerra del Pacífico*, vol. 2, Santiago de Chile:
Imprenta Universitaria, 1919, pp. 131-135.

    14. Lopez, p. 112.

    15. Bader, p. 207.

    16. Collier and Sater, p. 132.

17. U.S. House of Representatives, *Miscellaneous Documents*, Document 30, 40th Congress, 2nd Session, p. 27.

18. Caceres, p. 13.

19. Fredrick B. Pike, *The History of Modern Peru*, New York: Praeger, 1982, p. 142.

20. Ibid., p. 14.

21. Victor Villanueva, *Ejército Peruano: Del Caudillo Anárquico al Militarismo Reformista*, Lima: Libreria Editorial Juan Mejia Baca, 1973, p. 106.

22. Ibid., p. 12.

23. Jackson, p. 33.

24. Lopez, p. 99.

25. Bulnes, vol. 1, p. 125.

26. Lopez, p. 103.

27. Ibid., p. 104.

28. Roberto Querejazu Calvo, *Guano, Salitre, Sangre: Historia de la Guerra del Pacífico*, La Paz: Editorial Los Amigos del Libro, 1979, p. 344.

29. Ibid., p. 263.

30. Ibid., p. 348.

31. Andrés Lizardo Taborga, *Apuntes de la Campaña de 50 Días de las Fuerzas Bolivianas en Calama con Motivo de la Invasion Chilena*, Sucre: Tipografia de la Libertad, 1879, p. 3.

32. Ibid., p. 290.

33. Bulnes, p. 119.

34. Lizardo, p. 6.

35. Querejazu, p. 294.

36. Bulnes, p. 119.

37. Querejazu, p. 303.

Chapter Five

Decision at Sea

Of Admiral Jellicoe, comander of the British Grand Fleet during the First World War, it was often said that, with literally millions of men fighting and dying in the trenches throughout Europe, he was the one man who could lose the war in an afternoon. Perhaps Rear Admiral Juan Williams Rebolledo had the same vision of his role at the outset of the War of the Pacific. An efficient, energetic, and successful naval campaign could go far to advance Chilean fortunes in the war, but could not win it alone, while a major defeat could eliminate any chance for a Chilean victory in the long run. Williams' actions, or rather lack of action, as commander of the Chilean battle squadron certainly implied a strictly defensive attitude and a firm conviction that his primary role was to avoid losing rather than to attempt to achieve victory.

As the earlier discussion of the geography of the Atacama region illustrates, control of the sea lanes along the coast would be absolutely vital to the success of a land campaign there. The few roads, rail lines, and even mule tracks in existence in 1879 all ran from the tiny guano ports inland, none of them paralleling the coast through the inhospitable, waterless, and unpopulated terrain of the Atacama. It would thus be virtually impossible for a land force of any size to carry sufficient water, supplies, and fodder for its animal transport from the population centers of either Peru or Chile to the theater of combat. Consequently, all significant transportation would have to be conducted by sea, and the side that was able to dominate the sea would effectively strangle its opponent's armies in forward positions. At the same time, superiority at sea would enable that side to descend at any point along the enemy coast, well behind the opponent's field army, forcing the enemy either to withdraw from the Atacama to defend its homeland or to disperse its army in an attempt to cover every possible landing site. Since it was Chile that proposed to advance into Bolivian and then Peruvian territory, this ability to leapfrog along the coast was even more necessary, and Williams therefore was extremely, possibly excessively, protective of his fleet.

The Pinto administration in Santiago was aggressive enough in its outlook regarding the war at sea. In a style typical of bureaucrats who had paid good money to purchase these powerful warships, it seemed wasteful not to put them to use. Following a state council meeting on 28 March, Minister of War Belisario Prats ordered, via Rafael Sotomayor, the "advisor" to both fleet and army, that the fleet should sail north and directly attack the main Peruvian port of Callao, hopefully to destroy the Peruvian fleet at anchor, within earshot of the capital at Lima, and possibly putting a quick and decisive end to the war in a matter of hours. At the very least, the Peruvian warships could be blockaded there, allowing Chilean transports the run of the coast for hundreds of miles, cutting off Peru and Bolivia from their only sources of foreign armaments coming from Europe and the United States via Panama, and simultaneously ensuring that Chile's own imports through the Straits of Magellan would be unmolested.[1] Since war had not yet been officially declared, the orders were held in abeyance until a subsequent message was sent by Prats to the fleet at Antofagasta on 5 April: "Declaration of war against Peru. Godoy and Lavalle [the Chilean and Peruvian envoys in Lima and Santiago respectively] will be withdrawn tomorrow. Proceed according to plan."[2] Presumably this referred to the proposed sneak attack on Callao.

Detailed reports had been provided to Santiago by Godoy, the Chilean envoy in Lima who, until his actual expulsion from the country in April, made good use of his presence in the enemy capital to obtain up-to-date intelligence on the state of the Peruvian fleet. It was thus well known, both to Williams and to La Moneda, that the Peruvian fleet was almost completely immobilized at the start of the war, with its most powerful ships sitting helplessly in drydock, their boilers completely dismantled and many of their guns dismounted. Pinto thus had trouble understanding Williams' reluctance to sail northward to seek out the enemy in his lair and crush him at will.

Williams, on the other hand, could not bring himself to take the plunge. His concept of campaign, rather than charging north with guns blazing was a rather more passive one of concentrating the fleet to blockade the port of Iquique where the allied army had begun to assemble. His vision was that, by cutting off the direct supply route to this army and simultaneously preventing Peru from exporting guano and nitrates through this port, and presumably, points south. He would thus deprive Peru of a considerable portion of the foreign exchange that the allies would need for the purchase of armaments abroad, undermining their war-making capability on a strategic scale. Ultimately, this slow strangulation would force the Peruvian fleet to sortie and meet his in combat at a time and place of Williams' choosing.

On a theoretical level, this was not necessarily a bad plan. Williams must have been conscious of the fact that the Spanish squadron had received a serious drubbing at the hands of the port defenses of Callao, and this before the arrival of Peru's ironclads, and it only made sense for the admiral to prefer to take on the enemy warships alone, where they would be deprived of the support of shore batteries. Also, he would have been aware of the inability of the two monitors, *Manco Kapac* and *Atahualpa*, to make the voyage to Iquique at all, much less to participate in a fleet action at sea, but their powerful armament outweighed any other pieces in either squadron, and it would be just as well to deal with the rest of the Peruvian fleet out of range of their massive ship-killers. Lastly, an action that much closer to Chilean territory would increase the chances of any damaged Chilean ships being removed to safety and that of any Peruvian casualties of facing the option of either capture or being scuttled.[3]

The only flaw in Williams' reasoning was, of course, that the Peruvian fleet, during the early months of the war, was physically incapable of sailing out of port to offer battle on the admiral's terms. Such an error in judgment might have been excusable had the immobility of most of the Peruvian ships been a closely guarded secret, but Godoy had reported the fact in good time. Naturally, Williams might have discounted this report, made as it was by an inexperienced landsman, but there is no indication that Williams ever made any serious effort to confirm or deny this information on his own. At the time, and in fact throughout the war, this would not have been difficult to arrange, even for Chilean nationals, and officers of neutral vessels continued to ply between the ports of the belligerents, often passing on valuable tidbits of news. Since a project such as the dismantlement of a ship's boilers or the presence or absence of a ship in drydock was not something that the yards at Callao could keep secret, the status of the Peruvian fleet was something that Williams clearly could have ascertained, had he only possessed the initiative. Since the Peruvians simply could not sortie, regardless of the provocation, Williams' insistence that he await their doing so, however advantageous such an event might have been for him, can only be seen as ludicrous.[4]

Obviously, no Peruvian battle fleet ever appeared on the horizon at Iquique, so Williams, under increasing pressure from Santiago to do something, began a campaign of harassment up and down the coast on 15 April in order to draw the enemy out. While maintaining the blockade of Iquique itself with *Esmeralda*, he also began to send raiding flotillas out to attack any Peruvian shipping they might find and to ravage the other Peruvian ports, with a view to further cutting off Peru's revenue from nitrate exports and generally making a nuisance of themselves. He sent *Cochrane* and *Magallanes* north and took *Blanco Encalada*, *O'Higgins*, and *Chacabuco* south himself. He shelled the docks at the little guano port of Pabellon de Pica and captured a small steamer and twenty-one launches, used to ferry goods from ship to shore. The next day he made a similar raid at Huanillos, taking fifty-one launches and destroying the primitive docking facilities against no resistance. On the 18th the squadron attempted a landing at Pisagua which was beaten off, and Williams contented himself with shelling the burning the town, an act of "barbarity" that the Peruvians loudly protested in this innocent age of international conflict. A similar bombardment of the port of Mollendo by Commodore Simpson in *Cochrane* was also the subject of loud complaint by the foreign community there.[5]

In light of these Chilean depredations along the coast, the Peruvian navy was also under strong pressure from the press and the administration to sortie and confront the enemy. Williams may have been aware of his nation's decisive superiority to her opponents in the war, especially if the war lasted any length of time at all, and his potential for ruining everything by precipitous action, but the Peruvians were faced with the opposite problem. Rear Admiral Miguel Grau, who had overall command of the fleet, in addition to tactical command of the squadron composed of the two ironclads *Huascar* and *Independencia*, knew that the only chance his inferior force had would be to strike hard and fast and hope for a miracle that would tip the balance at sea against the Chileans. Caution would only lead to inevitable defeat, where audacity might unexpectedly pay off.

However, at this time only the small wooden corvette *Union* and the gunboat *Pilcomayo* were ready for sea, and Captain Aurelio Garcia y Garcia was placed in command of the little squadron and sent out to cause what trouble he could. Regular reports were being passed to the commanders of both fleets about enemy dispositions and expected movements by neutral merchantmen plying up and down the coast, and word reached Callao that the Chilean transport *Copiapo* would be carrying a load of troops, food, and coal from Valparaiso to the blockading squadron at Iquique. Garcia y Garcia thus was lying off Huanillos on the morning of 12 April when his lookouts spied smoke on the horizon.

The ship turned out to be *Magallanes* under Commander Latorre, carrying orders for Williams to begin planning for the invasion of Tarapaca with a force of five thousand men. The Peruvians immediately took up the chase of the woefully outgunned Latorre who ran hard for Iquique. Although the ships were fairly evenly matched for speed, Garcia y Garcia cut the distance from forty-three hundred yards down to twenty-three hundred in the course of a five-hour running fight during which *Magallanes* sustained a number of hits and lost a steam launch, blasted to splinters on its davits. However, *Pilcomayo* eventually began to lose steam pressure, and the Peruvians gave up the chase. The only real loss was that Latorre, fearing possible capture, had burned the orders he carried for Williams.[6]

Despite the lack of material damage, the incident was a humiliation to Williams in view of his superiority to the enemy fleet. His critics in Santiago were also quick to point out that his policy of focusing on Iquique to the exclusion of all else had allowed the Peruvians to shuttle unaccompanied transports down to Arica, and this port was now fully fortified and garrisoned and the Peruvian army in Tarapaca had been built up from barely eight hundred men to over four thousand, all under the noses of the Chilean fleet. This criticism reflected on the cabinet, and on 18 April the Prats cabinet fell and was replaced by one headed by Antonio Varas. It is worth digressing for a moment to mention that the Chilean political system was a unique combination of the presidential and the parliamentary, with a president popularly elected for five years but supported by a cabinet that could be dissolved in the face of a vote of no confidence by the legislature. This cabinet centered around the Minister of Interior, a sort of prime minister, and was composed of the coalition of political parties that supported the president. A change in the cabinet could be forced on the administration to reflect a realignment of forces within the legislature in support of or opposition to the government's policies. This change in administration, while still under President Pinto, now included General Basilio Urretia as minister of war and the navy, Jorge Huneus as minister of justice, Domingo Santa Maria as foreign minister, and Augusto Matte with the finance portfolio. The message the opposition was sending to Pinto was clearly that they expected a vigorous prosecution of the war and a quick and glorious victory.

Although Sotomayor may have been the political watchdog of the Pinto administration over the fleet and army at Antofagasta, it should be noted that he tended to support Rear Admiral Williams' refusal to move to an immediate attack on Callao, an order that was reiterated by the Varas cabinet at the end of April. By that time, Sotomayor realized, the Peruvian fleet was in far better shape to take to sea, thus making it more likely that they would come out to offer battle as Williams had hoped, and the defenses of both Callao and Arica had now been reinforced so that a raid by the fleet would likely involve more significant losses. However, in his typically contrary way, Williams had now come around to the idea of a sortie in his own right and, on 17 May, without advising Santiago (or consulting with Sotomayor), he got his anchors aboard and put to sea. Williams had hinted at his intentions some days before when Sotomayor was sailing down the coast to Antofagasta to meet with Francisco Puelma, another civilian envoy of the administration to General Arteaga, saying that Sotomayor should return quickly as, "It is probable that I will make an excursion to the north."[7] The admiral had also left a sealed envelope with Captain Arturo Prat of the *Esmeralda* with instructions not to open it until three days after the fleet had left Iquique. Inside was a note indicating that the purpose of his voyage was to attack the enemy at Callao and instructing Prat to send a copy of the note on to Valparaiso. Williams concluded with the comment, "If we do not see each other again, remember your friend." While the implication was that Williams, rather melodramatically did not expect to return, the note was grimly prophetic, and the two men would not see each other again.[8]

General Arteaga casually informed La Moneda on the 18th that the fleet had headed off toward the north (which was as much as he knew) and also that intercepted mail indicated that Peruvian President Prado had departed Callao with his fleet and 4,000 reinforcements for Arica. The government in Santiago would not have any definite knowledge of the whereabouts of its fleet until when Williams would send a message to Arteaga to have supplies sent up the coast to Iquique. The blockade of Iquique would be left in the hands of young Captain Arturo Prat, soon to become a legend in the military history of Chile, in command of the elderly *Esmeralda* and *Covadonga*.[9]

Williams' plan of attack at Callao was a multi-faceted concept that required that everything go like clockwork. The idea was for the *Abtao*, which had been converted into a floating bomb loaded with several tons of gunpowder, to race into the port under cover of darkness, before the Peruvians could be aware that his fleet was in the vicinity. She would steer for the nearest Peruvian ironclad and pull up alongside, at which point the crew would abandon ship and set the fuses. By the light of the subsequent explosion, *Cochrane, Chacabuco,* and *Blanco Encalada* would then steam in, blazing away with all guns and releasing a number of launches that would make use of the distraction to race up to any surviving Peruvian ironclad and place torpedoes against their hulls. *O'Higgins* and *Magallanes* would then join in, and the fleet would pound the city and forts at their leisure. The collier *Matias Cousino* would accompany the fleet to ensure an ample supply of coal for the duration of the operation.[10]

Things began to go badly almost at once. *Matias Cousino* failed to make the rendezvous at the Islas Hormigas on 21 May, but Williams determined to carry on with his plan. With any luck, there would be prizes taken in the harbor, and coal could be transferred to the fleet from them. At thirty minutes after midnight on 22 May, the lookouts of the fleet could make out the lights of Callao, and preparations were begun to lower the torpedo launches. Choppy seas and general confusion caused delays in this operation, however, and it was after 0430 hours, much later than expected, by the time the fleet reached the approaches to the harbor. In the early morning light, it soon became obvious that the Peruvians had spotted them, thus eliminating the element of surprise. Even so, Williams might have carried on had not the lookouts aboard *Abtao* signaled that they could not identify either *Huascar* or *Independencia* among the ships in the harbor. This information was then confirmed by an Italian fisherman who shouted up to the quarterdeck of *Cochrane* from his dinghy that the Peruvian ironclads had departed, heading south, four days before. Both Williams and Sotomayor immediately recognized the threat that was now posed to the small force that had been left at Iquique, and all further thought of attacking Callao was abandoned.[11]

It was now that the absence of the collier became significant as, faced with a fast passage south at the end of which might be a battle and/or a sea chase, precious time had to be spent transferring bags of coal from both *O'Higgins* and *Chacabuco* to the two ironclads. The former ships would have to make their way home as best they could under sail, while *Cochrane* and *Blanco Encalada* headed south under full steam. They would sight *Huascar* briefly on 30 May, north of Iquique and give chase in vain until their coal ran low again, and they dropped anchor in Iquique the next day. There they found the errant *Matias Cousino*, which had only just escaped capture by the *Huascar* earlier the day before and had been sitting at the fleet's first scheduled rendezvous at Camarones since 17 May, the captain not having thought it wise to sail alone to the very approaches of the enemy's main port. While a disappointment, this fruitless expedition might have been written off as nothing more than a waste of time and coal had not the war's first significant naval engagement taken place in the absence of the Chilean admiral. Here the Peruvians were finally doing precisely what Williams had hoped they would do from the start of the war, doing it in fact just as soon as they physically *could* do it, and Williams had missed it.[12]

The Peruvian decision to send out the bulk of their fleet actually had almost nothing to do with Williams' campaign of harassment. At a meeting of the council of ministers in Lima on 14 May, which was also attended by Bolivian President Daza, newly arrived from La Paz, his foreign minister Serapio Reyes Ortiz, and the combined general staffs of the allied armies, it was determined that the army then concentrated at Iquique was fast running short of supplies and would be faced with a tortuous retreat across the desert if not relieved soon. At the same time, President Prado feared that the fleet might be caught and blockaded in Arica if they did sortie. The decision was finally made, however, to move substantial reinforcements by sea to Arica, along with Prado and Daza, who would command their respective nation's armies in the field, with Prado in overall command while on Peruvian territory and Daza taking over if the campaign led them into what had been Bolivian territory. The convoy would be escorted by every major combatant of the fleet, and even the monitor *Manco Kapac* would be towed along to become a floating battery for the defense of Arica itself.

The expedition did not have an auspicious start on the 15th, as *Manco Kapac* nearly foundered, and the entire flotilla had to return to port and try again the next day. Still, the fleet arrived at Arica without further incident on 20 May, having passed Williams the night before without either squadron seeing the other as the Peruvians hugged the coast while Williams had swung well out to sea in an effort to avoid being spotted by coastal shipping. Heavy guns were unloaded to complete the defenses of Arica, and the transport *Oroya* continued down the coast with five hundred Bolivian troops for the garrison at Pisagua. Of greatest importance, the allies learned from the captain of an English steamer of the departure of Williams and his ironclads from Iquique, leaving only *Esmeralda* and *Covadonga* to maintain the blockade.[13]

Rear Admiral Manuel Grau needed no more encouragement than that. Born in 1834, Grau had entered the merchant marine as a youth before returning to Peru to enter the naval academy at the relatively advanced age of twenty. He had been expelled from the service in 1859 for supporting the losing side in a military rebellion and rejoined the merchant marine, travelling to India and China among other places before returning to the navy in time to fight the Spanish in 1866.[14] He was barrell-chested, with a balding pate and an impressive set of sideburns that looped up to join his moustache, and he was every inch a sailor.

If Williams had perhaps taken too much to heart the responsibility he held for avoiding defeat at sea, Grau espoused exactly the opposite philosophy. He knew that, unless he could take the war effectively to the enemy and inflict a telling reverse on him, the allied cause would be lost. Of course, it would be lost all the sooner if Grau were defeated, but the *only* chance for an allied victory in the war would necessarily involve aggressive action at sea. Since the Bolivians and Peruvians were defending their homelands, they would fight as long as they were able, while the Chileans, who had long since passed the limits of even their most ambitious territorial claims, might conceivably lose their appetite for the war if it became costly enough for them. But time was not on the side of the allies. With Chile already in possession of the nitrate-producing region of the Bolivian Atacama, and with Peru denied the revenue of her own nitrate exports by the Chilean blockade, Chile had the means of purchasing armaments in Europe at leisure and the avenue to bring them in safely through the Straits of Magellan, while the allies lacked the funds to buy much, and would have to bring any purchases they could afford through Panama, a route that could be cut off at any time if a strict policy of neutrality were to be adopted by the government there. It was with this thought in mind that Grau took *Huascar*, in company with *Indepenencia* under Commander Juan Guillermo Moore, and weighed anchor on the evening of 20 May for Iquique.

After a brief pause at Pisagua to pick up information confirming the presence of Chilean shipping at Iquique, and the absence of the enemy ironclads, Grau pressed on and arrived at dawn. The *Esmeralda*, under Captain Arturo Prat, and *Covadonga*, had learned of the Peruvian approach from the ubiquitous and talkative coastal skippers, and were as ready as they could be. *Esmeralda's* boilers had failed, leaving her capable of no more than two or three knots, so escape had been out of the question, and Prat had both ships anchored within a cable length of the town of Iquique on the theory that the Peruvian gunners would have to be especially cautious with their shooting for fear of shelling their own people ashore. Prat calculated that the occasional peppering his ships received from infantrymen in the town was worth this marginal measure of protection.

At 0820 hours *Huascar* opened the action with a spirited but totally ineffective fire, and *Independencia* soon joined in. The captain of the port had come out to the Peruvian ironclads and informed Grau that he believed *Esmeralda* to be protected by a screen of torpedoes, or what we today would call floating mines, and Grau prudently decided to stay at a range of five hundred to six hundred yards to open his bombardment.[15] It was now that the lack of training of the Peruvian crews, fleshed out at the start of the war with the conscription of hordes of landsmen with no naval experience at all, began to tell. The Peruvian shots consistently went wild, many landing in the town, and none hitting either enemy ship. The Chilean gunnery was substantially better, but the armor of the Peruvian vessels held up against the ineffectual barking of *Esmeralda's* Armstrong 40-pounder smoothbores, and no serious damage was done. After an hour of this exchange, *Covadonga* had had enough, and her captain cut her cables, and she slipped away south, sticking close to shore and taking advantage of her shallow draft in the hope of escape. At Grau's direction, *Independencia* turned in pursuit.[16]

It was not until 1000 hours, after dozens of shots, that *Huascar* finally scored her first hit on *Esmeralda*, starting a fire that was quickly extinguished. At the same time, Prat's crew was beginning to take casualties from rifle and cannon fire from the shore, and he concluded that he had no choice but to attempt to make a run for it as well. Grau was embarrassed at the poor marksmanship of his gunners, and took *Huascar* in close, now that the Chilean had moved away from any floating mines there might have been. He tried to ram, but *Huascar's* iron beak struck only a glancing blow, although, now at point blank range, even the raw Peruvian gunners could not miss.[17]

It is worth mentioning that Grau's decision to ram was not an act of desperation. For a brief period, after the advent of steam power and then the development of armor plating, ramming became a favored naval tactic in the mid-to-late 1800s. Ramming had been, along with boarding, the primary weapon of the oar-powered fleets of the Mediterranean powers for centuries, but the increasing reliance on sail made this technique unusable, and the development of increasingly powerful naval artillery made it suicidal. Now, however, steam-driven ships could achieve considerable speed in any direction, while armor plating temporarily made ships impervious to gunfire. A well-placed blow by a ram, backed by a ship of two or three thousand tons travelling at ten knots, was more than any armor could withstand, and many ships built in the 1860s through the 1880s came equipped with a menacing iron beak, protruding from the bow below the waterline for just this purpose. It would not be until a truly effective armor piercing shell could be developed near the end of the century that ramming fell out of vogue as a tactic in naval engagements.[18]

In any event, the two ships were now virtually touching, and the huge 250-pound Armstrong guns in *Huascar's* turret would be able to gut the wooden *Esmeralda* in a matter of seconds. Aware of this, Captain Prat, cutlass and pistol in hand, raced across the deck of his doomed ship and leaped aboard *Huascar*, shouting for his men to follow.

It should be noted that the decks of the two fighting ships at this moment had much more in common with those of Nelson's *Victory* at Trafalgar than with the largely bare, armored decks of the battleships that dueled at Jutland a generation later. Both *Esmeralda* and *Huascar*, although steam-powered, still had masts and rigging that were more than ornamental, and the decks of both ships were crowded with sailors manning light deck cannon and Gatling guns and marines blazing away at *the* enemy with rifles and hurling grenades when the opposing ship came within range.

With the incredible din of gunfire, the rumble of the engines, and the screams of the wounded, only a single sergeant, Juan de Dios Aldea, heard Prat's order and joined him in leaping across the gap onto the deck of the *Huascar*. Prat was a thirty-one-year-old naval academy graduate and veteran of the war with Spain who had been brought north by Sotomayor as an aide-de-camp and named to command of *Esmeralda* shortly before by Williams. Now he and Aldea found themselves alone on the enemy deck and both were quickly cut down by small arms fire, Prat dying immediately and Aldea lingering on for three days to die in a Peruvian hospital.[19]

Huascar came about and tried ramming again, and once more without result. This time, a Lieutenant Serrano and twelve sailors from *Esmeralda* followed Prat's example and attempted to board the Peruvian ironclad, but these too were quickly cut down by the fire of the Peruvian marines. As the ships scraped past each other again, *Esmeralda* fired a broadside directly into the hull of *Huascar*, but the shells simply caromed off harmlessly, sending up an impressive shower of sparks.

Finally, just after noon, Grau positioned *Huascar* for a third ramming run and this time plunged the long beak deep into the ribs of *Esmeralda*. When *Huascar* pulled away, *Esmeralda* immediately began to take on water and to list heavily to port. In a matter of minutes, the frigate slipped beneath the waves, leaving *Huascar* to rescue a total of only 63 out of a crew of 198. The Peruvian losses were only one killed and seven wounded, although the superstructure of the ship and the smokestack were riddled by bullets and shell fragments.[20] Had the day ended on this note, it would have been a signal victory for the allies, but there was still another drama to play out farther down the coast.

The tiny *Covadonga* (half the size of *Esmeralda* and one fifth that of *Independencia*) headed south at her best speed, just over ten knots, which was a little slower than that of the Peruvian ironclad, and *Independencia* gradually closed the distance as Condell, the Chilean skipper, was forced to hug the coast, trusting to his ship's shallow draft to stay out of reach of his pursuer, while Moore on *Independencia* could steer a straighter course, pounding away with all guns. The gunners on *Independencia* proved to be no better than those on *Huascar*, however, and not a single shot struck home. *Covadonga*, meanwhile, scored a dozen hits, dismounting a Parrott bow chaser and inflicting at least a few casualties on the ironclad's decks, even if she could do nothing to disable or slow her opponent. Moore tried desperately to get into a position to ram, but Condell had little trouble slipping his more nimble ship out of the way on each occasion.

The chase continued for several hours and, just after noon, when *Huascar* was meeting her fate at Iquique, *Covadonga* shuddered slightly as she scraped over a submerged rock that did not appear on any of Condell's navigational charts. No damage was done, however, and Condell must have smiled as he turned to watch as the huge Peruvian ironclad came charging on in *Covadonga's* wake. With a grinding screech, *Independencia* struck the rock, tearing a long gash in her hull below the water line and sticking fast. *Covadonga* now turned and began to rake the deck of *Independencia* with her lighter guns while the Peruvian's boiler room and magazines quickly flooded. Moore's men kept up their own fire with the deck guns until the ready ammunition ran low, and the lower batteries were put out of commission by the rising water.[21]

This one-sided duel went on for some time until the smoke of the approaching *Huascar* could be seen on the horizon, and *Covadonga* prudently retired. By the time the other ironclad came alongside, most of the crew of the fast-sinking *Independencia* had made their way to shore in the ship's boats, although Peruvian sources would later claim that *Covadonga* ungraciously shelled these survivors as well before fleeing. Grau pulled off the twenty remaining crewmen, including Moore, and ordered the helpless vessel burned to the waterline.[22]

Such was the sense of chivalry in this war, occasional accusations of atrocities notwithstanding, that, during a brief lull in the action, Grau took the time to write to the widow of Captain Prat:

Pisagua, 2 June 1879
Most Honorable Madam:
  A sacred duty obliges me write you, and I am deeply sorry if this letter, by reviving unpleasant memories, contributes to the increase in your pain that must rule you on this day. In the battle of the 21st just past, . . . your worthy and valorous husband . . . was the victim of his own terrible bravery in defense of the flag of his country. Deploring such a tragic event and joining you in your grief, I fulfill the painful and sad duty of sending you his effects.[23]

At noon Grau must have been congratulating himself on a glorious, if relatively minor, victory. The loss of *Esmeralda* hardly affected the Chilean naval superiority, but it might have pushed the already timorous Williams into an even more cautious strategy and at least given the Peruvians a little more time to make use of the sea lanes with relative freedom. At the same time, it is doubtful whether the entire Peruvian fleet could have survived a stand-up fight with the two Chilean ironclads alone, their best ships being decisively outgunned and under-protected, but a lucky turn of fate might have enabled the aggressive Grau to catch one or the other alone or might have seen *Cochrane* or *Blanco Encalada* fall victim to a whim of the sea as had occurred with *Independencia* now, in which case the playing field would have been almost leveled. However, in a matter of hours the Peruvian fleet had been converted from a contender for supremacy, albeit of the dark horse variety, into a mere nuisance, a force to be considered, to be sure, but not one that could seriously challenge any determined effort that the Chilean fleet might choose to make in the future.

Since the *Esmeralda* had been sunk within sight of the allied positions at Iquique, the news had been telegraphed immediately to the high command at Arica. President Prado, in that moment of elation, conceived of a plan to launch an amphibious assault directly against the occupied Bolivian Atacama near Antofagasta to destroy the invading army in one final battle. He had obviously not given any thought to how the invasion convoy might have been defended against the Chilean battle fleet, whose principal fighting power remained unscathed and substantially superior to that of the Peruvian, or if the army had managed to land intact, how its supply lines could have been kept open in the face of the undefeated Chilean squadron. In such an event, the most likely outcome would have been that the army, deprived of a reliable source of munitions, food, and even water, would have withered and been forced to surrender without ever having been brought to battle. This hardly mattered in the long run, as word of the loss of *Independencia* came in that evening, plunging Prado from the heights of elation to the depths of despair. He obviously abandoned his ambitious offensive plans, attributing this solely to the loss of the ironclad, and later claiming that this one event essentially lost the war for the allies.[24] The loss was certainly a hard blow, both morally and materially, but it is highly debatable whether the fortunes of the allies were decisively altered.

Prado may have lost his nerve at the news, but the loss converted Grau into a veritable dynamo. Instead of rushing home to protect the one ironclad still remaining to the navy, he sought to make use of this asset. On the 25th he sighted and captured the transports *Recuperado* at Antofagasta and *Clorinda* at Mejillones, being obliged to burn them as he had no crew to spare for the prizes. The next day he sighted two other transports, *Rimac* and *Itata*, transporting 2,500 troops to Antofagasta, but lost them and then, on the 28th, he dueled with the batteries at that port briefly and shelled the water distillation plant. The next day he found and cut the submarine telegraph cable to Valparaiso and, learning of the belated approach of the Chilean squadron, headed north, capturing the sailing ship *Coqueta* en route. The next morning Grau spotted smoke from the Chilean ironclads, but he was able to evade them for seven hours when Williams was obliged to suspend the pursuit for lack of coal, and by 1 June *Huascar* dropped anchor in Arica to take on coal and supplies and put her wounded and prisoners ashore.[25]

Arguably, the Chileans should have considered the 21st of May a highly profitable day for their war efforts. They had, in effect, traded an obsolescent wooden frigate for one of the only two ships in the enemy fleet that even stood a chance of contending with their own ironclads. Of course, the favorable outcome was ultimately a question of the purest chance rather than the result of a calculated plan, but even the sinking of *Esmeralda* had provided the Chilean cause with a martyr and a symbol of national pride that survives to this day in the person of young Captain Prat.

However, the focus of the Pinto administration was on Rear Admiral Williams whose own actions had only proved sterile or disastrous. His sortie to Callao, which was conducted without consulting with, or even informing, Santiago, had not only resulted in a wasted voyage, it had as an added embarrassment the image of *O'Higgins* and *Chacabuco* inching their way home under sail due to Williams' sloppy logistical planning. For the moment, he was still in too strong a political position for the administration to risk replacing him, but his days would certainly be numbered if another failure could be attributed to him.

And Grau was just the man to provide that pretext. Hardly pausing at Arica, on 3 June he was at sea again, hoping to find *O'Higgins* and *Chacabuco* still limping along under sail, but he ran into *Blanco Encalada* and *Magallanes* at Huanillos instead. Hopelessly outmatched, Grau turned tail, leading his pursuers on an 18-hour chase. At one point *Blanco Encalada* managed to pull within gun range but was unable to score any hits, and when her captain reduced speed in an effort to improve his aim, *Huascar* was finally able to escape. By 7 June she was back in Callao for some hasty repairs, and this phase of the naval war appeared to be over.[26]

But Grau was not finished yet. By the 11th he was again cruising off Iquique and this time spotted the transport *Matias Cousino*, whose absence from Williams' squadron may have saved *Huascar* from destruction the month before. She surrendered, and Grau took her under tow, again lacking enough spare men to fit out a prize crew. A few hours later, however, he spotted smoke and ordered the transport sunk to free him to face this new threat.

It turned out to be *Magallanes*, and the much smaller, and unarmored, Chilean ship gamely came up to offer battle, probably due to word getting around about the abysmal state of Peruvian gunnery. After half a hour of futile firing and a failed attempt by *Huascar* to ram, *Cochrane* appeared hull down on the horizon, and Grau was again forced to head north for the safety of a friendly port.

Even while he was bearding the much superior Chilean fleet in its den, Grau was obliged to deal with much more mundane and frustrating problems. In his correspondence to the ministry of the navy he complains of the inferior quality of the coal, supplied by civilian contractors, that fouled his engines and of the sorry state of his crews' uniforms, no replacements having been received since the fleet was first mobilized in February. He also complained about the salaries of many of his sailors being anywhere from one to three months in arrears. From his letters one notices the large number of non-Peruvians serving in the fleet as he lists names such as: Doward, McCarley, McCollum, Carlson, Ray, Chambers, Martin, and Glaspy, most of these being American or British adventurers in the Peruvian service.[27]

Despite the loss of *Independencia,* Grau had managed to put the superior Chilean fleet on the defensive. At the same time as Grau's ranging along the coast, the gunboat *Pilcomayo* under Captain Ferreiros had also been cruising and had captured two merchantmen, one flying the Nicaraguan flag and one the British, but a quick study of the ships' papers revealed them to be Chilean, and both were sent to Callao as prizes. Ferreiros sank three other small enemy transports and numerous launches and generally raised alarms up and down the coast before being chased back to Arica by *Cochrane* and *Blanco Encalada* on 7 July.[28] But Grau was quickly back at sea and, on 10 July captured the transport *Matias Cousino,* although he was forced to scuttle his prize after taking off the crew, when a Chilean squadron headed by *Cochrane* came up on the horizon, and Grau deftly evaded them once more.[29]

Williams was clearly at a loss for any fresh ideas as to how either to deal with the aggressive actions of the Peruvians or how to take advantage of the sudden windfall presented to him with the sinking of the *Independencia.* The best he could come up with was to take *Blanco Encalada* and *Magallanes* to bombard the port of Iquique, leaving *Cochrane* and *Chacabuco* at Antofagasta, along with the now extensive shore defenses as protection against the depredations of the Peruvian raiders, a clear indication of the exaggerated sense of fear that Grau had managed to instill in his opponents, since *Cochrane* alone would have been more than a match for the entire Peruvian fleet at that point. Williams conducted his bombardment on the 16th, but the only significant result was a storm of protest from the various foreign consuls, including the American, German, Italian, Austrian, and Argentine, over the wanton destruction of neutral, private property.

Meanwhile, Grau took the hastily reprovisioned *Huascar,* in company with the *Union,* out of Arica on the 17th and spent the next five days ranging up and down the coast as far as Antofagasta, taking no less than three prizes, all Chilean vessels falsely flying the Nicaraguan flag, two loaded with copper and one with coal for the enemy fleet, and sent them to Callao as prizes. Apart from the loss of the ships and their cargoes, this was another slap in the face for Williams and a mark of Grau's disdain, that he would put his little force in a position where the Chileans stood between Grau and his base.

On the 23rd, however, off Antofagasta Grau scored his greatest coup of all. To cover more territory, *Huascar* and *Union* had split up, and in the pale light of the early dawn Grau could make out two smokes on the horizon. It turned out to be *Union* in pursuit of a Chilean transport, and *Huascar* was able to move into position easily to cut off the prey and force *Rimac* to surrender. Rather than coal or copper, *Rimac* was transporting a full squadron of cavalry, the "Carabineros de Yungay," 240 men and 215 horses, in addition to three hundred Comblain rifles, 200,000 rounds of ammunition, and four hundred tons of good English coal, part of the build-up of Arteaga's forces in the Atacama. Considering the lack of significant ground action to date, this single capture resulted in the largest loss the Chilean army had thus far suffered in the war.[30] More than satisfied with his achievement, Grau then escorted his prize back to Arica and took a few well-earned days of rest. To make matters worse, *Cochrane*, under the command of Captain Simpson, had been supposed to be escorting *Rimac* with her important cargo, but Simpson had expended his coal stores in a fruitless pursuit of the gunboat *Pilcomayo* and spent the crucial days of the 22nd and 23rd in Antofagasta harbor restocking.[31]

The loss of the *Rimac* was more than public patience in Chile could tolerate. It would be a solid week before Santiago got definitive word of the fate of the transport, but when it arrived, mass demonstrations swept the capital, and General Urrutia, the Minister of War was stoned at the doors of the Senate. The press, whether of the opposition or not, was full of criticism of Williams for being made a fool of once more by the Peruvians, and, far from achieving any signal victory, had blundered from one fruitless endeavor to another while Grau sailed rings around his superior force.

A series of resignations quickly followed. Urrutia went first, followed by Admiral Altamirano, commander of the navy, General Echaurria Huidrobo, intendant general of the army and navy, with Rear Admiral Jose A. Goni and General Vicente Davila Larrain taking their places, and finally Williams himself fell. On 3 August Williams unilaterally decided to abandon the blockade of Iquique, again without consulting with Santiago, although he did pay Santa Maria, then minister of war and the navy, the courtesy of sending a note to this effect, and returned with his fleet to Valparaíso. He offered his resignation, claiming "health reasons," although he commented that he had planned to divide the fleet into two divisions, each with one ironclad and attending vessels which, "made unnecessary my presence and that of my staff [at sea], being more of an inconvenience for the direction of the ships."[32] His resignation was accepted with unseemly rapidity, and the admiral was called to the capital to "explain" his actions, particularly his unapproved sortie and his equally unapproved abandonment of the blockade.

Finally, the entire Varas cabinet was obliged to resign, although Domingo Santa Maria was called upon to take over the portfolio of minister of interior and form the new one. Arguably, then Minister of War Santa Maria may have been ultimately responsible for the *Rimac* disaster, having held her in port, causing her to miss sailing with a small convoy that would have provided some measure of protection and then sending her north without escort and with all lights blazing when *Huascar* was widely known to be on the prowl, but it was Williams and the military hierarchy whom the people viewed as the culprits in this crime.[33] The new Santa Maria cabinet included Miguel Luis Amunategui as foreign minister, Rafael Sotomayor as the secretary of war and the navy, Jose Antonio Gandarillas for justice and education, and Augusto Matte as the only survivor of the old cabinet in his post at finance.[34]

Back in Arica, Grau was probably unaware of the stir caused in Santiago by his latest exploits, and he did not feel he could rest on his laurels. As gratifying as his unanswered series of blows against the Chileans must have been, Grau was aware that only through the destruction of one or more of the enemy ironclads could he hope to give his country any chance of victory in the war. Consequently, on 1 August he was again at sea following a report that *Cochrane* was alone at the anchorage of Caldera. Grau hoped to hit the ironclad by surprise and use launches equipped with torpedoes to disable her in a night attack. Unfortunately, the report turned out to be false, and the anchorage was empty. Grau had to content himself for the moment with destroying a few enemy launches in small ports on the way back north, being lucky to survive a severe storm before arriving back at Arica.[35]

The principal focus of naval operations at this time was the effort to provide cover for the movement of troops along the coast, allied reinforcements for the advanced posts in the Atacama, and Chilean plans for a major invasion of Peruvian territory, and the continuing hopes of both sides to shift the balance of naval power decisively through the destruction of the irresistible ironclads. One other aspect of the naval war is worthy of mention, and that is the protection of supply lines to the belligerents from the arms markets of Europe and the United States. As it began to look as though the war would not be as quick a campaign as both sides had originally hoped, the need for resupply of military materiel took on increasing importance. As noted previously, Chile started the war with an adequate stock of modern weaponry, but Peru and Bolivia lacked the arms to bring to the field the numbers of recruits available and thus to take advantage of their numerical superiority, and the allies thus had to buy sizeable lots of weapons abroad. Chile had the undeniable advantage in this regard, being able to bring in new weapons directly by sea through the Straits of Magellan. Bolivia and Peru, however, could not take advantage of this southern route, and had to transship all merchandise in Panama, crossing the isthmus by train and reloading it on ships on the Pacific coast.

The semi-autonomous status of Panama posed a complex problem. Panama officially supported the cause of the allies while the government in Bogota had declared its neutrality in the conflict, and money freely changed hands in both places as Chilean and Peruvian agents desperately tried to bribe officials either to facilitate or hinder the passage of allied arms shipments. On 2 June 1879, a joint Colombian-Panamanian resolution declared the free transit of goods across the isthmus without distinction to the origin, destination, or type of shipment. Less than a week later, however, a coup ousted Panamanian President Casorla, and the new President Ortega decreed a prohibition on the embarkation of arms for either of the belligerents, a move that obviously hurt the allies much more than the Chileans, giving rise to rumors that Chilean money had helped finance Ortega's rise to power.[36] Notably, press reports from April 1880 implied that Chilean envoy Francisco Valdes Vergara had paid Ortega as much as $10,000 to enforce the prohibition of Peruvian arms shipments across the isthmus.[37]

This was only the official position, of course, and weapons and equipment purchased in Europe and the United States by Peru's agents, the firm of Grace and Company, continued to flow along the railroad with the complicity of venal local officials. As early as July, since the Peruvian government had begun to purchase and ship arms and munitions from Europe as soon as war with Chile appeared imminent, the Peruvian envoy in Panama, Jose Antonio Miró Quesada arranged for passage of 757 crates containing six thousand French rifles and one million rounds of ammunition through Colon.[38]   Subsequently, in early September, the transport *Oroya* loaded two Herresford torpedo boats, four thousand rifles, three million rounds of rifle ammunition, six Krupp cannon, and forty shells in Panama despite protests by the Chilean consul Jimenez Arce. Having failed to block the shipments through legal means, the *O'Higgins* was sent north in a fruitless effort to catch a loaded transport after a tip-off by Jimenez Arce, and in December the armed Chilean transport *Amazonas* manage to seize a small torpedo boat en route to Callao off Ecuador. But, despite its inconveniences and close calls, this route of supply was to remain open to the allies, in addition to small lots of aged rifles they were able to purchase in Honduras and Costa Rica and ship directly south without passing through Panama.[39]

Chilean purchases in Europe went ahead apace under the guidance of former Minister Alberto Blest Gana. As the crisis with Bolivia appeared headed toward war in February of 1879, he contracted for three million rifle rounds in Paris, with another order of that size in March and double it in early May, doubling the order yet again at the end of the month. Making full use of the credit the Europeans were willing to advance Chile on the weight of her apparent acquisition of the nitrate-rich Atacama region of Bolivia, Blest Gana purchased no less than 145 cannons, including Armstrong coastal defense guns, Krupp field and mountain guns, and another one hundred older muzzle loaders at knock-down prices, in addition to the new Gatling and Hotchkiss machineguns. He bought thousands of slightly obsolescent rifles from Comblain of Belgium, and Beaumont and Grass of France tooled to the same caliber, eight thousand cavalry sabers from Germany, besides ten thousand full uniforms with material for another ten thousand from England.[40]   In short, while money would eventually become a serious problem for Chile in prosecuting the war as it dragged out month after month, during its first year Chile had little trouble finding and obtaining the means to arm its forces, while the situation for the allies steadily deteriorated from marginal to worse over the course of time.

Back at the front, a general lull continued over activities. During the first half of September, *Cochrane* had been taken out of action to go into drydock for extensive repairs, and *Blanco Encalada* was put strictly on the defensive, guarding against any aggressive moves by the markedly inferior but feared *Huascar*. These repairs included a quick scraping of the ship's bottom, since the richness of marine life in the region, that which attracted the clouds of birds that deposited the guano that formed the basis of the dispute over the coast, tended to manifest itself in thick encrustations of barnacles and other animals and plants on the hull of any ship within a matter of weeks while at sea, a process that took much longer in other waters, and this severely restricted the speed of the ship. When *Cochrane* again put to sea, she could make 12 knots and was now equipped with electric lights and new Gatling guns on deck. It was then *Blanco's* turn for refit at Mejillones, a less substantial job, but one that enabled her to do nine knots reliably by the start of October, now under the command of Captain Galvarino Riveros, while Captain Latorre took over *Cochrane*. In keeping with the Pinto administration's policy of providing political "commissars" to the major military commands, Eusebio Lillo, a confidant of the new Minister of Interior Santa Maria, was named "secretary" to the fleet, allowing Sotomayor to concentrate on the land campaign in the future.[41]

Finally, on 30 September, Sotomayor learned from his network of agents ranging north into Peruvian territory that *Huascar* had come down to Arica. A council of war was quickly called aboard *Blanco Encalada* including that ship's commander, Riveros, and his second in command, Guillermo Peña, Latorre from *Cochrane*, and Captains Mont of *O'Higgins*, Molina of *Loa*, Manuel J. Orellana of *Covadonga*, as well as Lillo and Sotomayor. They agreed that the defenses of Arica, now including the monitor *Manco Kapac*, would make a direct assault a bloody one, but that a surprise torpedo boat strike under cover of darkness might just disable the Peruvian ironclad, their only real competition along the coast. When the fleet arrived on station off Arica on 5 October, new intelligence informed them that *Huascar* was no longer in port. Riveros, in nominal command, although never having been given the same authority that Williams had enjoyed and made so little use of, had *Blanco Encalada* and *Covadonga* remain at Arica awaiting *Huascar's* return, while *Cochrane* and *O'Higgins* swept well out to sea to the south in hopes of either intercepting Grau or driving him into the waiting arms of Riveros.[42]

Grau had been in Arica on the 30th right enough, but he set sail that same day, in company with *Union* to escort the captured transport *Rimac*, now in the Peruvian service, with a contingent of reinforcements for the garrison at Pisagua, and the rival squadrons had passed each other on the night of 2 October, separated by sixty miles of wine dark sea. After dropping off the troops, *Huascar* and *Union* moved on to the port of Sarco where they seized the *Chala*, a ship currently flying the British flag, but Grau knew that she had been Chilean-registered before the outbreak of the war and considered her good prize. After some hurried repairs on the engines of *Huascar*, which were starting to show the strain of months of constant cruising, the Peruvian squadron headed north again.[43]

The key development now was that Sotomayor's intelligence network, including well-paid merchant ship captains and fishermen up and down the coast, was able to confirm that *Huascar* was to the south of the Chilean squadron, implying that Grau would have to make his way past it in order to return to his home port, and Riveros was promptly advised of this discovery. Specifically, Grau was expected to try to slip past Antofagasta on the night of 7 October. Sotomayor, using the authority of the minister of war and the navy, ordered Riveros to load coal at Caldera and take position off Antofagasta with *Blanco Encalada*, *Covadonga*, and *Matias Cousino* by the 7th while Latorre with *Cochrane*, *O'Higgins*, and *Loa* would cruise off Mejillones to the north in the hope of catching the slippery Peruvian raider between them.

During the day on the 7th, *Huascar* again had to heave to and make temporary repairs on her engines, as well as to transfer three hundred sacks of coal from *Union*, before getting under way again. At midnight, the two ships came in sight of the lights of Antofagasta and continued past at between two and three miles of the shore. All was quiet until 0430 hours on the 8th when Captain Garcia y Garcia of the *Union* saw *Huascar*, which was leading the formation, pour on coal and raise signal lights indicating "enemy ships," before turning out to sea. In the light of a full moon, Garcia y Garcia could make out, once *Huascar* had moved out of the way, three or four columns of smoke at about three miles distance, in toward shore, at least one of which would be a Chilean ironclad (*Blanco Encalada* and her escorts). Despite the jury-rigged engine, *Huascar* was making nearly eleven knots at 0715 hours when lookouts spotted another three columns of smoke, these to the northwest. Grau was finally caught in the trap.[44]

Latorre steered an interception course as Grau angled to get out to sea and past him, and by 0930 hours the range had dropped to twenty-three hundred yards, at which point *Huascar's* gunners opened fire. *Union*, although she had been wrapped with layers of chains as a sort of homemade armor, had no hope of inflicting any damage on either of the Chilean ironclads, and Garcia y Garcia turned aside and used her greater speed of up to 13 knots to flee, with *O'Higgins* and *Loa* in pursuit. He would later claim that Grau had raised a signal for him to make use of his superior speed to escape, while Lieutenant Garezon, his second-in-command denied this, but there would have been little *Union* could realistically have been expected to accomplish in the battle of the ironclads that followed.[45] Riveros had also spotted the Peruvians, as well as Latorre's squadron up ahead, and came on at full steam, despite problems *Blanco* had been having with her own boilers that made her speed frustratingly slow.

A running fight went on between *Huascar* and *Cochrane* for some forty minutes off Punta Angamos, as the battle would eventually be named, as the range continued to decrease to about two hundred yards, at which point Latorre's guns opened up. At this range the 250-pound shells could and did penetrate *Huascar's* thinner armor, less than half that of the *Cochrane*, even though it was backed by nearly a foot of solid teak. Even on the Chilean ships, a shell clanging off the armor plating could incapacitate any seaman unfortunate enough to be touching a bulkhead at the moment, and loose rivets could be sprayed about the interior like rifle balls. The first shot from *Cochrane's* guns penetrated the armor of *Huascar's* turret, killing a dozen sailors, and the second volley smashed *Huascar's* bridge, killing Grau instantly, leaving only a bloody foot and a few teeth embedded in the paneling, along with his aide, Lieutenant Diego Ferre, who was on the deck below, receiving Grau's steering instructions through a metal grate as he manned the tiller. Captain Elias Aguirre assumed command and attempted to ram *Blanco Encalada* unsuccessfully before he, too, was killed as was his replacement, Lieutenant Meliton Rodriquez, shortly thereafter. At one point both *Cochrane* and *Blanco* attempted to ram *Huascar*, but the Peruvian ship's erratic course, still at considerable speed, made this impossible.[46]

Another broadside from the *Cochrane* destroyed the chain that controlled *Huascar's* rudder, sending her into a tight turn to starboard caused by her twisted beak, bringing her within range of *Blanco's* broadside as well. The same volley also started a fire in her engine room and in the officers' quarters. At this point, Garezon and three of the surviving officers agreed that the time had come to scuttle the ship, and young Ensign Ricardo Herrera was sent below to open the sea cocks. But by now the Chileans had closed with and boarded the crippled Peruvian ship, sloshing through up to four feet of water in the hold to force the Peruvian engineers to start up the pumps and close the cocks.[47]

The battle was over, although the *Huascar* apparently never struck her colors, and a seaman, Enrique Palacios, suffered no less than nineteen wounds in attaching the flag to the stump of a mast after it had been shot away. *Union* had escaped, and her captain would be criticized for failing to stand and fight alongside Grau, although it is hard to imagine how such a gesture might have affected the outcome, since his 70-pounders could hardly have done what *Huascar's* own 250s failed to accomplish, and this would also have added the fire of *O'Higgins* and other Chilean ships to the enemy's total. The big nine-inch Pellisser guns of *Cochrane* and *Blanco Encalada* had fired a total of only eighty rounds, most at point-blank range, and inflicted losses of thirty-five killed out of a crew of two hundred, most of whose survivors were also wounded. *Huascar's* poor gunnery record had not improved, and only five hits were scored on *Cochrane*, causing minor damage, with nine killed and one seriously wounded, and no hits at all on *Blanco Encalada*.[48]

The *Huascar* survived and was towed back to Valparaiso, her decks still scored from shell and rifle fire, and she was refitted to reinforce the Chilean squadron for the northern campaign later in the war. *Huascar* remains in Valparaiso today as a floating naval museum. Her arrival was greeted with wild euphoria in Chile, enhanced by the fearful reputation she had earned under the aggressive command of Grau and by the fact that this was the first bona fide victory of Chilean arms in the war. The occupation of the Bolivian coast had hardly been contested, the martyrdom of Prat a noble gesture, and the sinking of the *Independencia* an act of God, and there had been numerous humiliations at sea to deplore. But this was a clear triumph, albeit of a rather one-sided battle, and everyone was eager to take credit for it, notably the Pinto administration, who made it clear that Sotomayor had essentially been the intellectual father of the victory with his brilliant two-pronged strategy, which the naval officers had simply carried out. The implication was that this sort of victory might have been achieved at a far earlier date and lesser cost had only Admiral Williams followed the sage advice of his civilian advisor/secretary.

Conversely, the news of the battle was greeted in Peru and Bolivia as a cause for national mourning. As long as the odds had been before against the allies, they seemed truly insurmountable now. The Chileans would now be free to transport their army up and down the coast in a matter of hours, landing behind any force the allies dared to advance to the south, and it was not even just a question of how much longer travel by the land-locked allied armies would take, but whether much of the barren terrain could be crossed at all on foot. Peru's ports could be conveniently blockaded, cutting off supplies from abroad and any revenue either allied state could hope for from mineral exports or even more traditional sources such as sugar from plantations in the north of Peru. Even if the allies did manage to inflict a reverse on the Chilean army in the field, the survivors could always be whisked to safety by the enemy fleet and the blockade continued until a refurbished army could be dropped anywhere along the coast, even at the gates of Lima itself. In other words, the allies could easily lose the war with a defeat on any battlefield, but they could no longer win it no matter how well their troops fought. It is hardly to be wondered at, therefore, if the allies looked forward to the next phase of the campaign with little enthusiasm.

NOTES

1. William F. Sater, *Chile and the War of the Pacific*, Lincoln: University of Nebraska Press, 1986, p. 19.

2. Jacinto Lopez, *Historia de la Guerra del Guano y el Salitre,*. Lima: Editorial Universo, S.A., 1980, p. 110.

3. Ibid., p. 111.

4. Gonzalo Bulnes, *Guerra del Pacifico*, vol. 1, Santiago de Chile: Editorial del Pacífico,1955, p. 130.

5. Lopez, p. 115.

6. Ibid., p. 123.

7. Bulnes, vol. 1, p. 172.

8. Ibid., p. 173.

9. Cesar A. Bazo, *La Guerra del Pacifico*, Lima: Litografia e Imprenta Badiola y Berrio, 1905, p. 59.

10. Bulnes, vol. 1, p. 175.

11. Lopez, p. 147.

12. Bazo, p. 63.

13. Ibid., p. 157.

14. Roberto Querejazu Calvo, *Guano, Salitre, Sangre: Historia de la Guerra del Pacifico*. La Paz: Editorial Los Amigos del Libro, 1979, p. 402.

15. Miguel Grau, *Diario Abordo del Huascar*, Buenos Aires: Editorial Francisco de Aguirre, S.A., 1880, p. 5.

16. Bulnes, vol. 1, p. 182.

17. Jose Rodolfo del Campo, *Campaña Naval 1879*, Lima: Instituto de Estudios Historicos-Maritimos del Peru, 1976, p. 91.

18. James Phinney Baxter, *The Introduction of the Ironclad Warship*, New York: Anchor Books, 1968, p. 74.

19. Lopez, p. 163.

20. Ibid., p. 169.

21. Campo, p. 86.

22. Lopez, p. 187.

23. Querejazu, op. cit., p. 359.

24. Lopez, p. 188.

25. Ibid., p. 195.

26. Ibid., p. 200.

27. Grau, p. 57.

28. Lopez, p. 205.

29. Grau, p. 107.

30. Campo, p. 127.

31. Bulnes, p. 230.

32. Lopez, p. 265.

33. Sater, p. 20.

34. Bulnes, p. 252.

35. Ibid., p. 243.

36. Lopez, p. 232.

37. Rafael Leiva Vivas, *Posicion de Centroamerica en la Guerra del Pacifico*, Tegucigalpa: Universidad Nacional Autonoma de Honduras, 1989, p. 48.

38. Leiva, p. 46.

39. Ibid., p. 251.

40. Ibid., p. 258.

41. Bulnes, p. 253.

42. Lopez, p. 299.

43. Ibid., p. 304.

44. Campo, p. 167.

45. Benjamin Vicuña Mackenna, *Historia de la Campaña de Tarapacá*, vol. 2. Santiago de Chile: Imprenta Editora y Litografia de Pedro Cadot, 1880, p. 381.

46. Bulnes, p. 290.

47. Querejazu, op. cit., p. 407.

48. Lopez, p. 321.

Chapter Six

Coming to Grips

Although no serious combat took place on land from the outset of the war until after the threat of the Peruvian fleet was finally eliminated at the Battle of Angamos in early October, neither side had completely wasted its time. All of the belligerents were essentially undertaking the war from a standing start, and time would have been required in any case to mobilize, arm, and train the forces that would participate in any campaign and then to move them considerable distances to the theater of the conflict.

In response to the collapse of the Prats cabinet that signaled the loss of patience of the government with further lethargy in the prosecution of the war, Arteaga finally moved his headquarters from Valparaíso to Antofagasta, bringing with him twenty-seven hundred additional troops in preparation for an invasion of Peruvian territory. However, like Williams, Arteaga was not one to be hurried in what he considered his professional duties, a personal attitude that was aggravated by his inability to work more than eight hours a day, due to his age. He began issuing demands for more of everything before he would consider moving an inch, and, as has often been the case with civilian governments in other wars, the administration was reluctant to refuse him anything lest he be able to blame any future failure on a lack of support. Arteaga estimated the allied forces at six thousand men at Tarapacá and another fifty-seven hundred at Tacna, and he wanted at least a further twenty-five hundred men (which would give him at least ten thousand) before he would even consider offensive action.[1]

He also wanted more ammunition, an increase of his stock of two million rifle rounds to eight million (about eight hundred per man if he got the reinforcements he requested) with proportionate increases to his supply of artillery shells. The government considered these demands excessive, since it had only been recently that soldiers armed with muzzle-loaders would normally march into battle with forty to sixty rounds in their belt pouches, but with nearly all the troops now equipped with repeating rifles, commanders in this war would find that even allotments of one hundred fifty to two hundred rounds per man would prove inadequate after a few hours in some of the more intense battles. Thus a demand for a stockpile of ammunition for what might be four days of combat might not seem out of line. In addition, there was no calculating how many thousands of rounds men in both armies would expend in training or simply discard by the roadside to lighten their loads during their repeated forced marches through the Atacama desert, since virtually all of the combatants were new to war as were their officers. On the other hand, the allied army at this stage had a total stock of less than half a million rifle rounds available at the front, barely a quarter of the amount held by Arteaga.[2] More men would be forthcoming as soon as they were available, but Pinto pointed out to Arteaga that the country simply did not possess and had no means of producing that much ammunition and to await delivery from Europe would delay the operation for months. He promised to double the general's current stock from existing supplies, stripping government arsenals bare, and, as we have noted, Chilean agents in Europe were actively seeking new supplies to supplement the modest amounts of ammunition that could be produced by Chilean industry at this point.[3]

Arteaga, a rather small, prim man, still vigorous and sharp despite his advanced age, who struck one more like a French diplomat than a man of war, had not exactly wasted his time since the start of hostilities. He had spent the months since the creation of the Army of the North over which he presided with rigorous drill of the troops and classes of instruction for all officers in military tactics, logistics, and the other arts of war in which they had such limited experience. He had made great strides toward incorporating the thousands of new recruits into the ranks and organizing them into usable military formations. Like General George B. McClellan, commander of the Union Army of the Potomac in the early stages of the American Civil War, however, Arteaga's skill in creating an army did not translate into an ability to make effective use of the weapon he had forged.

By the end of May, the Chilean army numbered upwards of eighteen thousand men, ten thousand in Arteaga's Army of the North in and around Antofagasta, and another eight thousand in the Army of the South under Colonel (later General) Cornelio Saavedra in Chile proper, either watching the frontiers, guarding Valparaíso and other ports, or serving as training cadres for still more units en route to the front. The nearly tenfold expansion of the peacetime military establishment had been accomplished without the benefit of a law permitting actual conscription, because all able-bodied males technically belonged to the National Guard, which the government now called into service. The ranks of officers of the new regiments or greatly engrossed regular units were provided by gentlemen volunteers who were given ranks more or less in accordance with their social standing as opposed to military experience and whose names were not entered on the official *escalafon*, the almost sacred catalogue of regular officers used for determining seniority for promotion and assignment. When the war ended, these officers would presumably return to civilian life immediately without salary or pension.[4]

As the southern winter approached in early June, the debate over the future use of the army centered on four basic plans. The most ambitious, which had been sponsored by former Minister Varas and President Pinto, called for a bold stroke, lifting the bulk of the army far to the rear of the allied forces gathering in the Atacama, for a descent on Callao and Lima itself, to bring the war to a swift close by decapitating the enemy at one blow, following the precedent set by San Martín during the Wars of Independence in 1820 and Bulnes in 1832. Arteaga and Williams had scoffed at this idea, especially as long as the Peruvian fleet remained even a remote threat, as being a physical impossibility, and the idea was quietly shelved for the moment.

The second plan called for a slightly less daring move, an invasion of the Peruvian province of Moquegua and a drive on Tacna. This would still put the Chileans well to the rear of the main allied force concentrating at Tarapacá, shielded from them by many days' march across inhospitable desert. Between the dominant Chilean fleet at sea and this army sitting astride the only possible land route of resupply and reinforcement for the allied army, the enemy would either be forced to surrender or to march north to meet this threat and fight a decisive battle with exhausted troops, cut off from supplies of food, forage, and ammunition. There was some objection to this proposal from the Foreign Ministry in that the bulk of the enemy troops present in the Tacna area were Bolivian, and there was still hope in Santiago that an agreement could be reached with La Paz over a break-up of the alliance in exchange for a trade of Bolivian territory to Chile with yet-to-be-conquered Peruvian territory going to Bolivia. The somewhat illogical rationale was that a serious defeat of the Bolivian Army, far from encouraging President Daza to settle the dispute amicably, would damage a potential ally while leaving the primary Peruvian enemy untouched. President Pinto tended to agree with this latter view as he held the Bolivian negotiations very dear and was reluctant to abandon them.[5]

A compromise plan, one that seemed to be everyone's second choice, involved an amphibious assault, but much closer to the Chilean bases, with a landing around Tocopilla and then an advance on Tarapacá. Thus a decision would be forced with the main allied army, an encounter that few Chileans had any doubt would result in a total victory, and the richest Peruvian nitrate-producing region would then be occupied by the advancing army. Peru would be deprived of all revenues on which its war-making capacity relied, and these resources would simultaneously be added to the Chilean coffers. If the enemy were foolish enough to insist on prosecuting the war after such a loss, it could be done at Chile's leisure with the nitrate industry footing the bill, probably exclusively, from the conquered territories. This approach seemed to minimize the risks of landing an army too far from its sources of support while boding well toward a decisive move toward ending the war.

The only problem with this plan was that Arteaga apparently held the navy in such low esteem that he was unwilling to trust it to move his army securely any distance at all or to be able to supply it reliably once ashore. His own plan called for an invasion of Tarapacá, but overland from Antofagasta, involving a march of two to three weeks, at least, over the worst terrain in the entire region, roadless, waterless, and without an ounce of forage for the hundreds of horses and mules that would have to haul the army's equipment. In presenting this plan, Arteaga also chose this moment to unilaterally inflate his own estimate of forces available to the allies to thirteen to fourteen thousand men in Tarapacá itself with another five thousand on hand in Tacna available to reinforce them on relatively short notice. No advance at all would thus be possible until further reinforcements reached him at Antofagasta along with the material to create a huge supply train off which his army could live for weeks at a time.[6]

Negotiations over the future campaign went on through June, with Arteaga sending his personal secretary, Colonel Donoso back and forth to Santiago to meet with the Council of Ministers, and arguing endlessly with Rafael Sotomayor in Antofagasta. Pinto had confirmed Sotomayor in his position as intermediary between the government and the army on 11 June, formally naming him *comisario general* of the government to the army and the fleet. However, in the face of Arteaga's objections, no progress had been made on even deciding on a plan of campaign by 17 July when Pinto's patience finally ran out, and Arteaga was summarily removed, being replaced with General Erasmo Escala.

At fifty years of age, Escala seemed likely to breathe fresh vigor into the Chilean campaign after the dapper but aged Arteaga. He was a life-long military careerist and had lost an arm at the battle of Loncomillo, albeit nearly three decades before, although he lacked much experience in the command of large numbers of troops, as did most of his compatriots. He had a reputation as a severe disciplinarian, a perfectionist when it came to drill and presentation, but his most singular characteristic was that he was a devout Catholic who insisted on dedicating time each day for the troops to hear Mass and who had a tendency to spend hours in prayer over his campaign plans that others might have spent in professional study on a more mortal plane.[7]

Regardless of the changes in the command of the army, most of the actual planning still centered around Minister of War Sotomayor who, by the end of September, had come around to the idea of an overland campaign. The *Huascar* was still on the loose, and the capture of the *Rimac* had sensitized Santiago, perhaps overly much, to the dangers of sea transport without complete domination of the coastal waters, although adequate convoy, which the Chilean fleet was certainly capable of supplying, would have obviated this problem. Sotomayor threw himself into planning for this operation, performing the function that he had originally been designated to do for the army in the field, and he soon came to the conclusion that the success or failure of such a campaign, involving many days' marching over barren desert, would center on the supply of water. He calculated the amounts of water that would be required by the troops, searched out columns of wagons to carry water tanks, purchased water distilling equipment, and scheduled shiploads of water to be sent up the coast for resupply.

Before this project got too far, however, Sotomayor's estimation that 1.5 liters of water per day per man would be more than sufficient for marching troops was discovered to be in error, fortunately in time. A reconnaissance in force by two regiments out into the desert from Antofagasta, with each man carrying two liters of water, demonstrated that the poorly disciplined and thirsty troops had gone through their ration before 1100 in the morning and had barely dragged themselves back to their base camp, tongues swollen, and with men already dropping out of the column from fatigue.[8] This implied that the required amount of water would have to be doubled, at least, and this would have involved a prohibitively large supply train, one in which the mules, horses, and oxen could not physically haul enough fodder and water for themselves, much less enough to supply the entire army. It became clear, therefore, that the only viable way for the Chilean army to get at the allies would be by amphibious movement up the coast.

By that time, however, the elimination of the *Huascar* had completely changed the strategic outlook. There was no longer any need to consider any movement that did not involve transporting the army by sea, and it only remained to determine where they would disembark. Even without a serious threat from the Peruvian navy, the Pinto administration had come around to the idea that a direct invasion of the heartland of Peru would be to risk too much, and the capture of the province of Tarapacá was decided upon as the logical next step in the war. The key consideration for the Chileans was that they needed to take a usable port, ideally one with railroad communications into the interior to facilitate onward movement and resupply, and a location that would put the army in a position to cut off General Buendía's army at Iquique and/or that of the Bolivians that was concentrating around Tacna farther to the north. Arica was considered too much of a gamble, since thousands of allied troops were gathered there, and the port was by now heavily fortified with strong shore batteries and the monitor *Manco Kapac* in the harbor that would confront the Chilean fleet with a real battle just to get the assault force into position. Iquique, likewise, although far closer to the Chilean bases, was strongly held by a major portion of the allied army, making any landing a risky proposition, since the troops would be going ashore in small launches and ships' boats, not the mission-designed landing craft that would not be developed until World War II. The small nitrate port of Patillos, the option that Sotomayor favored, was closer yet to Antofagasta and virtually undefended, but this would leave the army still with an imposing march across forbidding terrain before even coming within range of the nearest allied force.[9]

Pisagua seems to have been everyone's fall back choice. It had a protected harbor adequate for the invasion fleet, and it also boasted a railroad line running some 50 miles into the interior. Pisagua was defended, but only by a relatively modest infantry force that would not involve the invaders with a set-piece battle starting right at the water's edge. A landing here, followed by a rapid advance along the rail line, would put the Chilean Army in a central position to turn either south to attack the allied army at Iquique or north against the one in the Tacna/Arica area and defeat each in turn before they could unite. Consequently, after extended consultations between the high commands of the army and navy, Sotomayor, and Pinto in Santiago, Pisagua was chosen as the landing site, and the fleet was concentrated.

Fourteen steamers and one sailing ship were loaded with some 10,850 troops and 853 horses, plus guns and mountains supplies under the escort of *Cochrane*, *O'Higgins*, *Magallanes*, and *Covadonga*. To deal with the ever-present concern over the supply of water, the fleet was equipped with stills capable of producing 3,850 gallons of drinking water per day.[10]

In a possibly exaggerated form of operational security, Minister Sotomayor had chosen not to divulge the details of his invasion plan to any of the army or naval officers involved until after the flotilla had set sail from Antofagasta on 28 October. He then called a council of war aboard the transport *Amazonas* at which he revealed that he hoped for a surprise assault on the allied defenses at Pisagua with a pre-dawn landing of nearly five thousand troops on 2 November with a view to catching the defenders asleep and to capturing the rail line and rolling stock before the defenders could sabotage either. As an added guarantee of success, a simultaneous landing by a further two thousand men would take place down the coast at the undefended port of Junín, located some eight miles south of Pisagua, from which a flying column would proceed overland to take the allied forces at Pisagua in the rear, enabling the landing troops there to establish a secure beachhead and proceed with rapid exploitation. Another twenty-five hundred men would be held aboard ship as a floating reserve. The naval portion of the landing would be under the command of the formerly disgraced Captain Enrique Simpson, who had returned to the bridge of the *Cochrane*, and it was expected that the entire operation would only take a matter of hours.

And Sotomayor's assessment did not appear to be overly optimistic. The port of Pisagua consisted of a handful of hastily and poorly constructed buildings crowded between the crescent beach and a steep rise to a plateau of three to four hundred meters immediately behind them. A small sand-bagged fort crowned the tip of the headland marking the southern end of the shallow bay, sporting a single 115-pound Parrot rifle, with a similar redoubt on the headland at the northern end, both manned by a detachment of Peruvian sailors numbering not more than two hundred men plus perhaps as many as three hundred more locally raised militia of indifferent quality. A Bolivian infantry force consisting of the regiments "Victoria" and "Independencia" garrisoned the town itself with some nine hundred men, with another two regiments theoretically within two to three hours' march of the town. Neither the Peruvian commander for the region, General Buendía, nor the most senior Bolivian officer in the area, General Pedro Villamil, would be on hand to supervise the defense, at least in the early stages of the assault. Since Sotomayor estimated that the boats available to the fleet could land 900 men in each wave under close artillery support of the warships, the attackers would be fighting at relatively even odds from the outset, and this would evolve steadily in their favor as more troops came ashore and as defenders were drawn off to deal with the flanking attack from Junín.[11]

But nothing worked out quite right on the morning of 2 November. Through an error in navigation, the Chilean fleet rendezvoused at a point sixty-two miles from Pisagua, not fifty as had originally been planned the night before, so the sun was well up on the horizon when the dark warships and transports finally pulled into sight of the port. The Bolivian infantrymen who had been stationed at the railway station of El Hospicio at the summit of the switchback railway line up the escarpment from Pisagua itself, hurriedly stood to arms and raced down the hill, taking up strong defensive positions behind the stacked bags of nitrates awaiting export, and coal for use by the railroad, that littered the dockside area. They also dug in along the railbed itself, which gave them a series of terraced, parallel lines covering the bay and providing perfect protection from fire from below. The Peruvian naval gunners in the forts also manned their pieces and opened an enthusiastic, if largely ineffectual, bombardment of the fleet as it stood in to shore.

Cochrane and *O'Higgins* took on the southern fort, and their first rounds struck home, dismounting the gun and killing several officers, with the surviving gunners taking quickly to their heels. *Covadonga* and *Magallanes* likewise took the northern fort under fire, where the defenders had ceased replying by 0800 hours, and the Chileans suspended their own bombardment after lobbing a few shells into the vicinity of the town itself, attempting to avoid damaging the railroad station or any equipment that might be located there. Had the landing party been ready to move forward at this time, the battle might have ended there, but the inevitable confusion of loading and dispatching the boats in the heavy early morning fog wasted more than an hour, during which time the Peruvian gunners in the northern fort were rallied and returned to their weapon, opening a ragged fire that had to be suppressed once more before the defenseless boats could be risked.[12] The confusion was further aggravated, allegedly, by the drunkenness of Captain Simpson who was in charge of the landings.[13]

It was not until 1000 hours, therefore, that the first wave of boats began pulling for the shore under a covering fire from the smaller guns of the fleet. However, instead of carrying nine hundred men, as Sotomayor had foreseen, only 450 soldiers were aboard. It is possible that the minister had failed to account for the oarsmen who would have to remain with each heavy boat and take it back out to the waiting ships to load the successive waves, but, for whatever reason, the attackers were now going up against roughly twice their number of infantry, largely untouched by the bombardment and ensconced in strong defensive positions.

Still, two companies of the Chilean "Atacama" Regiment and another of sappers made for the rocky beach and flimsy quay under cover of the fire of a Gatling gun mounted in one of the boats for close-in support. As the sailors hunched over their oars, the infantrymen peppered the defenders with rifle fire and then splashed ashore, winning a narrow beachhead to which they clung while the boats made their painstakingly slow way back out to pick up another load. The second wave consisted of the rest of "Atacama" plus one company from "Buin" and some elements of the 2nd Line Infantry, and by the time the third wave landed, the Chileans had pushed the Bolivians out of the town, much of which was already in ruins from an earlier bombardment by the Chilean fleet back in April, and were gradually clawing their way up the escarpment, with assault parties taking the lower end of each switchback of the rail line and then rolling up the defenders' position while other companies poured in covering fire from the front to keep the defenders' heads down on the higher switchback levels.[14]

General Escala, possibly feeling marginalized by Sotomayor's monopolization of the command function, had made an effort to climb down into one of the landing boats to join his men, but Sotomayor had demanded that he remain with the fleet, arguing that his loss would be a tremendous coup for the enemy and a blow to the Chilean cause. When Escala insisted, Sotomayor simply ordered him to remain aboard, "in the name of the President of the Republic," and Escala obeyed, grudgingly. By 1400 hours, the attackers had reached the shabby buildings of El Hospicio at the crest of the escarpment, and the remaining defenders, allegedly headed by Generals Buendía and Villamil themselves, escaped pell-mell toward the town of San Roberto, some sixteen miles into the hinterland at which point Bolivian reinforcements were beginning to gather from nearby garrisons.[15] Buendía had allegedly ordered the destruction of all rolling stock, supplies, and water pumping equipment in the abandoned town, but his engineers apparently did not carry out this assigned task before escaping along with their general. The desertion of the bulk of the two Bolivian regiments at Pisagua reportedly soured Buendía on his allies, and, since most of the troops immediately at hand were Bolivian, no serious thought was given to a counterattack to attempt to drive the Chileans back into the sea, and Buendía ordered a concentration of his forces at Agua Santa about fifty miles to the southeast.[16]

The Chilean losses totaled only about fifty killed and 170 wounded, and allied battle casualties numbered about the same, although only some 240 members of the Bolivian "Victoria" regiment and barely two dozen from "Independencia" ultimately rallied to the colors, implying that most of these losses were undoubtedly due to desertion, with only some thirty prisoners left in Chilean hands, and most of these wounded. More importantly, the rail line had not been damaged, and several locomotives and freight cars, albeit in bad repair, had been captured, and a team of Chilean engineers whom Sotomayor had had the foresight to bring from Valparaíso were quickly put ashore to set them in working order.

Interestingly, while Sotomayor's grand strategy had called for a simultaneous landing at Junín, the ships with the troops designated for this disembarkation only moved off from Pisagua at 1100 hours, long after the battle had been joined, thus nullifying any effect they might have had in distracting the defenders there. They duly landed at Junín, scattering the handful of cavalry posted there by 1700 hours, and sent a column marching to El Hospicio, which they reached hours after the place had fallen to direct assault.[17] By evening the entire Chilean force was ashore and prepared for a further advance inland.

The next phase of the campaign would center on the control of water supplies. Perhaps overly affected by the previously mentioned bad experience of the reconnaissance force from Antofagasta in the desert, Sotomayor concentrated his effort in this area. Pisagua did not have a water still as did Antofagasta when the Chileans had captured that port, and had always depended for its supply on water brought in by sea or by rail from the wells at Dolores located some thirty miles inland along the rail line. Sotomayor had begun the construction of a still at Pisagua and had ordered another from Santiago besides keeping the stills on the ships anchored in the harbor working at full capacity. But he determined that, in order to gain the initiative, it would be necessary for the Chilean army to seize the wells at Dolores, both to support their own army as it advanced to the south to deal with the Buendía's forces and to deny this source of water to the enemy.[18]

A loop of railroad had been planned for this section of the coast before the war. Starting at Pisagua, it headed east to Dolores and then southeast through Santa Catalina to town of Pachica, for a total of perhaps sixty miles. A spur line would have eventually tied Pachica to the provincial capital of Tarapacá just to the east. The other end of the line began at Iquique and headed east to Noria, then north to Almonte, leaving an unfinished gap of about forty miles to Pachica. Both armies were obliged to make what use they could of this limited facility, Buendía's to facilitate his movement up from Iquique, and Escala for his advance inland from Pisagua, and the route of the line more or less inclined the Chileans to take care of the southern allied army first before turning on Daza's forces coming in from the north. The first order of business for the Chileans, therefore, was to determine the exact location of the two allied armies, to confirm that they had not yet effected a juncture, and to bring them to battle, if possible, before that time.

At this point Colonel Luis Arteaga, nephew of the former army commander, was at El Hospicio with the advance guard of the Chilean force, and he sent the former secretary, José Francisco Vergara, now in the role of a simple cavalry commander, with three mounted riders to scout the route forward. There had been a report that an enemy army of six thousand men was already at San Roberto, within easy striking distance of the wells at Dolores or of Pisagua itself, but Vergara proved this to be false.[19]

General Escala, who had now come up to El Hospicio himself, sent the energetic Vergara off with two companies of cavalry for further reconnaissance. On 4 November Vergara was able to confirm that the allied army under Buendía was concentrating at Agua Santa to the south, with another under Bolivian President Daza allegedly coming down from Arica via Camarones to the north which would give the allies, if the two forces effected a juncture, a considerable numerical superiority. On the 5th, Vergara found the water pumps at Dolores to have been left in working order, probably on the presumption by the Peruvians that they would be needing the wells themselves to support their counteroffensive, and he duly transmitted this information back to Escala on the coast.[20]

The next day the dashing Vergara's troop encountered a mixed force of Bolivian and Peruvian cavalry of slightly less strength at a small oasis/ranch called Germania. Although the fifty Bolivian and fourteen Peruvian troopers had time to dismount and take up defensive positions on a low hill, the charge by the Chilean troopers thoroughly routed them, leaving sixty killed, mostly during the wild pursuit, and the remaining four as prisoners of war. The Chileans lost only three men killed and six wounded in the spirited little action that did much to boost the morale of the Chileans and to undermine that of the allies.[21]

It is worth a brief digression at this point to delve more deeply into the nature of the hero of Germania, the ubiquitous José Francisco Vergara, as illustrative of the tenuous relations between the Chilean government and its military high command. Born in 1833 to a moderately prominent landed family, Vergara had been active in politics since his early youth. In the elections of 1871, he worked vigorously against the candidacy of Errazuriz but fervently welcomed the new president's conversion to increasingly Radical views (in party terms, as opposed to his original Conservatism). Vergara then worked even more fervently for the candidacy of President Pinto and endlessly complained in his memoirs about how, when he was the "only" person who supported Pinto at great sacrifice to his own time and treasure, the administration still seemed to look at him as an outsider, almost as an enemy.[22]

This attitude of paranoia and martyrdom was typical of Vergara's view of the world. He would always seem to be surrounded by imbeciles who did not have the wit to accept his sage advice and who actively worked to bring about his downfall. This, in turn, justified Vergara to engage in the most unscrupulous back-stabbing, both in the written word and in his actions. While he may have been an intelligent and energetic man, eager to serve his country, and a cavalry commander in the style of the dashing J. E. B. Stuart of the Confederacy, there could hardly have been a worse choice made of an individual for a position of trust and discretion.

And yet, he was chosen. He was first approached by Justo Arteaga, the newspaper editor son of the first commander of the Chilean expeditionary army, as a confidant and advisor to help his father at the front, and Vergara enthusiastically accepted the assignment, also at the urging of President Pinto, who wanted Vergara's candid view of the state of the army. No sooner was Vergara at Antofagasta, however, in mid-May of 1879, than he began to write the most cutting assessments of his commander.

Arteaga had not set the stage very well himself, apparently resenting Vergara's (and Sotomayor's) presence at his headquarters, since he may have been on in years, but he was not totally senile and readily understood their expected role as in-house critics of his actions and informants on behalf of the government. The old general joked with his officers when welcoming Vergara, who had an incredibly inflated opinion of his own value to any conceivable profession or situation, as someone with "long experience in the naval cavalry," an apparent reference to Vergara's total lack of military background. Vergara responded by beginning a clandestine correspondence with President Pinto, even over the head of War Minister Santa Maria, describing Arteaga as indecisive, forgetful, and timorous. Pinto, in his turn, accepted Vergara's comments at face value on the assumption that "if someone so close to the general (through Vergara's ties to

Justo Arteaga) expressed himself in such terms, there must be a serious reason."[23]

In response to Vergara's communiqués, Santa Maria traveled to Antofagasta in June 1879 and set up an informal civilian council there to discuss the actions of the military. This included Vergara, Rafael Sotomayor, and Isidoro Errazuriz. Vergara himself commented on the irony of this packet of bourgeois lawyers and politicians sitting about and discussing purely military matters as if they were "Wellingtons and Napoleons," but that did not keep him from participating in their deliberations.

Later, Vergara would be instrumental in convincing Santa Maria to accept Arteaga's resignation, arguing that, apart from the old general's apparent unwillingness to fight, there was the issue of the general being able to mobilize his political resources in opposition to the administration, a point that struck home to the politically astute Pinto. This same group of civilians, Vergara, Sotomayor, Errazuriz, and Santa Maria would select Escala as Arteaga's replacement, with the stipulation that Vergara would move over to become Escala's secretary. Apparently, the new commander had another young official in mind for the position, but Vergara claimed that Escala's ambition for the command won out over his personal preference, and he accepted the condition. This sounds suspiciously like a case of "projecting," in which Vergara attributed to others his own baser motives.

Almost immediately upon the new commander assuming his post, Vergara began a stream of scathing reports about him to President Pinto. He described Escala as "a good man" but totally incompetent. He stated that Escala possessed an "exuberant stupidity" and "a mind incapable of producing, or even receiving, the most elementary abstract idea," presumably ideas generously provided by Vergara himself. He went on to agonize over the "most cruel torture that a mortal can experience," that of a man of honor, such as himself, being obliged to serve an unworthy superior loyally while being honor bound to report candidly to his ultimate superior back home. It would be part of Vergara's martyrdom that he would never find a commander who quite measured up to his own lofty standards, and his account of the campaign, while insightful in many ways, must always be taken with a large grain of salt. He would describe scenes involving each officer under whom he served, in which everyone around him was overcome with shuddering, babbling fear and stupidity only to be rescued by Vergara's intelligence and bravery. For example, he claimed that, the night prior to the Chilean landing at Pisagua, Minister Sotomayor came to him in a total panic, insisting that the expedition was about to run out of water and that all that remained to do was to return in disgrace to Valparaíso. Fortunately, Vergara calmed the man down, got him to measure the amount of water in the immense cisterns carried by the fleet, and convinced him that there was more than enough water on hand for the operation, thus single-handedly averting a disaster for the expedition.[24]

In any event, Vergara, who made it a practice of conducting extensive personal reconnaissance patrols over any area in which he was posted, a habit that showed that he did have some basic military talents lacking in some of his professional colleagues, was given the task of guiding Colonel Domingo Amunátegui's 1st Division, comprising the 1st and 4th Line Regiments, plus the "mobilization" regiments "Coquimbo" and "Atacama" and a single battery of guns to Dolores on 6 November. Two days later these troops were joined by the 2nd Division under Colonel Urriola with the 3rd Line, "Valparaiso" and "Navales" Regiments plus another battery, giving a total of some six thousand men. Escala remained at El Hospicio with a reserve division under Colonel Luis Arteaga with the 2nd Line, "Zapadores," "Chacabuco," "Bulnes," the Naval Artillery Brigade, and another battery for thirty-five hundred men. Why Escala would remain this far in the rear with over a third of his force protecting a town that could amply be covered by the overwhelming firepower of the fleet, especially when an attack at Dolores was expected by the approaching allied armies at any moment, has never been fully explained.[25]

Meanwhile, on the allied side, the Chilean invasion, while hardly unexpected, had sown discord and confusion. Having been obliged to spread their troops out along the coast to guard against a Chilean descent at any point, the allied armies, under the nominal command of the two Presidents Prado and Daza, were divided into two main groups. In the south, General Juan Buendía, a sixty-five year old veteran of dubious military capacity, had left a garrison of fifteen hundred men at Iquique and was marching painfully north with about nine thousand men and eighteen guns including some five thousand Peruvians and four thousand Bolivians after reaching the end of track at Almonte.[26]

Another Bolivian force under Nicolas Campero had been concentrated in the Bolivian hinterland with a general idea of driving down to the coast through the former Bolivian territories. With only two to three thousand men, no artillery, and little cavalry, there was no hope that Campero could confront the main Chilean army directly. Rather, it was hoped that, once the Chileans moved north into Tarapacá, as they were presumed to be planning to do, Campero could sweep through the thinly held territory, and mop up isolated garrisons, unless Arteaga (or later Escala) found himself obliged to divert substantial forces to defend the new conquests, which would serve the allied purpose very well. However, the little army lacked virtually everything from sufficient weapons to uniforms, pack animals, shoes, and supplies for such a campaign. Through August, September, and October, Campero's column marched about aimlessly, sometimes heading toward the coast, sometimes retreating, covering literally hundreds of miles for no purpose, while suffering substantial losses to "wastage" from sickness, cold, and desertion in the process. Ultimately, only the Regiment "Chorolque" would eventually reach the allied army in Tacna, long after the loss of Tarapacá.[27]

In the north, President Prado, in nominal overall command, had ordered President Daza, in command of the Bolivian forces at Tacna, to move to Buendía's support, as their combined strength would give them a substantial advantage over Escala's army. On 8 November Daza set out from Tacna with 2,350 men, including Daza's favorite "Colorados" Regiment, "Sucre," the three regiments of the Cochabamba Division, a section of Gatling guns, and the hundred-man mounted "Bolivian Legion." At Arica the column paused briefly to await the arrival of the *Pilcomayo* with a shipment of fifteen hundred new rifles and six Krupp field guns, since the Cochabamba Division was still largely unarmed at this point.[28]

With no chance now for sea movement and no rail line paralleling the coast, the Bolivian army was faced with a lengthy march over virtually uninhabited desert. Prado strongly recommended that Daza march his men at night to avoid the worst heat of the day, but Daza pompously declared that he "was experienced in the handling of troops and that the Bolivian soldier could march for days together, under any conditions, without suffering the least fatigue." In his wisdom, Daza made no effort, nor did any of his officers, to review the troops, examine their packs or dictate what should be carried or left behind. Instead of being issued rations for the march, the troops were given a small amount of cash with which to purchase food from the handful of sutlers who traditionally accompanied the column, at whatever prices the merchants chose to set, and many of the raw troops chose to empty the water out of their canteens and replace it with wine before departing Arica. As was typical with raw troops, many of the Bolivians loaded up with useless gear while failing to take sufficient food, water, or ammunition. Prado had also recommended that Daza only take a thousand men with him, as the inadequate Bolivian pack train could not carry supplies for any more, but this advice was also ignored.[29]

Not surprisingly, the Bolivians ran out of water quickly, along with everything else of use in keeping them alive in the wilderness as the column snaked its way off into the choking clouds of alkali dust. The march from Arica to Camarones, some forty-five miles in length, should have taken two to three days, but Daza's column departed on the morning of 10 November and only arrived on the evening of 14 November.[30] Men began discarding their weapons and packs, and desertions had reached over two hundred, many of whom probably wandered off to perish in the desert, by the time the column straggled into Camarones, still barely halfway to their goal of juncture with Buendía's forces and without yet having come within sight of the enemy who now occupied a central position between the two armies.

Daza's attitude now changed completely, and he began to send Prado a stream of panicky messages about the state of his troops. He claimed that he had consulted with his officers, which he had not, and that they had unanimously advised against continuing the advance. He complained about a total lack of supplies, although Camarones at least had ample water and forage, and about his ignorance of the exact positions of either Buendía's army or that of the enemy, making it appear foolhardy to advance, possibly unsupported, against a Chilean army that would certainly outnumber his own.

On a more candid level, Daza had received word of the organization of strong political opposition to his regime back home, and it occurred to him that risking his beloved "Colorados" Regiment in combat with a real army was not the most efficient use of this political resource. He was quite aware that he only held power through coercion, and the means of this coercion was provided by the loyal "Colorados," whom he pampered and supported blatantly. Daza had already been obliged to compromise his long-standing policy through the demands of the war by raising and adequately arming thousands of new troops, thus giving some other ambitious commander the opportunity to seek the same road to the National Palace, through the barracks yard, that he had taken. It also struck him as unlikely that his popularity with the "Colorados" would survive any significant bloodletting in a real battle, especially an unsuccessful one. Consequently, he began to succumb to the urge to take his new army home, with the bright new weapons they had received from their Peruvian allies, and to use them to crush the opposition, a desire which was substantially stronger in Daza than his desire to recover Bolivia's lost coastline.[31]

One Bolivian author has suggested that President Prado was aware of and fully concurred with Daza's decision to withdraw his army from the campaign out of a selfish desire not to share in the glory of what would undoubtedly be a victorious battle against the Chileans, but there is no support for this wild theory.[32]   After all, if Daza were inclined to betray Peru to this extent, why would he have been so adamant in rejecting Chile's offer of Peruvian territory in exchange for the Bolivian Atacama?

Some Bolivian officers suggested at least sending out a reconnaissance to establish the location of both Buendía's and Escala's armies, but Daza ignored their objections and their appeals to the nation's honor and was insistent that retreat was the only option, and it was so ordered on 15 November. Daza later claimed that President Prado advised that he had given Buendía the order to attack with or without Daza's support, so the Bolivians could not have reached the battlefield in time in any event.

It is true enough that *after* Daza had made it clear to Prado that he had unilaterally decided to withdraw his forces from Camarones, Prado acceded. In a note to Daza dated 15 November, Prado wrote: "Seeing that you cannot advance with your army, the council of war that I called last night has resolved that Buendía attack the enemy tomorrow [the 16th]; thus it is not only dangerous but unnecessary for you to continue your march to the south." Rather than a hope to gain full responsibility for the coming victory, Prado's decision may have had more to do with a fear that, if he opposed Daza strongly, Daza might be tempted to withdraw the several thousands Bolivian troops already serving with Buendía.[33]

So the bedraggled Bolivian army shuffled back through the streets of Arica, to the bitter catcalls and pelting with garbage of the Peruvian populace, without having fired a shot. Daza himself remained at Camarones and even took the Bolivian Legion, his small mounted bodyguard, on a brief reconnaissance to the south, primarily to distance himself, physically if not morally, from the opprobrium of the retreat. Obviously, had there been any military purpose to the reconnaissance, it would have been done *before* the withdrawal of the army, when Daza was complaining bitterly about his lack of information on the locations of both the Chilean and Buendía's armies. In any event, Daza soon learned of the fate of Buendía's army at San Francisco and eventually returned to Tacna himself on 23 November.[34]

Meanwhile, Buendía's army of nine thousand men straggled north across the desert in search of either a battle with the Chileans, junction with Daza, or both.

Unlike Daza, Buendía did take Prado's advice to do his marching in the cool of the night, averaging about twelve miles at a stretch until arriving at the outpost of Negreiros on the morning of 18 November. Despite taking some care with the condition of his troops, the force had already dwindled to just over 7,400 men, about 4,200 Peruvians and 3,200 Bolivians, with eighteen guns and including about six hundred cavalry, with a disproportionately large number of the losses among the Bolivian troops who had taken the occasion to drift away over the passes of the Andes and back to their homes, particularly after the army had come across dozens of bloated, blackened, and rotting corpses strewn across their line of advance, the remnants of the allied cavalry troop massacred at Germania.[35] Oblivious to the view that Peru had only entered the war to support Bolivia against the Chilean invasion, many of the rank-and-file and even the officers in the Bolivian army apparently considered their own coastal territories definitively lost and that they were now fighting exclusively on behalf of the Peruvians. Even before Daza's retreat, there had never been anything like a close working relationship between the forces of the two allies. Buendía felt obliged to disperse his Bolivian forces among his own troops in the hope that this might put more mettle into his allies and prevent an entire sector of his line from simply vanishing in battle. The proud Bolivians understood his actions but resented his attitude during the length of their grudging cooperation in the field.[36]

After resting his troops all day on the 18th, Buendía called a council of his senior officers that evening. Although, at this juncture, Buendía was still under the impression that Daza's army could appear on the field at any moment, the decision was taken to assault the Chilean position at Dolores as soon as possible that day or the next rather than awaiting definitive word of the whereabouts of the Bolivian army. Scouts had accurately reported that the enemy had only about six thousand men or less at the wells, but it was also known that reinforcements could be moving up from the coast by train at any moment, and the allies would never have a better opportunity to catch the Chileans at a disadvantage. While there was still no sign of Daza's approach, Buendía felt that he had no choice but to seek battle. The Chileans at Dolores already sat between his army and friendly territory to the north. With the Chilean fleet unchallenged on the sea, the allied forces in the south would only grow weaker with time and eventually be forced to surrender for lack of supplies. If the enemy could be decisively defeated, however, the situation would change radically. If the expedition were destroyed, there would be the basis for a negotiated peace, even if the allies could not hope to move an army overland to reconquer the lost territory to the south directly. At the very least, driving the Chileans back under the guns of their fleet at Pisagua would open up the road north and enable Buendía to reunite with the allied forces in the Arica-Tacna area for further campaigning.

Chilean cavalry scouts had reported the enemy approach on the 18th, and Colonel Emilio Sotomayor, brother of the minister, chief of staff of the army, who had been placed in overall command of the forces at Dolores, wanted to send the army out to meet the allies on the plain at Santa Catalina. General

Escala had determined that there was not enough food and water at Dolores to support the whole expeditionary force, at least this was his claim after the fact, although it would seem that the rail line could have been used to provide the forces at Dolores with perfectly adequate supplies, and the wells there produced ample water. In any event, he kept some four thousand men idle at El Hospicio and, chose to remain there with them until after the battle had been decided.[37]

Sotomayor duly sent the 4th Line Infantry Regiment, supported by a cavalry squadron and eight guns, in the direction of Santa Catalina in the early evening, followed later by the "Atacama" Infantry Regiment. If we are to believe Vergara's account, he argued vociferously with Sotomayor against dispersing his force in such a way, as did Colonel Amunátegui, who was to command the advancing column. Vergara had taken the time since first arriving at Dolores to conduct personal reconnaissance of the entire area, something Sotomayor had apparently not done, and he had determined that there was no better defensive position than that already occupied by the army, and, given the superiority in numbers of Buendía's forces, even without Daza, the Chileans would need a strong position, from which their substantial artillery could be used to full effect. Sotomayor relented and, after just arriving at Santa Catalina at dawn, the weary Chilean regiments were obliged to about face and march back to their starting point, straggling into line just before the battle, having had no sleep, no food, and having marched for nearly eighteen hours without rest.[38]

That much is known, although Vergara's actual role is open to some question. As an indication of the kind of working relationship he had with his colleagues, he had just returned to Dolores after having threatened to resign from the army and return to Chile. Apparently, Colonel Urriola, who had operational command at Dolores prior to Colonel Sotomayor's arrival, had telegraphed Escala about a shortage of food, something that would have been Vergara's responsibility as his local chief of staff. When Sotomayor arrived shortly thereafter, Vergara allegedly demonstrated to him that there was abundant food, water, and forage, and Sotomayor cabled Escala, "Have arrived and resolved problem." That bit of cheek already enraged Vergara, but Escala's response that "I expected no less of you. I am glad to see that your presence has sufficed to make the difficulties disappear," was just too much for the vain Vergara, and he simply mounted up and galloped back to Pisagua, planning to take the first ship back home and end his escapade of military tourism. Again, according to Vergara, Escala begged, cajoled, and pleaded with him to keep this valuable officer in the field, claiming that he had only been stroking Sotomayor's ego and that he was quite aware that Vergara had personally seen to all of the army's needs, ultimately convincing him to take command of a squadron of cavalry for a reconnaissance of Daza's approach.

Vergara finally agreed and led a column of one hundred horsemen north to the town of Tana. There he observed a force of enemy cavalry about equal to his own and prepared an assault, but, just then, he spotted another column of cavalry off to his right and, assuming them to be the enemy, thought better of it and withdrew to join the army at Dolores. When he later learned that the first cavalry force had actually been President Daza and his escort and that the second had been a troop sent out by Sotomayor from Dolores *without having informed Vergara,* he was absolutely furious and could barely be persuaded to speak to the man thereafter. He would often refer to Sotomayor's "mental problems" which apparently manifested themselves in the latter's critical references to young civilian gentlemen posing as military officers through their political connections. Since the ill feelings were thoroughly mutual, it is questionable, therefore, how much influence Vergara actually had on Sotomayor's actions regarding the deployment of the army at the approach of the allies on the 19th.[39]

In any event, the key to the position at Dolores as it finally shook out was a collection of hills rising some two hundred meters from the surrounding plain, the Cerro de San Francisco in the south and the Cerro de los Tres Clavos to the north, both located parallel to the Pisagua rail line which ran along the eastern base of the hills. The town of Porvenir was located on the rail line just south of the southernmost edge of the hills, with that of San Francisco perhaps half a mile to the north, with Dolores still farther north on the flank of the Cerro de los Tres Clavos. The Chileans had set up their defensive position along the southern edge of the San Francisco hill, with their thirty-four guns arranged in a fan along a shelf of raised ground running from the rail line to the western edge of the hill, providing an excellent field of fire over the open ground over which the allies would have to approach. The infantry was deployed to support the guns, with the cavalry held back in the saddle between the Cerro de San Francisco and Tres Clavos.

On the Chilean right, facing more or less to the west, Urriola had the regiments "Navales," "Valparaiso" and the 1st Line with two Gatlings, a six-gun mountain battery under Captain Roberto Wood and a four-gun field battery under Captain Eulojio Villarreal. In the center, Colonel Amunátegui had "Coquimbo" and "Atacama" plus four Krupp guns and four French bronze muzzle loaders under Major Juan de la Cruz Salvo. Straggling out onto the plain to the east of the hills, running perpendicular to the rail line, Colonel Velazquez had the 3rd Line and the remaining artillery, plus a Gatling gun with some skirmishers and a squadron of cavalry covering his open flank.[40]

The flaw in this arrangement was that Sotomayor apparently counted on Buendía mounting his attack against the southwestern face of the hills west of the rail line when there was no good reason why the allies could not have just as easily swept to the east of the line, occupied the town of San Francisco, and forced the Chileans to redeploy hastily at the moment of the assault. Buendía had no reason to be concerned about his own line of communications back to Iquique, which was already isolated in any event, but he could easily have maneuvered to cut Sotomayor's rail link to Pisagua. This would have had the added benefit of simultaneously opening up Buendía's own route of retreat to Arica in the north. It would have been even more telling had Daza actually completed his march and come in to support Buendía's right, and it is hard to imagine how Sotomayor could have counted on Daza's bizarre decision to retreat just prior to the battle. Fortunately, for Sotomayor this option did not occur to General Buendía either.

If part of the Chilean army was fatigued from their fruitless wandering of the night before, the entire allied army was hardly in better shape after their weary approach march across the desert. They were very short of water and the barren plain in front of the Chilean position brought no relief. It was generally flat but pockmarked with countless pits dug by the nitrate miners making enough of a moonscape to make the proper alignment of troops very difficult, and the alkaline dust kicked up by the marching men soon covered men, animals, and guns with a caustic white coating that burned the eyes and parched the throat. The allies moved up in a rough arc with the right resting on the rail line with the Peruvian divisions of Bustamante and Dávila and the Bolivian division of Villegas. The left half of the line was formed of the Peruvian divisions of Velarde and Bolognesi with Villamil's Bolivians stretching out to the west and north with Caceres and the Peruvian 3rd Division in reserve. The full battery of eighteen guns, barely half the firepower of the Chilean artillery, was located behind the right wing, where it appeared the direct frontal thrust was intended, straight up the rail line, but General Buendía had positioned himself on the left and seemed to be envisioning a broad sweeping maneuver around the Chilean right, although this brought his force within the range of every Chilean gun without taking any advantage of the shortness of the Chilean line to get around their flanks and placed the full line of the San Francisco hills between him and the vital Chilean rail link back to the coast.[41] That this also happened to coincide with Sotomayor's estimation of allied intentions could not have been known to Buendía, but that did not improve the chances of success.

While Buendía's choice of his axis of attack might have been debatable, what followed was simply incomprehensible. Many battles in history have been what are euphemistically referred to as "meeting engagements" which means that neither general had a clue as to the proximity of his opponent, and the two armies merely stumbled into each other. Here, however, both commanders were fully aware of the location and disposition of his enemy, but neither apparently had any intention of joining battle on this day. The weary allied troops formed into their rough lines and advanced across the foul-smelling nitrate fields as soon as the fog burned off at mid-morning after having a brief rest from their night march. Then, when they had reached within two kilometers of the Chilean lines, they halted.

There is some confusion about just when Buendía learned of Daza's retreat, although it was probably during the course of the morning of the 19th, which implies that President Prado was not overly efficient in passing this word along, since it was known in Arica three days before, so the general may still have been hoping for a juncture with the Bolivian army, although even the most rudimentary scouting by his cavalry would have told him that no forces were close enough to support him on that day. It was also quite visible from the allied position that Chilean reinforcements continued to hurry up from the coast by train, disembarking at the little station at San Francisco under the very eyes of the attackers throughout the battle, so further delay was clearly tilting the numerical odds in the favor of the defenders. Buendía commented that the troops needed to rest after their exertions, but it would have seemed that the logical time for this would have been at the point where they halted at the end of the night march, well out of range of enemy guns and observation instead of under the merciless Atacama sun among the foul-smelling nitrate pits. Had they stopped in the hills before descending to the plain, they could have made camp and at least prepared themselves a hot meal. But stop them he did, just a few hundred meters short of the Chilean lines, and the two armies just sat and stared at each other for several long hours.[42]

At this point, it occurred to Buendía to send forward troops on the right to take possession of the wells at El Porvenir, several hundred yards south of the nearest spur of the San Francisco hills, in order to supply some water to the thirsty army, and Bustamante's "Exploradora" Division and Villegas' 1st Bolivian Division were chosen for the task. It should be noted that all of the armies involved in this war were extremely cavalier in their labeling of military units. The terms battalion and regiment are used more or less interchangeably but essentially correspond to a unit of regimental size typical of the American Civil War, anywhere from four to twelve hundred men. A "division" would have been more like a brigade, containing from two to four regiments.

The allies also sent forward four companies of their best troops as skirmishers on the right, one each from the Peruvian regiments "Zepita" and "Ayacucho" and two more from the Bolivian "Illimani" and "Olaneta" Regiments.[43] Skirmishers were still a necessary formation at this point in military evolution because, despite the lessons of defensive firepower from the American Civil War, the belligerents in the Atacama continued to send troops into battle arrayed in long lines, shoulder-to-shoulder, only slightly less densely packed than in Napoleon's time, and with no thought to making use of available cover for individual fire and movement. While the terrible casualties of Gettysburg and Antietam had been due to a marginal improvement in infantry firepower, with the cap and ball musket having an effective range of up to four hundred meters compared to barely one hundred of the "Brown Bess" of the Revolutionary War and a slightly improved rate of fire, the weapons in the hands of the Peruvian, Bolivian, and Chilean combatants were of a far higher lethality. The Chassepot and Comblain rifles were rapid-fire breech loaders accurate out to six hundred meters and still deadly to twice that distance,[44] and the artillery employed almost exclusively breech-loading Krupps many times more rapid that the old 12-pound Napoleons widely used just a decade before. Then again, it is perhaps unfair to expect these largely inexperienced South American commanders to have learned a lesson that would continue to escape the commanders of the armies of the supposedly "advanced" European countries throughout the hell of the First World War a full generation later.

In any event, while the bulk of the advanced allied troops busied themselves with filling canteens and casks with water at El Porvenir, the skirmishers, perhaps three hundred men in all, spread out in a rough line under the command of Major Espinar, moving forward from the low mud brick buildings toward the hills that rose suddenly from the barren plain. It was at this point that chaos set in. It would be well to be able to say that the plans of the opposing commanders fell apart, but it would be stretching the truth to imply that anyone had any

particular plan *to* fall apart. The only specific intention of both sides appeared
to be that neither expected the battle to begin that day. It was already mid-
afternoon. Buendía was allowing his troops the poor rest they could get under
the guns of the enemy, although these had not opened fire as yet, and
Sotomayor, not about to initiate combat until Escala and the rest of the army
could come up from El Hospicio, was spending his time in the telegraph office,
over a kilometer to the rear of the front lines, communicating with his
commander.[45]

But it is impossible to keep large numbers of armed men in close proximity to
each other for any length of time, especially when all of them have been stirred
up by patriotic propaganda and who have endured considerable hardships just to
get to that point. Apparently, some of the allied skirmishers opened fire on the
Chilean guns facing them at around three o'clock in the afternoon, which, in
turn provoked a desultory bombardment of their position by the Chilean
gunners. With the common sense typical of the infantrymen, the Bolivian and
Peruvian skirmishers quickly realized that their greatest safety lay, not in
hugging the featureless ground down on the plain in full view of the enemy, but
to rush to the base of the hill, where the Chilean guns could not be depressed
enough to reach them, and this they did in short order. Then, having made it this
far, it occurred to them that it might be a good thing to silence the guns once and
for all, and they charged, barely three hundred against twenty times their
number, without orders or support of any kind.[46] This placed them on the slope
beneath the battery of Major Salvo, who had advanced his guns to a little spur of
the hill mass that would give him an excellent flanking fire on any force
advancing on the right side of the Chilean line, but it also placed him well out in
front of the covering infantry force.[47]

General Buendía saw what was happening on his right, and quickly ordered
two Bolivian regiments of General Villegas' division, "Ayacucho" and
"Illimani" and the Peruvian "Puno" Regiment, plus the bulk of his cavalry,
forward to support the advance by sweeping around the Chilean left to the east
of the railroad, which he should have done from the outset. But these troops
fired wildly at the hills, striking some of their own skirmishers in the back.
Most of these reinforcements were then pinned down by fire from Salvo's guns
in the mud huts of Porvenir, although a few men made their way forward to join
the advance up the hill.[48]

Soon firing became general all along the line. The "Exploradora" Division
under Dávila tried to move up along the rail line itself but was taken under
heavy fire by the Chilean artillery and driven back. Farther to the allied left,
Velarde's and Bolognesi's divisions were pounded in the open by the rapid fire
of the Chilean Krupp guns that the allied artillery was powerless to silence, and
Villamil's Bolivians on the far left were stopped within a thousand yards of the
hill and routed, also by long range artillery fire, without the Chilean infantry
even taking part as yet.

Meanwhile, the allied skirmishers had actually overrun several of the Chilean
artillery pieces that had inexplicably been left without direct infantry support,
defended only by the sixty-five gunners of Captain Salvo's battery. The closest

Chilean infantry was the "Atacama" Infantry Regiment, which sent over two companies to join in the bitter hand-to-hand fighting around the guns. A single company of the Bolivian "Dalence" Regiment managed to reach the hill and come up to Espinosa's support on the allied side, but hundreds of Chileans were quickly being fed into the battle, and the attackers were soon driven back over the lip of the hill.[49]

Villegas and Colonel Ramírez de Arellano gathered up a scratch force of remnants of several Bolivian and Peruvian regiments on the right and made use of dead ground to push up past the town of San Francisco itself with a view to turning the Chilean line from the east. However, they suffered heavily from flanking fire from the remaining Chilean guns on the hill, and, as the columns turned to storm the high ground, the Chilean 3rd Line rose up from a depression in which it had been concealed out on the plain, and poured a murderous volley into their backs. At the same time, Regiment "Coquimbo" had come into position along the hilltop and swept the slope with accurate rifle fire, completing the destruction of the only allied force to conduct a serious attack that day, and expending some 112 rounds per man in the process.[50]

The rest of the allied line was pinned down on the plain. The soldiers had ready-made foxholes in the form of the shallow nitrate pits, and they dived into these and kept up of steady long-range fire on the Chilean positions, but they could not advance. Then the line began to crumble. First, the allied cavalry, that might have been of use in sweeping around the Chilean rear, at least to cut the rail line to prevent further reinforcements from riding directly onto the battlefield, simply deserted en masse, with each trooper taking advantage of the mobility provided him by his government to take himself all the way home, either to Bolivia or Peru. Only a single Bolivian squadron made an effort to support the infantry before the first Chilean volley sent them into headlong retreat as well. Next the Bolivians, with the exception of the "Loa" Regiment and the skirmisher companies still entangled with the Chileans on the slopes of the hill, fired off a few more ragged volleys and then decamped shouting, "To Oruro! To Oruro!" and disappeared from the campaign for good.[51] Peruvian General Bustamante, along with regimental commanders Mori Ortiz, Prado, and Zabala, had fled ahead of their troops, not stopping until they reached Arica, although Zabala would ultimately redeem his honor, dying in the battle for El Morro at Arica. Caceres, in command of the reserve division, was preparing to march forward to the sound of the guns, when Chief of Staff Suárez came galloping up and urged him to save his troops and the artillery and to pull back as all was lost. Instead of retreating, however, Caceres deployed his division on line as a rear guard, allowing the rest of the battered army to withdraw through his position to the south.[52]

About this time, just after five o'clock, General Escala arrived from El Hospicio, his entourage preceded by a huge banner of the Virgin and with his spiritual advisor, Friar Madariaga riding at his side. It is still hard to imagine what task the Chilean commander found so compelling on the coast that he would leave the direction of the bulk of his forces, in contact with the bulk of the enemy army, to his chief of staff for the whole day. Even though a large portion of the Chilean infantry and all of the cavalry had not even been engaged to any significant degree, and with a full infantry regiment, "Bulnes," arriving with Escala from the coast, Escala did not choose to pursue the retreating allies. Only two or three companies ventured forward from their entrenchments, and these were turned back at the first determined volleys by Caceres' troops out on the plain.[53]

The allied retreat at first went well enough, unmolested as it was by a determined pursuit. A brief council of war was called, and the commanders, except for General Buendía and Colonel Velarde who had "gone on ahead," agreed on a retreat to Arica via Tiviliche to the north. An order of march was set up with the artillery leading the way, followed by the divisions of Dávila, Bolognesi, and Velarde (under the command of Colonel Herrera as Velarde had absented himself), with Caceres bringing up the rear. Suárez, as chief of staff, was in overall command, but he lacked accurate maps, or even a compass, to provide direction. Fortunately, a soldier of the "Zepita" Regiment had worked for years as a digger in the nitrate fields hereabouts, and offered to serve as a guide with Dávila's scouts.

It was an extremely dark night, and this was made worse by the sudden descent of an impenetrable *comanchaca* fog that shrouded the entire region. The weary troops trudged on, each man hanging on to the pack of the man in front, until sometime after midnight, a warning ran through the column that unidentified troops were marching off to their left. Suárez, his nerves already taught from the day's unsuccessful battle called for an increase in speed, and the artillerymen cut the traces to their guns and caissons, mounted their mules, and raced off into the night. Suárez was then obliged to give orders for burying the artillery to facilitate the escape of the rest of the army, but Caceres investigated and discovered that their "pursuers" were actually the "Cabritas" Regiment from Herrera's division that had gotten separated at a rest stop and had taken off on a parallel course from the rest of the army.[54]

The total confusion of the army convinced the commanders to call a halt in the hope that daylight would make things easier. To their consternation, when the sun rose and began to burn off the fog, they found themselves still within sight of the San Francisco hills, having stumbled around in a circle, and heading southeast toward Tarapacá instead of north toward Tiviliche. Apparently the guide had been no more able to find his way in the fog than anyone else, and Dávila's constant roaring at him had only addled the simple man's brains, leading to more confusion. Now, with no concealment of the night, there was no way that the army could simply stroll past the Chilean Army that sat astride their line of retreat, and it was decided to continue south to Tarapacá with a view toward swinging eastward into the foothills of the Andes and skirting the Chilean positions on that side. With no further misadventures, the demoralized troops finally arrived at Tarapacá on the evening of 22 November, after marching for days in 100° temperatures with only brackish water to drink, and little of that, where they collapsed along the banks of the muddy, alkaline stream that ran through the narrow valley and waited for their commanders to decide what to do.[55]

But the allied army had been virtually destroyed. After departing Iquique with over nine thousand men barely two weeks before, less than three thousand fatigued and dispirited troops were gathered in the narrow valley of Tarapacá. The actual battle losses at San Francisco had been about five hundred dead for the allies compared to only sixty dead and about twice as many wounded for the defenders (nearly half from the Regiment "Atacama" alone, showing the lack of involvement of most of the defending army), and some prisoners had fallen into Chilean hands, but the bulk of their losses had been through the near total defection of the Bolivian army and sizeable units of the Peruvian. The army was now also without any artillery or cavalry and, even after Buendía ordered Colonel Ríos to bring his fifteen hundred men, mostly locally recruited militia and sailors now incorporated as infantrymen, up from Iquique, the combined force was woefully inferior to anything the Chileans were likely to send against them and in dire risk of being surrounded and destroyed before a juncture could be effected with Prado's army at Tacna.[56]

Meanwhile, back in the Chilean camp, General Escala had been having trouble deciding just what to do with his army's victory. Despite the fact that the Chileans had ample cavalry forces at hand, and the allies had none to oppose them, he made no effort to pursue and destroy the retreating army or even to keep in contact with it. Instead, the Chileans limited themselves to patrolling out to Porvenir where they rounded up some eighty wounded allied soldiers, including General Villegas, and digging up the abandoned allied guns.[57]

This gave Buendía the gift of several vital days in which to rest and reorganize his scattered forces, which they desperately needed after marching and fighting, being virtually without sleep or food for some fifty-one hours. Escala offered various explanations for this lapse including that he was under the impression that the alkaline dust of the plains hurt his horses' hooves. On another occasion he offered that the disintegration of the allied army had left him without a single viable target at which to aim his own army, and lastly that Minister Sotomayor had specifically ordered him not to conduct such a pursuit. Sotomayor replied to this last point denying that he had issued such orders, although admitting that he had not specifically ordered Escala to press after the allies and destroy them as it would have been "offensive to presume to tell a general something that any corporal should have known."[58]

Escala did take the opportunity to capture the now undefended port of Iquique, traveling there himself by sea to get as full credit as possible for the coup, although leaving his army in the field again under his chief of staff for days as a result. Peruvian General Lopez Lavalle, prefect of the province, had taken refuge aboard the British ship HMS *Turquoise* in the harbor upon the departure of Colonel Ríos and his garrison, leaving the fire brigade as the only organized body of men in uniform in the town. For fear of looting by the many stragglers from the allied army that prowled the streets, a delegation of the foreign consuls, including the American, British, Italian, and German missions, were rowed out to the *Cochrane* to ask for troops to come ashore quickly on 22 November. Sensitive to Escala's desire to be present at the "capture" of the port, 125 armed sailors were quietly put ashore, but they generally stayed out of sight, apart from freeing forty-seven survivors of the *Esmeralda* and escorting them out to the blockading fleet where they were received as heroes. Escala then took formal possession of the port the next day.[59]

As if these events weren't bad enough for the allies, Peru suffered yet another disaster at sea. Although incapable of seriously challenging Chilean naval dominance, the frigate *Union* and the gunboat *Pilcomayo* had sallied from Arica in the hope of scooping up some unescorted transports and generally making a nuisance of themselves. At dawn on 18 November, the two ships were off the mouth of the port of Ilo when they spotted a smudge of smoke on the horizon that was soon identified as the ironclad *Blanco Encalada*. At first *Union* offered herself up as bait, relying on her superior speed to evade pursuit later, but Riveros on *Blanco Encalada* was not so easily distracted and set his course to intercept *Pilcomayo*, knowing that he enjoyed a one-knot speed advantage over the gunboat.

By 0930 hours, with the enemy still five miles off, Comandante Ferreiros on the *Pilcomayo* called a council of war of his officers and determined to scuttle the ship. He opened fire at maximum range, with no effect, while crewmen splashed coal oil and other combustibles about the deck and the engineers opened the sea cocks below. As the Chilean came closer, Ferreiros ordered abandon ship and set the superstructure ablaze, but a motivated Chilean boarding party swarmed up the sides, extinguished the fires and were able to stop the flooding. After a night of steady work at the pumps, the *Pilcomayo* was taken in tow and brought into Iquique on the 20th as another prize for the navy.[60]

Back on land, true to his nature, Jose Francisco Vergara had been lobbying incessantly for an aggressive pursuit of the enemy, and Escala finally granted him permission to take four hundred cavalrymen in the direction of Tarapacá on 24 November to determine the state of the enemy's forces. Concealing his men in one of the narrow valleys west of Tarapacá, Vergara had occasion to see a column of enemy troops, actually Ríos' men from Iquique, dejectedly shuffling toward the town. From the sorry condition of their uniforms and their lack of march discipline, Vergara assumed this to be the bulk of the defeated allied army and sent word back to Dolores that this last remnant of the enemy could easily be swept away, possibly bringing the campaign to an early and successful conclusion. Escala promptly reinforced him with eighteen hundred men under Colonel Luis Arteaga, nephew of the former army commander, and eight guns, bringing the total Chilean force to 2,285 men, more than enough to deal with the fifteen hundred stragglers Vergara had estimated to be at Tarapacá.[61]

Actually, together with a number of stragglers who had come in by twos and threes since the battle at San Francisco, and with Ríos' division, Buendía now had over forty-five hundred men ready for duty, nearly all Peruvians with the exception of the Bolivian "Loa" Infantry Regiment that had remained faithfully with the colors. It should also be noted that hundreds of other Bolivian soldiers had been incorporated into various Peruvian regiments after their parent regiments had disintegrated, so the total allied force present may have been more evenly divided.[62] It was true that Buendía still had no guns or cavalry, but the morale of the little force was on the mend as the men at least now had had a chance to rest, eat, and drink to their satisfaction after weeks of deprivation. The ragged look of Ríos' column, that had convinced Vergara that the entire allied army was on the verge of collapsing, was due to the fact that they were largely militia, poorly equipped to begin with, who had just come off four days of hard marching through the desert. But the Chileans were about to learn that this was an army that still would require defeating, not merely rounding up.[63]

Vergara's account of the battle stands in marked contrast to his version of the other actions in which he participated. For one thing, he characterized Colonel Arteaga as an "excellent officer," the only positive word he had ever to say about any officer with authority over him in the field. He then goes on to state casually that, since Arteaga had been given command of the force as a full colonel in the regular army compared to Vergara's commission as a lieutenant colonel in the National Guard, he, Vergara, reverted to the status of a simple soldier during the course of the battle. This would have been the first time that Vergara would voluntarily relinquish command, no matter what authority issued the orders, but this view conveniently relieves Vergara of any responsibility for the outcome of the battle, which he also does not find it worthwhile to describe.[64]

In any event, Arteaga came up with a rather complicated plan of attack, one focused more on preventing the escape of a band of refugees than the defeat of a substantially larger armed force (although at least one source claims that the plan was Vergara's, a point he modestly refrains from making).[65] Buendía's army was encamped in and around the town of Tarapaca, a modest collection of adobe houses and a single stone church on the banks of a narrow stream that had carved a gully some three hundred meters below the level of the surrounding plain, not unlike the dozen or so other small settlements that dotted the stream's course from the foothills of the Andes down toward the sea. Comandante Ricardo Santa Cruz was to take the "Zapadores" Regiment, a company of the 2nd Line, a squadron of the "Granaderos" Cavalry and four Krupp mountain guns, a total of five hundred men, on a sweep along the high ground west of the town and the narrow valley in which it nestled to the village of Quillahuasa at a point north of allied position, thus blocking any possible retreat up the valley. Lieutenant Colonel Eleutero Ramírez would take the remaining seven companies of the 2nd Line and the squadron of the "Cazadores" cavalry with two bronze naval guns directly following the winding river itself up to the town, driving the Peruvians back against the blocking position occupied by Santa Cruz. Arteaga himself would take the "Chacabuco" Regiment around the right flank of the allied position, but inside the arc of Santa Cruz's march with the idea of dislodging any line the enemy might set up blocking the valley against Ramírez.[66]

The individual elements of the force would be from one to two miles from each other over very difficult, broken ground with no direct communications between them. Normally it is a truism of the military art that it is a fatal mistake to divide one's force in the face of the enemy, particularly if the enemy has an advantage in numbers. In Arteaga's defense, even though his scouts estimated that the defenders had as many as twenty-five hundred men on hand, up from fifteen hundred reported by Vergara but still barely half their actual number, Arteaga had reason to assume that he still had the superior force. Also, it should be noted that military history provides quite as many examples of decisive victories being won by inferior forces precisely by dividing to attack from different directions. Washington had done it at Trenton, Napoleon had done it on many occasions, and Lee had done it almost habitually. This is the way of military history. If a commander takes a gamble and succeeds, he is a genius. If he fails, he is a fool. But, unfortunately, Arteaga was not a Napoleon, a Lee, or even a Washington.

To make matters worse, the Chileans were not really ready for battle. Vergara's original excursion had been meant as nothing more than a reconnaissance, and the men had brought little in the way of supplies. He had hoped that Arteaga would have brought up a supply train with him, at least including some food, but this column had been put on the road hastily, and Escala had promised to forward food, water, and ammunition directly, but this had not arrived as yet. The men had been marching for the better part of two days, and some of them had not eaten for twenty-four hours, which did little to improve their fighting edge. However, such was the concern of both Arteaga and Vergara that the enemy would escape, that no thought was given to awaiting the arrival of more supplies or of giving their troops time to rest.

Most of the Peruvians, on the other hand, had had five full days to rest and recover from the trauma of San Francisco, with the exception of Ríos' men who had arrived on the 26th, but they had not been in a battle. Almost as if to even the odds, Buendía had sent Davila with his own "Exploradora" Division and the 1st Division on to Pachica, fifteen miles upstream to the northeast the day before to ease his own shortage of supplies, with plans for the rest of the army to follow that morning, and he failed even to post sentries around his encampment. This left him with about three thousand men immediately around Tarapaca, the 2nd Division under Caceres, the 3rd under Bolognesi, Ríos' 5th National Guard Division, and the "Vanguardia" Division. Buendía clearly had no inkling of an impending Chilean attack, which arguably gave the Chileans a fair chance at launching their surprise assault at dawn as planned.[67]

Since Santa Cruz's column had the farthest to go, it set off at 0330 hours, with the other two columns to start an hour later. In the pitch darkness and thick fog, however, Santa Cruz soon got lost, and when the sun finally burned off the mist around 0800, his men were revealed strung out on the open slopes of the hills just west of Tarapaca, instead of being a mile farther to the north in defensive positions blocking egress from the valley as planned. General Caceres, casually riding the lines as his troops breakfasted and prepared to decamp for Pachica later that day, spotted the enemy force and immediately took action. As he stood in the midst of his old regiment "Zepita," he formed it up into three assault columns of two companies each and rushed them at the Chileans who occupied slightly higher ground to the west. The "Dos de Mayo" Regiment joined in, and soon nearly a thousand Peruvians were charging the Chileans across open ground. At the same time, Buendía sent messengers galloping after Davila to bring his men back into the fight.[68]

Captain Fuentes, in command of the artillery section with Santa Cruz, recommended that the column stop and have the guns unlimbered, but Santa Cruz felt it his obligation to carry his out his orders and continue on down into the valley near Quillahuasa, abandoning the high ground to the Peruvians where Bolognesi's division had now come up to support Caceres, putting well over a thousand Peruvians in a position to fire down on the exhausted Chileans from as close as one hundred meters. The fight here lasted little more than half an hour, but Santa Cruz lost at least a third of his infantry, his cavalry having ranged on ahead before the Peruvian attack, and a rush by two companies of "Zepita" overran his four guns before they could deploy. Peruvian losses were substantial as well, including the commander of the "Dos de Mayo" Regiment and General Caceres' younger brother, Juan, a lieutenant in "Zepita."[69]

Arteaga and Ramírez were two to three miles southeast of Santa Cruz, having nearly reached the buildings of Tarapaca itself along the river valley, while the latter was actually cut off from the main Chilean force by Caceres' and Bolognesi's troops, but Arteaga quickly began marching to the sound of the guns, abandoning his own plan of advance. Santa Cruz gradually worked his way back through the maze of gullies to the west of Tarapacá to rejoin Arteaga and Ramírez, forming a rough line running east and west across the valley south of the town. At the same time the rest of Buendía's troops came into line as well, and they slowly pushed the Chileans southward through the morning, taking two more guns in the process.[70]

At about 1100, Santa Cruz's force of cavalry, only about 115 men, who had been setting up a now useless blocking position at Quillahuasa, came charging down on the right rear of the allied line, nearly routing the "Navales" Regiment and the Bolivian "Loa" Regiment, but a timely realignment of the Iquique militia drove off the attackers with a well-placed volley. Now, with both sides weary and having suffered heavy losses, a lull fell over the battlefield as the wounded were gathered in and the line solidified just north of the town of San Lorenzo. The merciless sun beat down, with temperatures reaching above 100° while most of the men on both sides were without water in their canteens.[71]

From the middle of the afternoon on, Buendía kept feeding fresh units into the battle as parts of his army returned from Pachica. Bedoya's 6th Division, which had just set off for the north when the Chilean approach had been discovered, came up on the Peruvian right. Davila's force arrived around 1630 hours and was also fed into the battle on the right, driving the Chileans completely from the field and capturing their last two guns before the firing finally died down at dusk. Buendía allowed only a desultory pursuit, lacking any cavalry for the job, and, despite the victory, determined to continued his retreat toward Arica the next morning on the 27th. General Baquedano quickly brought up five thousand Chilean infantry and five hundred more cavalry from San Francisco to reinforce Arteaga, and a reconnaissance of the battlefield soon turned up the eight captured guns that the Peruvians had buried, lacking any draft animals to haul them away, but the fighting here was over.[72]

In terms of the overall forces present in the Atacama, the Battle of Tarapaca could hardly have been seen as a decisive engagement. Of course, if Arteaga's assessment had been correct and he had bagged the entire allied force, the blow would have been of some importance; but even the annihilation of the entire Chilean force, barely a quarter of Escala's army, would have still left the invaders in a dominant position in the area.

The battle had widespread ramifications nonetheless. Obviously, it provided a much-needed boost to allied morale after the fiascoes of Pisagua and San Francisco and the disasters of the naval campaign, although the Bolivian role was minimal. It at least demonstrated that the Chileans were not invincible. More important, however, were the stunning losses, particularly on the Chilean side. The Peruvians lost about 230 killed and a like number wounded, probably many more actual battle casualties than they had suffered at San Francisco, although at that battle desertion had gutted the entire army. The smaller Chilean force, however, suffered well over five hundred killed and over two hundred wounded besides several dozen prisoners for a total of some eight hundred casualties out of 2,285 men engaged.[73]

The surviving Chileans had withdrawn in good order, and with the Peruvians moving in the other direction, happy to be allowed to get away, as there was no chance of the Chilean invasion being thrown back into the sea. But the true impact of the battle had to do with the horrendous losses and their impact on the close-knit Chilean society. Considering the size of the forces engaged, eight hundred casualties out of a force of only 2,285 represented an even higher percentage at nearly 35 percent than those suffered by either side at the battles of Antietam or Gettysburg, the bloodiest days in American military history. And with over five hundred *killed* outright, nearly one man in four, the "butcher's bill" for what amounted to little more than a skirmish shocked Chilean society to the core. In terms of percentage of population, the Chilean losses represented nearly double the ratio of that of the Union losses at Gettysburg. There were few families in Santiago or Valparaíso that did not suffer a loss at Tarapaca.

Sensitive to public criticism of its running of the war, the Pinto administration kept news of the disaster out of the press for some days, but given the imperfect nature of censorship of the mails coming back from the front, the tight-knit Chilean society soon learned of the scope of the defeat. The public had become used to the war as a kind of sport, with some losses to be sure, but hardly more than necessary to spice up the newspaper accounts and to provide the nation with a much-needed crop of martyrs and heroes. The Bolivian coastal territory had been taken almost without a shot being fired, the sea was under total Chilean control after a short period of doubt, and the landings at Pisagua and the San Francisco campaign had pushed the front line far away from the nation's boundaries. The only question then had been how much more the enemy could take before succumbing, and revenues were already starting to come in from the conquered nitrate fields to begin to offset the cost of the war. Tarapaca, however, brought home to the Chilean public that this was a real war after all, that there would likely be a great deal more fighting to come, and more of the "bloody math" to do before the end.

Also, while there had been occasional stories of looting and the shooting of prisoners and wounded, rumors of atrocities became more marked now. The

Chileans claimed that the Peruvians had torched a house being used as a field hospital that was full of Chilean wounded during the latter stages of the battle,[74] while the Peruvians insisted that Lieutenant Enrique Vargas had been shot dead under a flag of truce while attempting to negotiate the surrender of the house, thus justifying his enraged troops for burning it down.[75] Thus, far from being an adventure, a lark, the war was beginning to turn ugly with no end in sight.

There was a great deal of scrambling in the aftermath of the battle to place and misplace the blame. Escala demanded reinforcements and a formal statement of absolution of responsibility for the defeat from the government, which might have been justified since this was the third battle in which his army had been engaged without his direct involvement, while Minister Sotomayor demanded exactly the opposite sort of statement. Vergara took the occasion to resign his commission and return to Chile, where he was shocked at the reception he received from his supposed friends, harsh criticism instead of the adulation and honor that he felt he deserved for his sacrifices for his country.[76] He would eventually return to the army, again as Escala's civilian secretary, and Sotomayor managed to obtain the creation of the formal post of chief of staff for Escala, given to Colonel Pedro Lagos over Escala's objections, on the assumption that even closer supervision would prevent such disasters in the future.[77]

What was clear was that the hope of the alliance simply falling apart after the occupation of the Bolivian coastal province had dissipated. Likewise, the hope that a single, decisive battle in Tarapaca province would knock one or both allies out of the war had proven illusory. True, the Bolivian contingent with Buendía's army had disintegrated, but another Bolivian army was still sitting in Tacna, with reinforcements from both Bolivia and Peru steadily reaching the concentration points. Talk in Santiago now was for outright conquest of Tarapaca, although Chilean propaganda to date had been that this was not a war of territorial aggrandizement, only the "recovery" of Chilean territory usurped by Bolivia. The nitrate revenues of Tarapaca would become the reparations that Peru would have to pay for forcing such a war on Chile, and, beyond this, Tacna and Arica should also be taken, either to offer Bolivia as compensation for the Atacama or to serve as a buffer for Chile's new revenue producing territories. In any case, this would involve further invasions of Peruvian territory and a much larger military commitment by Chile, but events soon transpired within both of the allied governments that briefly called into question whether either could long continue the war.

NOTES

1. Gonzalo Bulnes, *Guerra del Pacífico,* vol. 1, Santiago de Chile: Editorial del Pacífico, 1955, p. 162.

2. Benjamin Vicuña Mackenna, *Historia de la Campaña de Tarapacá*, vol. 2, Santiago de Chile: Imprenta y Litografia de Pedro Cadot, Editor, 1880, p. 52.

3. Jacinto Lopez, *Historia de la Guerra del Guano y el Salitre,* Lima: Editorial Universo, S.A., 1980, p. 138.

4. Bulnes, p. 209.

5. Ibid., p. 216.

6. Roberto Querejazu Calvo, *Guano, Salitre, Sangre: Historia de la Guerra del Pacífico*, La Paz: Editorial Los Amigos del Libro, 1979, p. 410.

7. Bulnes, p. 308.

8. Ibid., p. 267.

9. Ibid., p. 292.

10. Ibid., p. 297.

11. Andres Avelino Caceres, *La Guerra del '79: Sus Campañas*, Lima: Editorial Milla Batres, S.A., 1973, p. 21. Note that Peruvian sources place Peruvian strength at 250 total, including gunners and National Guardsmen, and estimate Chilean forces at fifteen thousand.

12. Bulnes, p. 311.

13. William F. Sater, *Chile and the War of the Pacific*, Lincoln, NE: University of Nebraska Press, 1986, p. 21.

14. Caceres, p. 22.

15. Bulnes, p. 314.

16. Mariano Felipe Paz Soldan, *Narracion Historica de la Guerra de Chile contra el Peru y Bolivia*, vol. 2, Lima: Editorial Milla Batres, 1979, p. 31.

17. Ibid., p. 316.

18. Ibid., p. 320.

19. Sater, p. 21.

20. Bulnes, p. 322.

21. Querejazu, p. 413.

22. José Francisco Vergara, *Memorias*, Santiago de Chile: Editorial Andres Bello, 1979, p. 26.

23. Ibid., p. 32.

24. Ibid., p. 34.

25. Vicuña Mackenna, vol. 2, p. 800.

26. Caceres, p. 20.

27. Vicuña Mackenna, vol. 2, p. 543.

28. Querejazu, p. 417.

29. Ibid., p. 421.

30. Paz, vol. 2, p. 43.

31. Querejazu, p. 423.

32. Edgar Oblitas Fernández, *Historia Secreta de la Guerra del Pacífico*, Sucre: Editorial Tupac Katari, 1978, p. 225.

33. Paz, vol. 2, p. 43.

34. Querejazu, p. 427.

35. Caceres, p. 25.

36. Paz, vol. 2, p. 47.

37. Bulnes, p. 342.

38. Vergara, p. 53.

39. Ibid., pp. 48-51.

40. Vicuña Mackenna, vol. 2, p. 904.

41. Caceres, p. 25.

42. Ibid., p. 26.

43. Paz, vol. 2, p. 52.

44. Michael Howard, *The Franco-Prussian War*, New York: Collier Books, 1969, p. 244.

45. Vergara, p. 54.

46. Caceres, p. 27.

47. Vicuña Mackenna, p. 920.

48. Ibid., p. 923.

49. Bulnes, p. 349.
50. Vicuña Mackenna, p. 936.
51. Querejazu, p. 434.
52. Caceres, p. 30.
53. Vergara, p. 56.
54. Caceres, p. 31.
55. Ibid., p. 32.
56. Barros, p. 139.
57. Vicuña Mackenna, p. 951.
58. Bulnes, p. 354.
59. Barros, p. 137.
60. Vicuña Mackenna, p. 972.
61. Barros, p. 141.
62. Oblitas, p. 254.
63. Caceres, p. 33.
64. Vergara, p. 58.
65. Vicuña Mackenna, p. 1033.
66. Bulnes, p. 370.
67. Caceres, p. 34.
68. Ibid., p. 39.
69. Bulnes, p. 374.
70. Ibid., p. 376.
71. Caceres, p. 41.
72. Ibid., p. 42.
73. Barros, p. 148.
74. Sater, p. 23.
75. Bulnes, p. 382.
76. Vergara, p. 62.
77. Sater, p. 25.

Chapter Seven

The Presidents Depart

The most direct route from Tarapacá to Arica measured some 130 miles and should have taken General Buendía's army no more than a week of steady marching to cover. However, although he still had over four thousand men available for duty, now mostly veterans, he had a dread fear of enduring another battle before rejoining the main army of President Prado to the north. Consequently, Buendía picked out a route that hugged the foothills of the Andes, well to the east of the nearest Chilean positions, both to avoid the cavalry patrols that swarmed the flatlands, and to give his men a respite from the harshest desert country. It was thus twenty-two days after the battle of Tarapacá, on the 17th of December, that Buendía's thrity-seven hundred men finally straggled into Arica, bringing with them hundreds of Peruvian civilians, who had chosen to accompany the army on the basis of terrifying stories of Chilean atrocities, and about seventy Chilean prisoners.[1]

Although Buendía was probably not expecting a hero's welcome after the defeat at San Francisco and the abandonment of the province of Tarapacá, despite his at least temporary victory over Arteaga's column, it must have come as something of a surprise that President Prado had ordered Rear Admiral Lizardo Montero to demand both his and his chief of staff, Colonel Belisario Suárez's swords and to place them both under arrest pending a court of inquiry into the conduct of the campaign. Of course, the Peruvian government had little to celebrate in the results of the southern campaign. The province of Tarapaca was lost along with a population of 200,000, nearly one-tenth of the Peruvian total, and an annual gross income of £28 million in nitrate production, virtually all of the country's export earnings. As it turned out, neither officer would be cashiered, Suárez soon returning to significant command in the field, and Buendía becoming a member of the military advisory staff of both President Prado and his successor, but the act of the arrest and the subsequent inquiry gave a clear indication that the government in Lima was far more interested in apportioning blame than in pursuing the war to a successful conclusion. The half-hearted efforts at mobilization of the Peruvian army, its dispersal along hundreds of miles of coast, and then the bizarre meanderings of the Bolivian army could hardly have been seen as a blueprint for victory, and yet it was only the commanders in the field who seemed to have been held responsible for the defeats.

Still, while the fortunes for the allies were rather bleak at this point, there was at least some hope for the future of their endeavor. The naval campaign may have been essentially lost, but that on land was far less decidedly bad for the allies. There had never been much hope of defending the Bolivian coastal region, and the Chileans had taken it and then gotten ashore at Pisagua. But their victory at San Francisco had been a clumsy affair that might easily have gone the other way had Daza shown up or Buendia handled his own army more adeptly. Then the sharp little action at Tarapacá had shown that allied troops, even largely demoralized ones, could fight well enough and win if given half a chance, their superior numbers being somewhat compensated for by lacking both artillery and cavalry, so the contending forces were fairly evenly matched. Now a new allied army was forming, mostly inexperienced but with a leavening of veterans from Buendia's original force who had met the Chileans and driven them from the field. It is somewhat puzzling, therefore, that the two allied presidents would both have suddenly lost faith in the war to such an amazing degree.

The first to break ranks was President Prado. Even before the battle at Tarapaca was fought, the day before in fact, Prado turned over command of the army at Tacna to Vice Admiral Lizardo Montero and headed to the port of Arica. Pausing there until 28 November, he boarded a blockade-runner for the trip to Callao, where he arrived on 2 December, and thence on to Lima. In itself, this was not particularly alarming. Although Prado had nominal command of the army in the field, and although he did have considerable military experience in his own right, there was still a country to run, and it might have been that a firm hand on the administrative tiller of the state, taking charge of the task of raising new troops, arming them, and seeing them trained and shipped off to the front, was of greater importance at this juncture. And this was precisely what Prado did over the next two weeks.[2]

He was met with widespread rioting in the capital in protest over the administration's abysmal handling of the war to date. Virtually under siege in the Government Palace, Prado responded by dumping his cabinet and calling upon Nicolas de Pierola to form a new one.[3]

On 18 December, however, without waiting for the new administration to form, much less to have any effect, Prado suddenly gathered up his belongings, and allegedly some six million pesos in gold belonging to the General Administrative Council for Donations for the War with Chile, and took ship from Callao for Panama.[4] In a statement to the Lima newspaper *El Comercio*, Prado announced his full confidence in Vice President La Puerta to handle the government while he, Prado, undertook the more urgent job of traveling to

Europe to oversee the purchase of new arms and warships for the nation. In a note to his comrade-in-arms, President Daza, Prado wrote:

Since my arrival in Lima, I have come to the conclusion that this war is essentially a naval one and, thus, without waste of precious time, I formed a plan of what was required to be done and adopted it with firm resolution. I embark on the 18th of this month with a destination of Europe. I imagine that my sudden departure from Lima will give rise to all kinds of commentaries . . . but, since this deals with the good of the nation, I will rise above it all, it mattering but little to me to sacrifice my name and reputation momentarily . . . If some could attribute my travel to narrow selfishness, let it suffice to note that I leave here my family and deliver myself alone to the whims of fortune.[5]

Prado made it clear that he expected the war to be a long one and that this both allowed the time and emphasized the necessity of obtaining new ironclads to challenge the Chilean mastery of the sea. He did not anticipate, he commented to friends and colleagues, being away from the country for more than four months.

Reaction to Prado's surreptitious abandonment of his post in time of war did give rise to all sorts of commentaries. Some of his contemporaries, such as Colonel Caceres, whose own valor or dedication to this country is beyond question, assumed that Prado was, indeed, acting in the best interests of the nation.[6] At least one American historian tended to support this view stating, "No evidence surfaced to suggest that Prado's decision was motivated by other than sincere, patriotic concerns and convictions, but his departure was a fateful political decision."[7]

To say the least. It is hard to imagine how Prado could have realistically expected his countrymen to see his departure as anything but desertion in the face of the enemy. With the war going badly, and having just removed his field army commander from his job, it would seem that a military man who was nominal commander-in-chief, especially with the war now to be fought exclusively on Peruvian soil, would have moved forward to take a more direct hand in the running of the campaign, not gone off on a shopping trip to Europe. One wonders what his family's candid views were of his having abandoned them to the fates of war along with his country, especially as he held this up as evidence of his own level of sacrifice. In any event, Prado's longer-term plans would never be put to the test.

At eighty-four years of age, Vice President General Luis de la Puerta was hardly in any condition to steer the ship of state through such a tempest. On the 21st, before Prado had even passed through Panama, the notorious Nicolas Pierola, ex-minister, ex-pirate, who had spent the early part of the war in exile in Chile, had returned at Prado's request and now raised the standard of rebellion. He gained the support of one battalion of the army garrison in Lima, who mounted an assault on the Palace of Government but were repulsed by troops led by Minister of War General La Cotera, leaving more than three hundred corpses strewn about the streets of the capital. The insurgents then retired to Callao where more rebel troops, including a battalion of militia under the newly created militia Colonel Miguel Iglesias, as well as Pierola's partisans in the navy had seized the port.[8] The next morning a delegation of bishops and notables from Lima society visited de la Puerta and convinced him to step down in order to avoid a full-blown civil war with an enemy army camped on Peruvian territory, and Pierola was declared the new head of state. Admiral Lizardo Montero, probably for the same reason, immediately recognized the new government as did the other military commands throughout the country, and on 23 December Pierola made his formal entry into Lima.[9]

Pierola, whose career had also included work as a newspaper editor following his abandonment of a religious education at a seminary, was nothing if not a political animal, and, even before looking to the conduct of the war, he set about entrenching himself in power. On the 27th, Pierola had already dictated a new constitution giving himself full powers as head of state, stripping all other branches of the government of all but ceremonial roles. Pierola's new constitution eliminated the legislature and replaced it with a council of state, including the Archbishop of Lima and nine other notables chosen for their subservience more than their political abilities and grandly named himself the "protector of the indigenous race," as part of his official title.[10] At the same time, he passed a decree which deprived Prado both of his rank of general and his Peruvian citizenship, although he was otherwise relatively moderate in his dealings with his political enemies for fear of alienating Admiral Montero, who was a long-time opponent of his, and the army Montero still controlled. He named a new cabinet including Pedro José Calderon as foreign minister and Miguel Iglesias as minister of war.[11] Pierola also declared a call-up to military service of all males from the ages of eighteen to fifty, although this was largely for form's sake, as the nation did not begin to possess the weapons or uniforms necessary to arm such numbers.

Pierola also undertook changes in the military command. He removed General Miguel Beingolea from command of the reserve army that was forming at Arequipa and replaced him with Colonel Segundo Leyva, whose only military qualification was having supported Pierola unstintingly in his recent coup d'état. Pierola also began an apparent policy of keeping Montero's army starved for new weapons and supplies in favor of Leyva's troops. There is a possible explanation for this in that supplies for Montero's forces could only be delivered by blockade runners at considerable risk, although the frigate *Union* had proven quite adept at this job and frequently made the run from Callao to Arica under the noses of the Chileans, taking advantage of her exceptional speed, her crew's familiarity with the inshore waters, and the frequent heavy fogs on this part of the coast. Reinforcements and supplies for Leyva, on the other hand, could make their way overland from Lima with only marginal delays and inconvenience. However, Montero's officers soon noted that, even when a ship did get through to Arica, the cargo would just as likely consist of shoes or uniform caps rather than the latest shipment of repeating rifles or artillery from Europe. While the army was in sore need of everything, the officers would have rather seen their men go barefoot and well armed than sporting new footwear while carrying unserviceable muskets. It was assumed that this was a conscious effort on Pierola's part to augment the power of the politically loyal Leyva while decreasing that of the potentially independent-minded Montero, even though the latter was the one likely to be in direct contact with the enemy.[12] These and other reassignments gave rise to fear in the Peruvian officer corps that Pierola might actually sabotage the war effort, wanting to avoid giving Montero, his political opponent, a chance to win a victory which would augment his political power. While none of these doings were likely to enhance the chances of the alliance in the battle with Chile, worse was yet to come.

Pierola also took action in regard to the Peruvian economy although it would be stretching a point to suggest that he improved the situation at all. On the other hand, there was little he could have done to worsen the situation. The Peruvian economy was essentially dead, with all of the nitrate lands now in Chilean hands and virtually no other Peruvian exports able to leave the country due to the depredations of Chilean raiders up and down the coast, even if a formal blockade only actually applied to Callao and ports to the south. As the intellectual father of the original Dreyfuss contract, the newly proclaimed dictator entered anew into negotiations with that firm, recognizing all obligations to Dreyfuss and promising full repayment although no new sources of credit were forthcoming. Chile, meanwhile, had announced the sale of one million tons of (Peruvian and Bolivian) guano, half of the proceeds of which to go to bondholders of the companies involved and the remainder to go to the Chilean government. Lima and La Paz vociferously protested this action, labeling it as little more than official government piracy, but it does not appear that either potential buyers or creditors in Europe paid much heed.[13]

As badly as President Daza's unilateral decision to retire with his army from Camarones, leaving Buendia to his fate, had sat with the Peruvian populace, it had hardly sat any better with his own countrymen. As mentioned previously, at least one explanation for Daza's retreat was that he had already heard rumors of oppositionists mobilizing back in Bolivia, and the general/president was eager to take his army back home to deal with them. Actually, Daza only trusted the three original line regiments of the Bolivian army, "Sucre," "Aroma," and his own beloved "Colorados," and he planned to take them, along with all of his artillery as well as all of the army's horses and mules, leaving the rest of his troops to fend for themselves in Peru, supporting the alliance or not as they chose. He particularly did not plan to take with him the "Bolivian Legion" cavalry regiment, as it was composed of the sons of La Paz high society, a group that Daza had always envied and hated and who tended to return his feelings of distrust and animosity. Daza had explained his planned move to Admiral Montero by claiming that he planned to link his forces with those of Campero's wandering 5th Division and mount an independent drive on the Chilean garrisons in the Bolivian Atacama from the area of Potosi to relieve pressure on Peru.[14] It is highly unlikely that Montero credited this statement, but he was undoubtedly far too occupied with Prado's departure and Pierola's coup, which were taking place at the same moment, to pay his ally's maneuvers much attention.

Although Daza made a concerted effort to keep the true details of his plans secret from the officers in his army whom he considered untrustworthy, word eventually leaked out. Colonel Eliodoro Camacho, Daza's chief of staff, had been a friend since long before Daza's rise to power and had supported him during the ouster of Melgarejo. Camacho had, however, done a poor job of concealing his discontent with Daza's own subsequent seizure of power and had been kept at the fringes of Daza's inner council ever since. But Camacho did discover the plot to abandon the fight with Chile, and on 26 December he called a clandestine meeting with two of the army's divisional commanders, Colonels Miguel Castro Pinto and Severino Zapata and other like-minded officers. They agreed that the only solution was the removal of Daza from power, but they saw no possibility of doing this as long as he was still firmly supported by the "Colorados," who still possessed the army's most modern weaponry and could likely produce as much firepower as the rest of the Bolivian army combined.[15]

In desperation, Camacho and the other conspirators turned to Admiral Montero for support. Although Montero refused to use Peruvian troops to intervene directly in internal Bolivian affairs, he agreed to participate if a plan could be conceived that would avoid bloodshed, particularly as Montero wanted to avoid a Bolivian civil war breaking out in the middle of the Peruvian city of Tacna where most of the army was bivouacked. As his part in the drama, Montero invited Daza to travel from Tacna to Arica to discuss the latter's proposed change in strategy, an all-day train trip that would oblige Daza to leave the protection of his loyal troops, and Daza accepted.

At 1000 hours on 27 December Daza boarded the train, suspecting nothing. At the same time, Camacho, as chief of staff, issued an apparently innocuous order for most of the army to stack arms and go down to the nearby Chaplina River to bathe and wash their clothes. Only the Bolivian Legion, another squadron of cavalry, and the "Loa" Infantry Regiment were to remain in camp, precisely the units Camacho had recruited to support his coup. At 1300 hours, riflemen from the Legion seized army headquarters, arresting Generals Arguedas and Alcoreza and seizing control of the artillery park, while Camacho led the other cavalry regiment to the barracks where they secured the bathers' weapons without resistance. An hour later, when the troops marched back into camp, all clean and refreshed, they found the grim ranks of "Loa" formed up under arms between them and their weapons, and they were advised that General Daza had been removed from office both as president and as commander of the army for sullying the honor of the nation. If Daza's lavish entertainments had purchased him any loyalty among the "Colorados," it was not enough to prompt them to fight for his honor with their bare hands against rifles and bayonets, and most of the men just shrugged and turned to making dinner, while others openly celebrated.[16]

Meanwhile, Daza had just boarded the train in Arica for his return to Tacna after a suspiciously brief and insubstantial meeting with Montero, when Colonel Ildefonso Murguía, commander of the "Colorados" rushed up with word from the telegraph office to advise Daza that he had been overthrown. Daza first rushed back to Montero's headquarters and demanded the use of Peruvian troops to crush the mutineers, but he was summarily refused. Daza then attempted to gain asylum aboard one of the neutral warships riding at anchor in Arica harbor, claiming that he feared imminent assassination, but he was again refused. Becoming more desperate, he then took horse for Mollendo with a handful of followers, and thence went by train to Arequipa, still hoping to raise support for a march on La Paz to regain power, but here he learned that La Paz, too, had declared for the insurrection. He then returned to Mollendo where he was finally able to board an English steamship and take passage to Panama and thence to Europe.[17]

Following Daza's removal, many stories began to make the rounds regarding his betrayal of the allied cause. According to one account, Daza had held a council of war on 11 November 1879, attended only by his most trusted subordinates, at which he announced his plan to take his army only as far as Camarones for fear of losing it in battle and that he never intended to join up with Buendia.[18] Another story that was given wide credence in Bolivia after the war was that Daza had actually been bribed by the Chileans to sabotage the allied war plan, to march to the theater of war and then abandon the Peruvians who would have made their own strategic deployments based on their expectation of his army's participation. This story was allegedly told to Eliodoro Camacho by then Chilean Minister of Interior Domingo Santa Maria while the former was a prisoner of war in Santiago following the battle of Tacna. However, since Camacho was the prime mover of the plot to overthrow Daza, one might suspect that he might have a greater than normal interest in discrediting the ex-dictator.[19]

While the objectivity of some of the sources might be questionable, there is some basis for believing that Daza had indeed entered into a pact with the devil and planned to betray the allied cause from the outset. Certainly there is nothing in Daza's career as a military coup plotter and political opportunist that would suggest that he was above such a thing. It is possible that, after having his bluff called by the Chileans in early 1879 over the ten *centavo* tax, Daza found himself holding a hopelessly weak hand and was desperate to come out of the game a winner, at least on a personal level if not on behalf of his country as a whole. The Chilean offer of a Peruvian port in exchange for the Bolivian Atacama must have been tempting, but Daza, even if not well educated, was politically astute enough to realize that this would be a hard sell in La Paz, giving up any of the national patrimony being the kind of mortal sin for which Melgarejo had been ousted just recently, and stabbing the nation's only ally in the back into the bargain would not have been a popular move. So, perhaps Daza did have the idea of making a show of supporting Peru, allowing a little Bolivian blood to be shed in the process, and then cutting out the props from the allied war effort at the last minute to insure defeat. This would at least explain Daza's bizarre behavior on his round trip march to Camarones, and, perhaps, he did expect, once the defeated Peruvians sued for peace, to be granted a strip of land running down to the coast for his country in addition to whatever personal remuneration the Chileans might have offered him.

This interpretation has a certain Machiavellian appeal, but a simpler explanation seems quite as plausible. Despite his long time in uniform, Daza had never really taken part in a real military campaign against a real, armed and trained enemy, and it is possible that the headaches of getting his army dressed and fed and on the road to the battlefield brought home to Daza just how woefully unprepared he was for this challenge. His bluster up to that point was neither more nor less than that engaged in by similar tin pot dictators before and since, but every mile closer to the enemy must have given Daza time to think. He certainly knew that his pampered "Colorados" were his only lock on the presidency, and their loyalty to him stemmed from the high pay and soft living he lavished on them, not something that was likely to survive a bloody encounter, especially if Daza managed to bungle his command. Thus it is credible that he simply lost his nerve and came up with any lame excuse that entered his head simply to take himself and his supporters out of the line of fire, and the consequences be damned. Since neither Daza nor Prado ever bothered to return to their homeland during the course of the war and never again held a position of authority, the reasons for their respective desertions are largely academic.

In any event, with Daza out of the picture, on 2 January 1880, a commission of notables in La Paz met and elected General Narciso Campero, commander of the 5th Division, as provisional president. It was not until the 19th that Campero arrived at Oruro from the frontier and was advised of his nomination, and he accepted the post until a national convention could meet to elect a permanent replacement for the dictator. Campero was a sixty-five-year-old career officer, trained at the French academy at St. Cyr, and who had fought with the French Army in Algeria before returning to Bolivia for the Battle of Ingavi in 1841. He had also served as ambassador in Paris in 1873, but he had never shown much interest in politics. One of his first acts was to reinstate the 1875 conscription law that obligated to military service all males from eighteen to fifty years of age with the exception of those who were married, widowers, only sons, those with a brother already in the army, those who had been previously wounded in military service, science professors, teachers, and Indians living on autonomous communes.[20] If one adds to this list those with sufficient political connections or the money to influence the local authorities, it is easy enough to understand why relatively few fresh troops accompanied Campero on his trip to join Montero in Arica where he finally arrived on 15 April. But, since the Bolivian economy was in even worse shape than the Peruvian, there would have been precious little in the way of new weapons or equipment with which to fit out new units, even though Bolivia did at least get a steady trickle of armaments coming overland from Europe via Argentina.

It was thus that, having just undergone a massive political trauma, both of the allied nations now had to gird themselves to face a new onslaught by the Chileans in what promised to be the decisive battle of the war.

NOTES

1. Roberto Querejazu Calvo, *Guano, Salitre, Sangre: Historia de la Guerra del Pacífico,* La Paz: Editorial Los Amigos del Libro, 1979, p. 442.
2. Frederick B. Pike, *The History of Modern Peru,* New York: Praeger, 1982, p. 145.

3. Gonzalo Bulnes, *Guerra del Pacífico,* vol. 1, Santiago de Chile: Editorial del Pacífico, 1955, p. 393.

4. Edgar Fernandez Oblitas, *Historia Secreta de la Guerra del Pacífico,* Sucre: Editorial Tupac Katari, 1983, p. 286.

5. Querejazu, p. 442.

6. Andres Avelino Caceres, *La Guerra del '79, Sus Campañas,* Lima: Editorial Milla Batres, 1979, p. 100.

7. Ronald Bruce St. John, *Diplomatic History of Peru,* Boulder, CO: Lynne Rienner, 1992, p. 114.

8. Bulnes, op. cit., p. 394.

9. Caceres, op. cit., p. 101.

10. Bulnes, vol. 2, p. 8.

11. Diego Barros Arana, *Historia de la Guerra del Pacífico, 1879-1881,* Santiago de Chile: Editorial Andres Bello, 1979, p. 168.

12. Oblitas, p. 293.

13. St. John, p. 115.

14. Querejazu, p. 452.

15. Barros, p. 170.

16. Querejazu, p. 456.

17. Barros, p. 175.

18. Arturo Costa de la Torre, *Diarios y Memorias de la Guerra del Pacífico,* vol. 1, La Paz: Biblioteca Paceña, 1980, p. 7.

19. Querejazu, p. 469.

20. Ibid., p. 518.

Chapter Eight

Tacna and Arica: The End in the South

Arguably, the Chileans were now in a position to sit back and let the war simply peter out of its own accord. Their land forces now had undisputed control over all of the territory from their original border up to within a few miles south of Arica including all of the nitrate-producing areas. Their naval forces had effectively swept the seas of the Peruvian fleet, with the exception of occasional nuisance raids by the frigate *Union,* and no goods could be sent into or out of either of the allied nations without running a gauntlet of Chilean warships, while the main ports of Arica and Callao were under sporadic direct blockade. The economies of the allies were in a shambles with no hope of improvement as long as the war continued, and there was no serious chance that an allied army could make its way into the conquered territories, by land or sea, to drive the invaders out. It seemed that it would be only a matter of time until the allies came to their senses and sued for peace.

And yet they did not. One of the first things that the new governments in both Lima and La Paz did was to declare their continued adherence to the alliance and to reject any contemplation of a negotiated peace as long as Chilean soldiers still camped on the soil of either nation. These were largely empty words, and there were few effective measures being taken to mobilize the kind of military support necessary to prosecute the war on a practical basis, but, as long as no peace was concluded, the Chileans could not rest secure in the possession of their new territories nor could they fully benefit from the economic bounty they expected to reap as a result.

More than that, the Pinto government and the Chilean military command pushed on with plans for a new campaign to a large extent because there was a score to settle. The stinging defeat at Tarapacá was not something that either the Chilean military or the administration could allow to rest as it was. Chile had entered the war with a clear sense of racial and national superiority that the relatively easy victories on the sea and at Pisagua and San Francisco had only reinforced. That a demoralized rabble, poorly armed and already in flight, had turned and bloodied a substantial combined arms force of Chileans was a blot on the honor of the army that would have to be washed out with blood. Consequently, regardless of the prudence of simply sitting back and letting the alliance starve and fall apart on its own, planning for a new Chilean offensive went forward apace.

Buendia's exhausted troops had only straggled into Arica on 17 December after their three hundred-mile march, and it would take them some weeks to rest and refit and be incorporated into the fresh army that Montero was forming, but the allied camp was almost immediately rocked by word of another disaster. In the early morning hours of 31 December 1879, Lieutenant Colonel Aristides Martinez had landed with the "Lautaro" Infantry Regiment and a small detachment of cavalry and engineers, about six hundred men altogether, at the tiny port of Ilo, nearly one hundred miles to the north of Arica. The oars of the landing boats had been wrapped in rags to muffle the sound as the Chileans came storming ashore from the transport *Copiapó* and covered by the guns of the frigate *Chacbuco*, but the ships were seen in the predawn darkness and the alarm spread. But the warning only served to allow the local prefect, Colonel Chocano, and his 450 militiamen to flee into the desert after loosing a few scattered rounds in the general direction of the ocean. The Chileans quickly established beachheads both north and south of the town, and captured a functional locomotive and rolling stock and cut the telegraph line before a warning could be given to the other allied forces inland.

The intrepid Martinez then loaded most of his men aboard the captured train and raced forty miles inland to within sight of the town of Moquegua, fired a few shots at the timorous garrison who, while enjoying a substantial numerical superiority, did not dare to challenge the Chilean advance, and then returned to the coast. Within a matter of hours the raiders had reembarked, suspiciously doing no damage to either the rail line or the port facilities, and disappeared back over the waves.[1]

The incursion had been meant merely as a reconnaissance in force, primarily aimed at capturing a shipment of arms and munitions that had been landed at Ilo from the *Union* a few days previously but which had been moved out of harm's way in time. But the raid illustrated dramatically how vulnerable the allied position at Tacna/Arica was. Even though the front line had been pushed north hundreds of miles closer to the Peruvian population centers, it was still not feasible to supply the army exclusively by land over the difficult terrain and almost non-existent road network. Meanwhile, the Ilo raid demonstrated that the Chileans were quite capable of landing their entire army in Montero's rear and forcing him to fight his way through them to reestablish his supply lines. The rain also served notice that the locally raised Peruvian militia were in no condition, either moral or physical, to stand up to Chilean regulars, even in roughly equal numbers, so there was no protection against such an end run at any time in the future. In fact, there was considerable concern in Lima that there was precious little to stop the Chileans from making a stab for the capital itself, its twelve thousand man garrison being composed almost exclusively of raw recruits, and Montero's army be much too far away to be of any concern to an attacking force.

In fact, it was precisely this plan that Sotomayor had been urging *La Moneda* for some weeks, a landing near the enemy capital, leaving five or six thousand men to garrison the conquered territories, and driving for a quick end to the war. President Pinto and his cabinet, however, favored a campaign in Tacna, both to crush the only remaining viable allied army in the field and to gain actual possession of the Tacna-Arica corridor that Santa Maria still hoped Bolivia would accept in exchange for abandoning the alliance, and this was the plan of campaign that was ultimately adopted.[2]

In the meanwhile, while the broader strategic goals of the campaign were being decided, Sotomayor was faced with the practical task of rebuilding and reorganizing the army for the next phase of the war. Not counting several thousand men still with the colors in Chile proper, on the Araucan frontier or garrisoning the coast or the thousands of men in the navy, the Chilean army in the field numbered only some 9,532 effectives at this point, having suffered over twelve hundred killed, one thousand wounded, and several hundred sick to date.[3] To make matters worse, the army, which was concentrated around Pisagua and Dolores, was suffering from the harsh climate, where temperatures often swung thirty degrees Centigrade in a twenty-four-hour period and where fevers were widespread. It was therefore of first priority to reinforce the army in the field and to organize the supplies and transport necessary to get it up the coast in preparation for taking on the main allied forces at Tacna.

But the atmosphere at the headquarters of the army in the field was hardly conducive to dynamic, efficient work. In mid-December General Escala came down with an attack of what was described as apoplexy, possibly a real or imagined resentment of Sotomayor's continuing role in running the army. Sotomayor, for his part, saw Escala's headquarters as a kind of debating society where nothing was decided, and the entire gaggle of officers was hopelessly divided into quarreling cliques, none of which were interested in the job at hand. To deal with this problem, Sotomayor had suggested the naming of a formal chief of staff, on the Prussian model, to handle the administrative and logistical business of the army, a role Sotomayor was largely performing himself, but Escala violently opposed the first two nominees, Generals Villagran and Velásquez, probably fearing them as potential replacements being groomed to take over his command. He finally accepted Colonel Pedro Lagos in the post in mid-January 1880, but with a very bad grace that would lead Lagos to offer his resignation more than once in the coming months.[4]

Sotomayor also engineered the reorganization of the army, something that would be required if the numbers of troops were to be significantly raised. He proposed the creation of four divisions, each with one of the original line infantry regiments plus between one to three of the reserve regiments raised since the start of the war. Each division would also have its own artillery battery and a squadron of cavalry, creating a true combined arms team, plus an overall artillery command at army level with additional batteries. He also created a corps of engineers, where only a collection of sapper troops and pontoon bridge builders had existed before.

As might have been expected, Escala violently opposed Sotomayor's initiative, less out of disagreement with the concept than over which officers would get the new divisional commands. President Pinto finally had to referee an agreement in February that gave the posts to Colonels Santiago Amengual, Mauricio Muñoz, Jose Domingo Amunátegui, and Pedro Lagos (later replaced by Orizombo Barboza when Lagos moved over to be chief of staff).[5]

With that issue finally decided, the debate now centered on what to do with the army. Sotomayor wanted to move quickly to take advantage of the disarray in which the allies still found themselves. He envisioned taking some seventy-five hundred men who were already on hand aboard whatever transports could be scraped together and putting them ashore near Ilo for a sudden thrust inland, with reinforcements to be brought up as soon as they could be organized. Escala, however, claimed that the allied forces in the Tacna-Arica area alone numbered at least fifteen thousand men with seven thousand more at Moquegua, two thousand at Ilo itself, and another five thousand on the march from Mollendo. He insisted, therefore on postponing the initial landing until at least ten thousand men could be lifted in the first wave with a substantial reserve on hand to build up the landing force immediately.[6]

Although Escala had easily doubled the actual number of allied troops in the region, the Pinto administration was reluctant to discount the possibility that he was right, and the assault troops did not begin to embark until 21 February, an operation that would take a full three days in itself. The initial wave would consist of ninety-five hundred men of the 1st, 2nd, and 3rd Divisions with the 4th Division to remain at Pisagua to come along in a second wave to bring the total invasion force to 14,800 men and sixteen guns. The invasion fleet consisted of some eighteen transports, both steam and sail, and was escorted by most of the Chilean warships available.

The fleet arrived at Ilo on the 26th and, expecting strong resistance according to Escala's intelligence reports, the "Esmeralda" Regiment was landed north of the town and the "Artillery Naval" (actually an infantry regiment) to the south, repeating the tactics of the December raid, but not even a detachment of skittish militia could be found in the port, and the rest of the army landed dryshod on the Ilo docks. Even the telegraph, rail line and rolling stock were still found to be in perfect working order.[7]

A separate squadron comprising the *Magallanes* and the *Huascar*, now in the Chilean service and equipped with two new English Armstrong 40-pound breach-loaders capable of reaching six to seven thousand meters were sent to hit the port of Arica. The purpose of the bombardment was both to cause actual damage to any supplies and blockade runners that might be in the port and to confuse the allies about the intended target of the invasion. As soon as the approaching Chilean warships were sighted, the aged monitor *Manco Kapac* came wallowing out to the edge of the harbor to offer battle, and the various forts surrounding the port also opened fire. In the brief but spirited engagement, *Huascar* suffered several hits which cost some seven crewmen killed, including her captain, Comandante Thompson, as *Huascar* was to prove a very unlucky ship for her skippers, and *Magallanes* also sustained some damage, and the attackers eventually withdrew. Once the landing area had been secured, other units of the fleet were sent ranging along the coast, shelling ports more or less with impunity, both to punish the Peruvians for continuing the war and in the hope of pinning more Peruvian troops down watching for amphibious raids farther to the north.[8]

The full disembarkation took several days to accomplish, along with the transfer of the 4th Division up from Pisagua, but no allied troops showed themselves in the meanwhile. While waiting for the army to concentrate, on the 2nd of March, the ubiquitous Vergara, back with the army on Escala's staff as a full colonel, along with General Baquedano and a number of other officers took one of the captured Peruvian trains on an excursion twenty miles into the interior of the province without encountering any Peruvian troops or obstacles to their progress. Given the lack of enemy resistance, Sotomayor was eager to send a large force inland to take up a strong defensive position that the allies could neither ignore nor bypass and force them to attack him there, much as had occurred (largely by accident) at San Francisco. Unfortunately, Escala was not ready.[9]

In the meanwhile, Sotomayor detached Colonel Orozimbo Barboza with a force of some twenty-one hundred men on 8 March on an amphibious expedition to Islai with the purpose of distracting the allied force gathered at Arequipa to prevent it from joining with that of Montero centered on Tacna. The force would then march overland to the port of Mollendo and destroy the docking facilities to obviate the need in the future for blockading that port, which was frequently used to smuggle supplies down from Callao to the allied forces in the region. There was minimal resistance at Islai and none at all en route to Mollendo, which Barboza's column reached on the 9th. The port, too, had been evacuated, including two coastal forts, and the Chileans disabled the guns they found there. Unfortunately, the troops also found considerable stores of liquor, and they engaged in several days of essentially unrestricted looting and burning, causing considerable embarrassment to the administration in Santiago and to the army.[10] The Chileans attempted to rationalize the poor discipline of their troops by claiming that the units involved contained a high percentage of men who had been laborers in Peru before the war and had been badly treated and then summarily expelled, giving them some justification for wanting to exact some personal revenge, but these arguments convinced no one.[11] In any event, this was another black mark against the comportment of the Chilean troops on foreign soil of which there would be more soon enough.

While the Chileans were consolidating their beachhead, the allies were scrambling to mobilize their forces to resist them. Contrary to Escala's estimates, there were at this point only about 2,500 Peruvian troops, eventually rising to four to five thousand, virtually all raw recruits, at Arequipa under the prefect, Colonel Carlos Gonzalez Orbegoso, soon to be replaced by Pierola's loyal supporter, Colonel Manuel Leyva. A further twelve hundred troops were at Moquegua under Colonel Andrés Gamarra, barely forty miles by rail from Ilo.

Montero had a total of some thirteen to fourteen thousand men, including about four thousand Bolivians in the immediate Tacna-Arica area. The combined allied total was thus somewhat higher than that for the Chileans, although not all of these troops would be available for field campaigning as garrisons had to be left at Arica and other points, and there was a distinct qualitative advantage on the Chilean side in both men and armaments.[12]

Beyond a lack of reliable troops, however, the main allied weakness was in the area of command. The original agreement between the two nations had been that the president of the nation on whose territory the allied army was fighting would assume command, since both were more or less experienced soldiers. This arrangement had largely gone by the wayside when both presidents essentially deserted the colors and fled to Europe. Pierola in Lima showed no sign of wanting to take to the field and would not have been a very qualified supreme commander in any case, and at the time of the Chilean landing at Ilo, Campero was only beginning his long trek down to the coast. That left Admiral Montero in nominal command, since the Peruvian contingent was by far the larger, pre-war agreements that Bolivia would provide the majority of the ground forces to compensate for Peru's contribution of her navy notwithstanding. However, Montero was loath to ignore the opinions of the Bolivian field commander, a post that had devolved upon Colonel Eliodoro Camacho since the coup d'état against Daza.

This might not have been a major concern in itself except that the two commanders were of widely divergent views on how to conduct the campaign. Montero saw the main Chilean goal to be the defeat of the allied army and the occupation of Tacna and Arica, and he opted to remain on the defensive, forcing the Chileans to come to him over difficult, waterless terrain and allowing him to fight the battle on the tactical defensive as well. Camacho, on the other hand, feared that time was on the side of the Chileans who now effectively sat astride the only viable supply line for the allied army, not counting a tortuous trail over the Andes to Bolivia, and the allies would only get weaker as the Chileans built up their own forces unhindered. He therefore wanted to move the bulk of the army to the valley of the River Sama, denying this source of water to the Chileans and force them to fight after having crossed a particularly barren stretch of desert, hopefully link up with Leyva's and Gamarra's forces, and concentrate the full force of the allied army in one final encounter.[13]

This disagreement prevented the allies from taking any significant action from the time of the Chilean landing at the end of February all through March and into April, but the arrival of President Campero at Tacna on 18 April at least eliminated this source of friction. Campero would take overall command, and both Montero and Camacho accepted the new authority with good grace. Unfortunately for the allies, the Chileans had chosen not to wait for them to sort out their leadership issues.

At fifty-four years of age, with an impressive handlebar moustache and smart dark blue uniform, the short, stocky Manuel Baquedano, recently promoted to general, could easily have passed for an officer in the armies of Grant or Sherman. He had been in the military since the age of sixteen, following in the footsteps of his father, also a cavalryman, and had fought in the 1838 war against the Bolivian-Peruvian Confederation. He was currently functioning in the post of commander of cavalry for the expeditionary force. At the urging of President Pinto, himself under intense pressure from the political opposition to get the campaign in motion, Escala ordered Baquedano to take Muñoz's 2nd division plus 18 guns, four Gatlings, and two squadrons of cavalry for a total of some forty-three hundred men, up the valley of the River Ilo on 12 March to assault the town of Moquegua.[14]

The purpose of the advance was to firmly occupy the entire coastal strip west of the Andes and ensure the isolation of the allied army to the south at Tacna as a first step to the Chilean army's own advance along the foothills of the Andes to bring the allies to battle. There was insufficient rolling stock on the rail line, which was still in good working order, to move the entire division, so the bulk of the troops would march, and it took until 20 March for Baquedano to occupy Moquegua itself, which he did against no resistance.

Colonel Gamarra, commander of the allied garrison, which numbered about fifteen hundred men, determined that the town of Moquegua was indefensible, surrounded as it was by high ridges that he did not have men enough to occupy. He therefore pulled back to a plateau just north of the town, a mesa with steep sides whose flanks were protected by two steep river gorges, known locally as Los Angeles. The site had a history, sometimes referred to grandly as the "Thermopylae of Peru," as the Spanish had held its easily defended ground during the wars of independence and Pierola had once beaten off an army led by General Buendia during one of the former's revolts in 1874. Gamarra did the best he could, deploying his scant force along the rim of the mesa with a strong central reserve to counter any Chilean breakthroughs, but his men were mostly raw militia, and he only possessed a couple of aged bronze cannons, no match for Baquedano's Krupps.[15]

Baquedano was aware of the site's reputation and, even though he enjoyed a nearly three-to-one superiority in numbers and an overwhelming advantage in artillery, he took some pains with his attack plans. He chose a battalion of rugged miners from Copiapo under Comandante Juan Martinez to infiltrate through the hills on the right of the Peruvian position while Colonel Manuel Muñoz took another thousand men, including some cavalry and a couple of mountain guns around the Peruvian left. Baquedano set up his own gun line directly facing the mesa, and the two flanking columns set out after dark on the 21st to be in position for an attack the following dawn. At about 0200 hours on 22 March Peruvian pickets opened a ragged fire, but Gamarra apparently attributed this to nervousness on the part of the green troops and took no action.

At first light, Martínez's miners suddenly sprang upon the Peruvian forward positions, having scaled the steep slopes in the dark, but Muñoz's column had had farther to march and had not arrived as yet. Baquedano opened fire with his artillery, smashing the Peruvian battalion "Grau" as it attempted to turn about to meet the threat from its right, and Martinez was finally able to get his men into position to support the attack with long range rifle fire that prevented Gamarra from shifting troops from this flank to meet the Chilean attack. Within an hour it was all over. The Peruvians were in full flight having suffered some one hundred casualties between killed, wounded, and prisoners, while the Chileans lost only nine men killed and about forty wounded. The rest of Gamarra's force simply disintegrated with relatively few of them ever returning to the colors in Arequipa. Pierola immediately ordered Gamarra arrested and tried for treason for his failure, while the Chilean troops returned to Moquegua and engaged in another sad display of looting by way of celebration.[16]

The Chilean command was now faced with a logistical and strategic problem. The Ilo River valley itself was agriculturally rich in forage and food supplies, but the allied army sat some sixty miles to the south across an area of arid desert and shifting sand. True, the rivers Locumba and Sama crossed this land, running east to west at more or less equal intervals along the line of march, but there were no roads worthy of the name, and it would take time to move the army with its guns and baggage between them. The longer the march took, the more water would be needed, and that meant that more wagonloads of casks of water would be required, plus more forage for the horses to pull them. The response to this problem was to engage in a round of bitter invective within the command staff.

As noted previously, General Escala had not accepted the minute guidance from Santiago, either directly from President Pinto or through Rafael Sotomayor, with good grace. Escala saw the role of the staff as aids to his exercise of command, not as partners in his decisions, and he missed few opportunities to show his displeasure. Unfortunately, Escala had no better relations with his subordinates. For example, in early March, he took exception to the way a Colonel Barcelo had disciplined his regiment and had him arrested. When Colonel Lagos, as chief of staff, objected to the action, Escala verbally castigated him and ordered that no further telegrams were to be sent to or received from Santiago without his personal signature, fearing that his officers were going behind his back to complain to *La Moneda*. In Santiago, meanwhile, reports of sloppy logistical arrangements on Baquedano's march inland and the long delay in preparing the rest of the army to move on Tacna had created the impression that Escala did not have a firm grasp on the tiller of command.[17] Escala's position was further weakened by the fact that he had not taken a direct role in any of the army's major battles do date, thus preventing him from taking personal credit for the significant successes that they had achieved.

In any event, on 18 March, Colonel Lagos resigned after Escala publicly blamed him for the rioting of the Chilean troops at Mollendo. Escala rejected the resignation until Lagos had formally accounted for all monies expended by the army during his tenure as chief of staff, a calculated insult to the very proper Lagos, and Sotomayor finally stepped in and ordered Lagos to Santiago in the hope of defusing the conflict. Escala, in response, offered his own letter of resignation, claiming that Sotomayor was interfering with his command authority, but almost immediately withdrew it and, instead, requested permission to travel to Santiago to explain his situation directly to the president. Pinto, with rather unseemly haste, approved this request, and Escala departed on 31 March, leaving Baquedano in temporary command. He would never return to the army in the field.[18]

As soon as Escala was safely aboard ship, Sotomayor entered into an intensive communication with Santiago regarding his permanent replacement. General Villagran was a leading candidate, due to his seniority, but it was well known that Villagran would never tolerate Vergara, who still clung to the staff in his semi-official position of civil-military gadfly. It was finally decided to keep Baquedano on. He was seen as rather dull, but he had proven himself as a combat commander to some degree and was well noted as being highly disciplined and could be expected to accept any conditions Santiago chose to impose on him for the post. And so the deal was done. When Escala arrived in Santiago to plead his case, he found himself already to be a man without a position, and the issue was closed once and for all.[19]

The focus of action for the Chileans then shifted from the conflict of personalities to overcoming the problems of geography. As a first step, on 7 April the ubiquitous Vergara was assigned to do what he did best, to conduct a reconnaissance with two cavalry squadrons from Moquegua south toward the Locumba River. At the same time, Colonel Rafael Vargas led two other squadrons south from Ilo along the coast to determine which might be the more feasible route. Meanwhile, the 1st Division was to begin its march south in Vergara's wake, using virtually all of the mules available to the army, setting up food and forage stockpiles at key points along the route for the troops that would follow.

Apart from one sharp skirmish, in which Vergara would rout a similar-sized force of Peruvian cavalry and infantry and for which Vergara would be rewarded with a promotion to the rank of General of Cavalry, the two scouting columns determined that there were no significant enemy troop concentrations in the area, but they also confirmed that the terrain was impassable to the army's artillery and supply wagons. The infantry and cavalry could use this route, but another means would have to be found to bring up the heavy trains.[20]

Consequently, the four divisions would be moved in relays over the barren stretch of ground from Moquegua to the Locumba River, with carefully regulated rest stops every half hour and ample water brought along by the mule trains, a process that took until the end of April. Even so, Barboza's 4th division suffered substantial losses from thirst and fatigue in the march, and these might have been worse had Colonel Bulnes not anticipated the problem and sent back a mounted detachment with a supply of water from the Locumba to meet the column. It should be noted that it was Barboza's men who had disgraced the army with their rioting at Mollendo, and this was another example of the colonel's lack of skill in commanding his troops.

The cabinet in Santiago had wanted at least one division left as a garrison at Moquegua for fear that the Peruvian forces under Leyva at Arequipa, now designated 2nd army, might fall on the expeditionary force from the rear. Sotomayor overruled this decision, however, having correctly read Leyva as being a man of little action and the terrain north of Moquegua as being even more difficult to traverse than that which faced his army heading south.

The second part of the plan called for the artillery to be re-embarked at Ilo and brought down by sea to the small port of Ite with a guard of about one thousand infantry. This would avoid much of the most difficult terrain south of Moquegua, but it still involved hauling the guns up the steep seaside cliffs behind Ite, using block and tackle from the ships, and then detailing much of the infantry force to road building to make the route inland passable for the guns. To make matters worse, a small pox epidemic was sweeping through the ranks with as many as four hundred cases being treated in the Moquegua hospital alone. Still, by 10 May the army had been reunited on the Locumba with 11,622 infantry, 1,200 cavalry, and 550 artillerymen with forty guns. They were now ready for the final drive on Tacna.[21]

But Sotomayor would not live to see the fruit of his efforts. On 20 May, the Minister of War and longtime guiding force of the army died of an apparent stroke. This loss had an immediate effect on the morale of the army, as Baquedano was not seen to have established his authority as yet, and Sotomayor was recognized by the rank and file, if not the officer corps, as the man responsible for most of the strategic planning for the campaign. Sotomayor's body would lie in state in the chambers of the Chilean Senate for several days. The obvious choice to replace him was none other than the aggressive, emotional, and energetic Francisco Vergara.[22]

Back in the allied camp at Tacna, the command crisis had passed, but things were still not going smoothly. President Campero had ultimately decided in favor of his countryman Camacho's plan to advance to the Sama River and to meet the Chileans there, with a trackless, waterless desert at their backs. The fact that the route from Tacna to the Sama was equally trackless and waterless had apparently not occurred to anyone, and the entire army fell in on 27 April with great fanfare to begin the march. The column came to a halt less than one kilometer from the city, however, as it became evident that there was a total lack of the necessary transport for even the minimum amount of supplies and water.[23] The contrast between this kind of blundering and Sotomayor's meticulous logistical planning could not have been more marked.

At this point the allied army numbered about nine thousand effectives, of which about two thirds were Peruvian, now called the 1st Army, the rest Bolivian. In addition Montero had left the 7th and 8th Divisions and some naval troops as a garrison at Arica under Bolognesi, for a total of some two thousand men, falling into the same trap as Buendia had farther south when he had been obliged to garrison Iquique, robbing himself of troops that would be desperately needed in the coming battle in order to protect a port that would fall on its own if his field army were to be defeated. There was also Leyva's 2nd Army at Arequipa of about thirty-one hundred men at this point, including the survivors of Gamarra's force, and these had been ordered on 14 May to move southward, sweeping up any isolated Chilean garrisons they might find around Moquegua and eventually join up with Campero. However, even though Leyva had been receiving the lion's share of what few new recruits and weapons Lima had been able to raise, he continually managed to find excuses for not moving his army, and they would not be within a hundred miles of the Chileans when the battle was finally joined.[24]

The allied army that would fight the Battle of Tacna now moved into its defensive position atop a low mesa to the north of the city, a strong position whose flanks were protected with deep arroyos with rough ground to the front as well that would limit the effectiveness of the superior Chilean cavalry. The mesa also had a natural lip that would protect the bulk of the defenders from direct fire by the Chilean artillery and infantry. The force was divided into six Peruvian and three Bolivian divisions, each of roughly a thousand men supported by twenty-two guns of which six were modern Krupps and eight British Blakeleys, and four Gatling guns.[25]

Perhaps the greatest allied weakness was in the area of intelligence. Even though the campaign was being conducted on Peruvian soil, and one might suppose that the local inhabitants would form a ready-made network of informants, the allied commanders were forced to do virtually all of their planning in total ignorance of Chilean army movements and dispositions. Thus, Baquedano was able to move his army up from the Locumba River to the Sama River, within twenty miles of Tacna on 22 May without hindrance by the allies. It may be true that the Chileans did have a superior force of cavalry at their disposal, but the difference was more in that the Chileans made aggressive use of the forces they had. For example, on 22 May, Baquedano sent forward a force of four hundred cavalry and two hundred mounted infantry with two Krupp guns under his chief of staff Colonel Velasquez to reconnoiter the allied line. This column moved close enough to provoke the allied artillery to open fire, their main purpose, and having determined that the range of the allied guns was inferior to that of the Chilean, they withdrew without losing a man or seeing even the dust of an allied trooper.[26]

To make matters worse, this brief incursion convinced Campero and Montero that the Chileans had lost heart and might be on the verge of retreat. Nothing could have been further from the truth, however, and on the 25th Baquedano moved up his forces to Quebrada Honda, barely five miles from the allied position, now officially dubbed the *Campo de la Alianza*, in anticipation of attacking early the next morning.

Given their conviction that Chilean morale was about to crumble, but also because the allied commanders were well enough aware that the Chileans had easily double their firepower in artillery, Campero, Montero, and Camacho agreed to attempt a surprise attack on the Chilean encampment for first light on the 26th. Consequently, the entire army was formed up and marched out of camp at midnight through the maze of gullies to the north and into a dense *camanchaca* fog. Not surprisingly, after two hours the force was hopelessly tangled and lost, and the order was given to return to their defensive positions, all except the Peruvian 5th Division which did not receive the order and stumbled into the Chilean pickets alone just before dawn and then beat a hasty retreat, arriving back at the *Campo de la Alianza* just moments ahead of the leading Chilean troops.[27] Thus, like the Chileans at San Francisco, the allied troops now faced a relatively fresh attacking force after having spent a fruitless night marching about in the desert. Unlike San Francisco, however, where the bulk of the Chilean infantry was not even engaged, the fatigue and confusion among the allied units would have a fatal effect in the coming battle.

As the sun finally came up and began to burn off the fog on the 26th, the allied soldiers wearily shuffled into their original lines, some pausing to build fires to make a quick breakfast while others did what they could to improve the fortifications. It is somewhat difficult to establish just how well dug-in the allies were, Peruvian and Bolivian sources wanting to minimize the impact of their defeat by implying that their troops were essentially as unprotected as the attackers, while Chilean sources tend to amplify the glory of their victory by implying that the allied position was little short of a Maginot Line. Narciso Campero wrote, in his formal report to the Bolivian legislature after the battle that he was convinced that the natural courage and elan of the Bolivian soldier did not suit him to fight from behind fortifications and that the existence of entrenchments would actually dilute the offensive spirit that marked the highland infantryman. He added, as a footnote, that after the night's march there was no time for the troops to dig in in any case.[28] One has to take this view with a grain of salt, however, as Campero, as commander-in-chief of a force that was in possession of the defensive position for some time prior to the battle (before the fruitless march to Quebrada Honda) would have been responsible to see that his troops did dig in. Since he apparently failed to do this, and since the battle was ultimately lost, it was in his interest to attempt to justify his actions as well as possible. In any event, it can be said that the position was naturally strong, with something like a natural entrenchment along the edge of the mesa, although the rolling ground to the front did allow the attackers to approach without exposing themselves unduly.

The allied position was laid out with Camacho on the left, where the allies expected the main Chilean attack to fall, commanding a division composed of nearly three thousand Bolivian troops, including a small cavalry squadron, backed by nine guns and two Gatlings. In the center, Bolivian General Castro Pinto had a mixed Peruvian-Bolivian force of about forty-five hundred with a single gun and two Gatlings, including a reserve composed of the Peruvian 5th Division that was only just coming in from its hapless night march. On the right Montero commanded a small force of twelve hundred men of the 1st and 6th Peruvian Divisions with another six guns and two Gatlings. Located just behind Montero was the allied reserve with about five hundred Peruvian cavalry, the Bolivian "Colorados" and "Aroma" Regiments, and a scratch force of some seven hundred gendarmes hastily brought up from Tacna itself. This gave the allies a total of between eleven and twelve thousand men and sixteen guns compared to about 13,500 effectives and forty guns for the Chileans.[29] The allies now sat down nervously to wait.

While the allied army was marching around in the fog, a considerable debate was going on in the Chilean headquarters at Quebrada Honda. True to form, Vergara strongly urged a broad flanking maneuver around the allied right to force them out of the strong *Campo de la Alianza* position, hopefully bringing battle on more open ground. This tactic would make the best use of the Chilean superiority in cavalry, Vergara's favorite arm. Baquedano, however, argued that such a move would take at least another full day, which the army could not afford as water was already running short. Furthermore, it would not be possible to drag the army's forty guns with it on such a move, and this would sacrifice one of his chief advantages over the allies, as Chilean intelligence estimated the overall size of the opposing forces to be approximately equal. Baquedano recognized that his cavalry would be largely useless in a set piece battle due to the broken ground on both of the allied flanks, but he planned to keep them in reserve for a pursuit if a breakthrough should be achieved.[30]

The Chilean line had Colonel Amengual's 1st Division on the far right to spearhead the assault with Barcelo's 2nd echeloned slightly back in the center of the line. Barboza's untrustworthy 4th Division was on the extreme left, held still farther to the rear and kept under Baquedano's direct orders as a kind of general reserve since most of the fighting was expected to take place on the other end of the line. Just behind Amengual was located Amunátegui's 3rd Division in position to support either Amengual or Barcelo, whichever assault division should appear to be making the best progress.[31]

The Chileans were in position by 0900, and the artillery opened up its initial bombardment. It immediately became apparent that the allied gunners had not divulged the full range of their weapons when scouted by the Chileans on the 22nd, and the defenders returned a more brisk fire than the attackers had anticipated, although the weight of the Chilean shelling silenced them sufficiently by 1000 hours for Amengual to send forward the "Valparaíso" Regiment as skirmishers covering the advance of "Esmeralda" and "Navales." These columns pushed forward over the open slope for more than an hour under heavy fire but quickly found themselves to be running out of ammunition, after having begun the advance with more than a hundred rounds per man, and the division was called back to resupply. This attempt was quickly followed by the 2nd Division, which also fought toe-to-toe with the defenders for more than an hour before it, too, was obliged to withdraw to obtain additional ammunition.[32]

Campero could see that the main enemy thrust was against his left wing, and he personally led his reserves to shore up the line, the "Colorados" and "Aroma" Regiments and the Peruvian 4th and 5th Divisions. At this point, the battle was going fairly well for the allies, but Colonel Camacho got the impression that the Chileans were beaten, unaware that they were merely seeking to replenish their ammunition, and he moved his division forward onto the open slope in pursuit.

This was a fatal error. Just as the allied troops advanced from the protection of the depression behind the lip of the mesa, Colonel Lagos brought forward three fresh regiments in support of the Chilean 1st and 2nd Divisions, who had refilled their cartridge boxes, and he temporarily took command from Colonel Barcelo who had been wounded. At the same time, Vergara came forward leading a headlong charge by 500 cavalry, trampling some of his own infantry in the process. Some of the allied units broke at the sight of the charge but several regiments, notably the "Colorados," quickly formed infantry squares in the Napoleonic style, actually three-sided boxes with massed rifles and bayonets facing outward that cut down the attacking horsemen in swathes. However, while the infantry square was a superb formation for dealing with cavalry in the open, it exposed the infantrymen to concentrated return fire, especially in this day of repeating rifles and rapid-fire artillery, and the allies suffered devastating losses.[33]

At the same time Amunátegui rushed forward with the remainder of his reserve division, and the allied line began to waver. The Peruvian "Victoria" Regiment broke, and Campero ordered the artillery to fire on the deserters without effect. Colonel Caceres was in the heat of the battle with his division, his own "Zepita" Regiment now down to less than one hundred men, and he attempted to rally the advanced troops that were beginning to stream to the rear. Camacho fell with a shrapnel wound in his stomach, from which he would later die in captivity, as his men tried to reform along their original line of defense, but the Chilean pressure was too great. At last, Barboza's 4th Division smashed into Montero's reduced forces, now just the Peruvian 1st Division and a handful of cavalry, turned both of his flanks, and drove up over the crest of the mesa. The allied army disintegrated with Montero and Campero calling for a retreat all the way to Tarata, some twenty miles to the northeast, with a hope of getting the survivors of the army back to friendly territory by skirting the region occupied by the Chileans through the foothills of the Andes as Buendía had done after San Francisco.[34]

By 1430 hours the field was completely in Chilean hands. The Chilean losses for the day were approximately two thousand killed and wounded, nearly all of them from the 1st and 2nd Divisions. Actually only about half of the available Chilean force had been actively engaged apart from the final moments of the battle, so the losses amounted to almost one quarter of these troops. Baquedano would take steps to prevent the bulk of his troops from entering the town of Tacna, in order to prevent the kind of looting that had occurred at Mollendo and Moquegua, but there was no thought by the local residents of attempting to resist his entry.

The allied losses, however, were far worse. The Peruvians alone lost nearly two hundred officers killed and wounded, along with ten guns captured, but the allied army essentially ceased to exist. Barely four hundred Peruvian soldiers eventually rallied to the army in Arequipa and a few more straggled into the defensive lines around Arica in the following days, but the rest of the army was gone. The Bolivian army, meanwhile, made its way as a swarm of fugitives over the passes leading back to their homeland, never more to take part in the war. There was no disguising the fact that the allied war-making capability had been dealt a disastrous blow.[35]

As a bizarre sidelight to this stunning victory, Santiago groaned for more than a week under the impression that the battle had been lost. This was due, not surprisingly, to the actions of the mercurial Francisco Vergara. Vergara had already been miffed that Baquedano had chosen to ignore his advice about a wide sweeping envelopment of the allied position, and his mood was hardly improved by the fact that Baquedano's straightforward tactics had managed to win a decisive victory without even fully engaging the army. Immediately after the capture of the main defensive works, however, Baquedano further enraged

Vergara by rejecting his call for an energetic pursuit of the fleeing enemy, the commanding general claiming that the troops had marched and fought hard and needed some respite, particularly the cavalry, and that, in any event, the allied forces did not appear to be in any condition to rally this side of Lima.

Feeling that the hard-won success of Chilean arms had been thrown away by the dullard commander, Vergara unilaterally withdrew, immediately took ship for Iquique, and from there sent in a scathing report of the battle. According to the version produced by Vergara, which was published in the newspaper *Ferrocarril* on 3 June and had already circulated widely even earlier by word of mouth, the Battle of Tacna was another bloody defeat along the lines of Tarapacá and that a possible victory had been wasted by Baquedano's gross mismanagement of the mounted arm. Hostile demonstrations against the government ensued, and the mood of Santiago, Valparaíso, and other cities was glum until, on 6 June, a more detailed and much more accurate report came in from Patricio Lynch in which it was learned that Tacna had been occupied and the entire allied army had ceased to exist. It was only then that bonfires of celebration illumined every street corner, and the balconies of the fine houses were festooned with bunting while bands blared out martial tunes. One might have thought that Vergara's political career would be over after such a blatant and public gaffe, but such was not to be the case.[36]

Although this battle marked the end of the active participation by organized Bolivian military forces in the war (with individuals drifting across the border to join the Peruvian ranks on their own until the end of the fighting), the odyssey of Campero's army had not quite run its course. After vainly trying to rally some of the fleeing troops during the late afternoon, Campero had met with Montero on the outskirts of Tacna, and both had agreed that further resistance at this point was useless, and both officers determined to return to their respective capitals with whatever of their national forces they could gather.

Campero was able to organize a column of about one thousand men, with a few dozen survivors of the "Colorados" in the lead and those of the "Grau" Regiment forming a rearguard. They also brought with them the only two Krupp guns salvaged from the field. Campero rode on ahead and, on 31 May learned that he had been formally elected president, no longer provisional, by the National Assembly, even though word of the defeat had reached La Paz by that time. The troops, however, had to endure the derision of the citizens of Tacna, who blamed the Bolivians for the defeat and then had to face a march of several hundred miles over brutal desert and then icy mountain passes reaching to well over ten thousand feet above sea level. Naturally, whatever food, supplies, and extra clothing the army had possessed had been abandoned with its wagons in the chaos after the battle, and dozens of men dropped out from illness, wounds, fatigue, and the bitter cold. Out of desperation, some of the men turned to stealing from farms along the route, and open combat was narrowly avoided on more than one occasion. After surviving this agony, the soldiers finally had to endure one final disgrace, to be confronted by a troop of cavalry sent out from La Paz to the border town of La Joya to forcibly disarm them before allowing them to enter the country. Apparently the authorities were concerned that the returning veterans, whom the government had no intention of paying their back salaries or subsistence allowances, might turn to brigandage if left in possession of their weapons. A similar scene was played out farther to the south where some seven hundred more survivors crossed into the country en route to Cochabamba. Thus ended the Bolivian adventure of the War of the Pacific.[37]

Montero would take his handful of survivors, less than a thousand men, back to Arequipa via Torata. At least he would be spared the indignity of a court martial, although the admiral was received with extremely bad grace by Pierola. This was due at least in part to the president's knowledge that Montero had been pleading for weeks for support from Leyva's army and for additional supplies and weapons to be sent to his army in the south, all of which had been studiously ignored by Lima.

Vergara's panicky report notwithstanding, Baquedano did not waste any time after the fall of Tacna in continuing with the campaign. The fortifications of Arica had been under intensive construction for months, and it was known that the coastal batteries installed around the port and on the Morro, the huge mass of rock rising some 268 meters from the edge of the sea and resembling a little Gibraltar, that flanked the harbor, had kept the Chilean fleet at bay since the start of the war. Baquedano realized that, while the defenders of the town could not expect any succor now from Lima, his best chance to take the place without a protracted siege or bloody assault would be to keep up the momentum of his advance and capitalize on the demoralization that word of the defeat at Tacna would undoubtedly bring to the Peruvian forces there.

The town of Arica itself had a population of only some three thousand, down somewhat due to the earthquakes and accompanying tidal waves of 1868 and 1877. The fortification of the port had been begun in 1865 during the war with Spain but subsequently abandoned. Admiral Montero had been originally placed in charge of the place at the start of the war, not because of his military qualifications as an artillerist or engineer, but to keep him away from the fleet for strictly political reasons. He had taken on the task with the same seriousness with which he had applied to all his duties, and he had begged, borrowed, and coerced the government in Lima to come up with the materials with which to do it. His first priority had been to defend the port from bombardment from the sea, a requirement that was enhanced by the eventual Chilean destruction of the Peruvian fleet. He installed three 70-pounders, a 150-pounder, and a pair of 100-pound Parrott rifled guns atop the Morro with a 250-pound French Vavasseur and another four 70-pounders at a lower battery. He also created two batteries on the beach, the "2 de Mayo" at San Jose with another 250-pound Vavasseur and another at Santa Rosa with two 150-pound Parrotts and another Vavasseur 250. The monitor *Manco Kapac* was also towed into the port to add its two 500-pound guns to the defensive fire.[38]

It was not until December 1879 that any consideration was given to the landward defenses, and the engineer Teodoro Elmore was given carte blanche to create an impregnable ring of steel. He set up batteries of three guns each on the hills Chuno and Aniani in sandbag redoubts and connected them with lines of entrenchments. His most innovative work, for the time, was the installation of hundreds of mines, both pressure-activated, and the very modernistic electronically detonated variety, in barriers covering the most likely approaches to the town by a land force. Unfortunately, the electronic mines were highly experimental and not at all reliable, but they also had the effect of thoroughly terrorizing the Peruvian soldiers on the line, some of whom had witnessed gory accidents during the installation process, and their presence discouraged any patrolling by the forward troops, without creating a similarly fearsome impression on the Chilean troops who either blithely ignored them, carefully disarmed them, or inadvertently detonated them without it having any effect on their military operations. Elmore also eventually established two more forts, one called the *"Ciudadela"* with one 70-pounder and two massive 300-pound Parrotts, and another simply referred to as the eastern fort with three 100-pounders. It was hoped that, with these heavy guns, which the defenders could employ as they did not have to worry about moving them, they would far outrange any artillery the Chileans could bring to their landward assault, while the Chilean fleet would also be kept at arm's length by the huge guns on the Morro.[39]

The command at Arica had been entrusted to Colonel Francisco Bolognesi, the sixty-five year old veteran of San Francisco and Tarapacá with some two thousand men of the 7th and 8th Divisions and some local militia at his command. Most of the gunners for the coastal artillery were provided by the homeless survivors of the Peruvian fleet, and command of the defenses on the Morro itself was given to Guillermo Moore, the unfortunate captain of the *Independencia*.[40]

On 1 June the first Chilean troops appeared within sight of the Peruvian defenses and began scouting the outer works. Baquedano was in personal command of the force, but he only bothered to bring with him the 1st, 3rd, and 4th Line Regiments, "Bulnes," one squadron of mounted *carabiñeros,* three batteries of field guns and one of mountain howitzers, for a total of approximately six thousand men, mostly those who had not taken part in the heaviest fighting at Tacna. Baquedano expected the fleet to be able to supply most of the heavy firepower for the bombardment of the fortifications, and a squadron composed of the *Cochrane, Loa, Magallanes,* and *Covadonga* were cruising offshore for this purpose. By the afternoon of 2 June the Chilean force was encamped on the Agufre River within a few miles of the entrenchments.[41]

Also on the 2nd a severe blow was dealt to the defenders when Teodoro Elmore, the designer of the defenses, was captured by a Chilean patrol while supervising the placement of his electronic mines. Unfortunately for the Peruvians, Elmore did not perceive his terms of employment to include the protection of privileged information, and he freely discussed with the attackers the location and nature of his mine fields.[42] It should be noted that, at this stage in the evolution of modern warfare, pressure mines and the command-detonated electronic versions were considered "infernal machines" by many professionals. Blowing up enemy soldiers with previously placed mechanical devices was seen as something dishonorable when compared to the more genteel dismemberment by long range artillery fire or the valorous bayoneting of men face to face. The use of these weapons tended to enrage the Chileans and had something to do with the alleged massacre of Peruvian prisoners and wounded after the battle, since even the full knowledge provided by Elmore did not prevent some casualties among the attackers from the mines.

In any event, on 5 June the Chilean preparations for attack were largely completed with the artillery dug into the hills east of the town, and the fleet in position to join in the assault. Baquedano sent in a delegation of parliamentarians to call for Bolognesi's surrender. Bolognesi had sent repeated messages to Montero, complaining of a lack of information on the likelihood of relief. The original plan of defense had called for resistance for some three or four months until a relief army could be organized, and there had never been any consideration of the garrison holding out indefinitely. Montero had not replied, but it must have been clear to Bolognesi from the reports provided to him by the survivors of Tacna who had straggled into the town that there was no chance that Peru could mobilize a force that would sweep away the victorious Chileans within the foreseeable future. Colonel Segundo Leyva, commander of the 2nd Army at Arequipa, had, in fact begun an advance to the south on 26 March, but he had retreated upon receiving news of the defeat of the allies at Tacna.

Now Bolognesi met in a large house on the outskirts of Arica with the Chilean delegation led by Major Juan de la Cruz Salvo, the commander of Chilean artillery who had earned his reputation at the Battle of San Francisco. When Bolognesi summarily accepted the terms of surrender, Salvo simply stated that his mission was then completed. Bolognesi hurriedly added, "You understand that this is my personal view and I must consult with my officers." He then asked for a delay of two hours to accomplish this.

Salvo refused, this being beyond his authority to grant. Bolognesi then held a quick conference with some of his officers in the next room and returned to confirm that the garrison would fight to the last round. While hardly changing anything, this brief vacillation did seem to rob the moment of some of its potential glory.[43]

At 0900 hours on 5 June the Chilean fleet and land artillery opened fire. Baquedano had a vague hope that the weight of fire would convince the defenders to accept terms and thus avoid the bloodshed of an infantry assault. The bombardment continued throughout the day without noticeable effect.

The shelling from both land and sea resumed the next morning, and the ships moved in closer in the hope of achieving greater accuracy. Again, however, the bombardment had no serious effect, although a shell from one of the forts struck the *Cochrane*, setting off some ready powder for the guns and inflicting nearly thirty casualties and causing the ships to pull back out of range once more.[44]

That evening, a second group of Chilean parliamentaries were escorted within the lines, this time accompanied by engineer Elmore. They again offered Bolgonesi the option of surrender, and he again refused, adding, "although we recognize the futility of our sacrifice."[45]

Baquedano had assigned responsibility for conducting the assault to Colonel Lagos. He assigned about nine hundred men to attack the ring of forts north of the city against the Peruvian 8th Division, with the main thrust to come from about nineteen hundred men who were to assault the hills and forts southeast of the port where the Peruvian 7th Division was positioned. He held another twelve hundred men in reserve to exploit any breach in the enemy lines. During the night of 6 June the Chileans were able to move to within one kilometer of the Peruvian lines, taking advantage of dead ground, their knowledge of the location of most of the Peruvian mine fields, and the reluctance of the defenders to send patrols outside of their own entrenchments.

In fact, the Peruvian sentries would not spot the advancing ranks of the Chilean 3rd Line in front of the eastern fort and the 4th Line at the *Ciudadela* until they were within some three hundred meters of the works at 0500 hours on the morning of the 7th. The first Chilean assault was repulsed, but it was quickly followed up, and the attackers soon gained a foothold in the first line of trenches. The commander of the 7th Division was killed in action, as was his replacement in short order, and, with Chilean troops now driving the defenders back, a sixteen-year-old corporal, Alfredo Maldonado, hurled a burning torch into the magazine of the *Ciudadela*, destroying himself, the fort, and inflicting heavy casualties on the Chileans. The eastern fort fell soon thereafter, and Bolognesi ordered the 8th Division to withdraw to the Morro, even though the Chilean attack on that front had not yet kicked off.[46]

Only some four hundred men managed to reach the Morro to reinforce the 160 naval gunners already there under Moore. The hill had virtually vertical cliffs on three sides, facing the sea, but its landward side was a broad, sloping plain up which the Chileans swarmed, hardly slowed now by the Peruvian entrenchments. Bolognesi was killed here, as was Moore, finally expunging any dishonor his loss of the *Independencia* may have caused. With them fell at least a thousand more Peruvians killed, all of the rest of the defenders being taken prisoner. The *Manco Kapac* in the harbor was scuttled as soon as the Chilean flag appeared atop the Morro, and the battle was over. The Chilean losses totaled some thirty officers and another 114 soldiers killed and nearly three hundred men wounded. The fighting ended by 0830 hours that morning.[47]

The allied military power south of Arequipa had now been entirely eliminated. More than that, Bolivia had effectively dropped out of the war, and virtually the entire Peruvian pre-war professional military establishment had ceased to exist. The Chileans were in full possession of all the lands they had claimed, Peru's nitrate-rich territory that had been seized as a bargaining chip, and the entire Tacna-Arica region to serve as a buffer for that province. It now appeared that it only remained for the diplomats to do their jobs, and the war would finally be over.

NOTES

1. Mariano Felipe Paz Soldan, *Narracion Historica de la Guerra de Chile contra el Peru y Bolivia*, vol. 2, Buenos Aires: s.n., 1884, p. 98.

2. Gonzalo Bulnes, *Guerra del Pacífico*, vol. 2, Santiago de Chile: Editorial del Pacífico, 1955, p. 11.

3. Ibid., p. 27.

4. William F. Sater, *Chile and the War of the Pacific*, Lincoln: University of Nebraska Press, 1986, p. 27.

5. Bulnes, p. 34.
6. Ibid., p. 46.
7. Diego Barros Arana, *Historia de la Guerra del Pacífico*. Santiago de Chile: Editorial Andres Bello, 1979, p. 189.
8. Mariano Felipe Paz Soldan, *Narracion Historica de la Guerra de Chile contra el Peru y Bolivia*, vol. 2, Buenos Aires: s.n., 1884, p. 106.
9. Bulnes, p. 68.
10. Sater, p. 26.
11. Bulnes, p. 81.
12. Andres A. Caceres, *La Guerra del '79: Sus Campañas (Memorias)*, Lima: Editorial Milla Batres, 1973, p. 50.
13. Martin Eduardo Congrains, *Batalla de Tacna*, Lima: Editorial Ecoma, 1972, p. 83.
14. Bulnes, p. 89.
15. Paz, p. 131.
16. Barros, p. 195.
17. Bulnes, p. 101.
18. Sater, p. 27.
19. Bulnes, p. 107.
20. Ibid., p. 134.
21. Barros, p. 215.
22. Sater, p. 28.
23. Barros, p. 220.
24. Paz, p. 163.
25. Caceres, p. 51.
26. Barros, p. 223.
27. Paz, p. 172.
28. Narciso Campero, *Diario de la Campaña de la Quinta Division del Ejercito Boliviano*, Sucre: Tipografia de la Libertad, 1882, p. 42.
29. Congrains, p. 90.
30. Bulnes, p. 160.
31. Congrains, p. 92.
32. Bulnes, p. 170.
33. Paz, p. 173.
34. Caceres, p. 61.
35. Bulnes, p. 177.
36. Ibid., 182.
37. Roberto Querejazu Calvo, *Guano, Salitre, Sangre: Historia de la Guerra del Pacífico*, La Paz: Editorial Los Amigos del Libro, 1979, p. 565.
38. Paz, p. 185.
39. Ibid., p. 187.
40. Bulnes, p. 185.
41. Barros, p. 250.
42. Martin Eduardo Congrains, *Batalla de Arica*, vol. 1., Lima: Editorial Ecoma, 1973, p. 74.
43. Ibid., vol. 2, p. 11.
44. Barros, p. 250.
45. Congrains, op. cit., p. 32.
46. Ibid., p. 74.
47. Barros, p. 256.

Chapter Nine

A Diplomatic Interlude

With the only viable war making capability of both allies now thoroughly destroyed, it was logical that the Chileans believed that the time had come to arrive at a settlement of the conflict. Their troops occupied all of the disputed territories, Peru's most valuable export-producing lands, and a generous buffer zone into the bargain, far more than the most optimistic strategic planner might have hoped. The Chilean army was larger and more experienced than ever and sitting within easy striking distance of Peru's main population centers and political heart. The navy, little the worse for wear, had actually been augmented by the addition of the refurbished *Huascar* and now had ample forces to blockade all of Peru's major ports and to cruise the coast in search of enterprising smugglers attempting to bring in military supplies. It only remained for the defeated allies to realize their situation and to come to terms.

Another factor working in favor of a quick settlement to the conflict was the influence of the neutral powers. Contrary to the concept of the "merchants of death," the arms manufacturers of Europe and the United States conniving to keep alive the conflict, from which they had earned some welcome sales of their merchandise, the most influential foreign businessmen and their respective consuls and ambassadors were the traders in nitrates and the holders of the growing stack of debts of all the belligerents. They were all aware that the only way they could hope to receive payment on their loans and earn the profits from the nitrate business was to see the war ended and trade resumed on a normal footing without legal disputes over ownership of the resources of the region hanging over their heads.

However, in spite of these expectations, no delegations of contrite and timorous allied officials appeared at Baquedano's headquarters nor were any humble telegrams received at *La Moneda* seeking peace on any terms. Instead, the same assembly that witnessed the swearing in of Narciso Campero as president in La Paz on 16 June 1880 voted in favor of a continuation of the war. This may have been a largely empty gesture, as the Bolivian treasury was empty and her army scattered to the winds, but it was an indication of the opposition of the Andean republic to accepting a Chilean victory. The National Assembly voted additional taxes for the war, and Melchor Tenazas, the new Bolivian Ambassador in Lima convinced Pierola that Bolivia would not abandon the alliance.[1]

On 11 June 1880 a document was signed in Lima, which would later be ratified by the legislatures of both Bolivia and Peru, declaring the creation of the United States of Peru-Bolivia, an "indivisible union." This, too, may have been no more than a gesture, as the document outlined very few details of creating a country. It envisioned a kind of federal arrangement with a single president serving for five years, Pierola to be the first, with Campero as vice president, but it left it to a future convention to pick a capital for the new nation. Some attention was paid to the important aspect of designing a new coat of arms and a new flag, which would have boasted thirteen purple and gold stripes, so it is perhaps just as well that no samples of this rather garish symbol were ever actually produced. The plebiscite that would have been required to put the protocol into effect was never held, however, and the concept was left unrealized.[2]

In the face of this intransigence, the Pinto administration, which was under constant pressure from the opposition parties to bring the war to a successful conclusion, felt it necessary to increase the pressure on Pierola, which would hopefully obviate the need for a full-fledged invasion of the Peruvian heartland. The first step in this process was to press home the rather casual blockade of the Peruvian coast that the Chilean navy had been carrying out since the start of the war. Since the Chilean advance up the coast had drastically reduced the number of ports that required monitoring, this task was feasible, although it involved long weeks at sea for the Chilean sailors, along a hostile coast often enshrouded in an impenetrable fog which both increased the danger to their ships and improved the chances of the blockade runners. Still, a pattern was set up in which the major combatants would patrol well off shore, leaving it to smaller frigates and a host of newly purchased or built steamers, lightly armed and with shallow draft, that could work in close to the shore and investigate suspicious vessels, calling on the heavier firepower of the ironclads whenever necessary.

The blockade had been formally announced on 10 April 1880, giving neutral shipping some two weeks to clear out of the combat zone, although the representatives of the nations with merchants interests in Peru, notably the United States, Britain, and France, protested against this policy, to no avail. The blockade was further reinforced with periodic bombardments by the fleet of Callao, Ancón, and other Peruvian ports, usually without much effect.[3]

The Peruvians could reply to attacks on Callao with the substantial armament around the port. Since the start of the war, the Peruvians had continually augmented the fortifications around the port and their weaponry, now including nearly fifty guns ranging from 32-pounders, to 300- and 500-pound British-made ship killers in addition to the twin 500-pound guns aboard the monitor *Atahualpa* and the guns of the notorious raider *Union* in the harbor itself. While the Chilean ironclads were more or less impervious to the shelling, all of the blockaders suffered casualties, and the commander, Admiral Riveros, was under strict orders to avoid running any risk of having one of his major ships sunk or, worse yet, captured. It is easy to imagine the sleepless nights the Chilean admiralty officers must have spent in Valparaíso dreaming of *Cochrane* or *Blanco Encalada* running aground in a fog and being seized by boatloads of Peruvians soldiers from the shore, thus potentially ending Chile's naval superiority and putting into question all of the conquests thus far in the war.[4]

The blockade dragged on, week after weary week, with little significant action to report until about four weeks after the fall of Arica. On the afternoon of 3 July the frigate *Loa* was on patrol off Callao when a lookout spotted a Peruvian launched anchored not far from shore and apparently abandoned. Captain Peña ordered a closer look, and it was discovered that the launch was loaded to the gunwales with fresh vegetables and meat, possibly being shipped to one of the outlying fort garrisons. Since one of the great hardships for the sailors on blockade was having to survive on ship's biscuit and salt pork and fish for weeks on end, the possibility of a windfall of fresh food was too good to pass up, and the captain ordered the launch tied off and the supplies transferred to the *Loa*, ignoring the suspicions of his first officer, Lieutenant Martinez. Just as the eager crewmen of the *Loa* clambered into the boat to begin off-loading, a tremendous explosion disintegrated the boat and tore a gaping fourteen-foot hole in the side of the frigate. Within five minutes *Loa* had sunk beneath the waves, taking her commander and over one hundred of her crew with her, leaving some fifty men to be rescued by a Chilean motor launch. Lacking a means of confronting the Chilean fleet in open warfare, the Peruvians had resorted to subterfuge to attempt to even the odds.[5]

There was an immediate howl for vengeance in the Chilean legislature and in the press. The Chileans chose to view the incident as a low blow, unfitting for civilized warfare. It was considered especially disgusting as the *Loa* had only recently delivered a number of Peruvian wounded from Arica to Callao. This had been done primarily to relieve the Chilean authorities of the need to care for these men who could be of no further use to the allied war effort, but it now took on the image of an unparalleled act of charity for which this treachery had been the repayment.[6]

One of the first results of this cry for revenge was the replacement of Minister of War Baldomero Lillo, who really had much more aptitude for diplomacy than war, with the ubiquitous Jose Francisco Vergara. While it might have been supposed that Vergara's shameful, panicky reporting after the Battle of Tacna might have doomed his political career, he was still associated with being a gadfly of the government on defense issues, always pushing for a more aggressive stance. This made him the logical choice to spearhead a renewed policy of forcing the Peruvians to see the error of their ways and come to the negotiating table. And one of the first acts of the new minister was to endorse a punitive expedition to the north of Peru, to bring the war to a part of the country that had thus far been spared, to attempt to destroy Peru's one remaining source of foreign exchange, its large sugar plantations, and to exact "contributions" from the *hacendados* to help defray the rising cost of the war.[7]

Patricio Lynch was actually a naval officer who had been in the service since 1838 when he fought against the Peruvian-Bolivian Confederation. He had then studied seamanship with the British Navy and had fought with them in the Opium Wars in China before returning to his native land. Earlier in the war he had held the unexciting post of commander of transports during the invasion of Tarapacá and had acted as military governor of that province since its conquest. With the elimination of the Peruvian fleet, however, Lynch found the scope of action far too limited for his taste, and he had transferred to the army and was now given command of the amphibious expedition to the north.[8]

Lynch's force consisted of the 1st Line Regiment and the Regiments "Talca" and "Colchaga," a battery of mountain howitzers, and a small cavalry squadron for a total of twenty-two hundred men. They were transported and escorted by the *Chacabuco, Amazonas,* and *Abtao,* departing on 4 September from Arica. The force landed six days later at the port of Chimbote, meeting no resistance from the local militia. His men immediately occupied the sugar plantations of *El Puente* and *Palo Seco* and demanded a "war tax" of 100,000 pesos to be paid over in three days or the buildings, crops, and equipment of the plantations would be destroyed.[9]

The reaction of President Pierola in Lima, rather than sending troops to deal with this relatively small Chilean force and to hurl it back into the sea, was to keep his forces in the immediate vicinity of the capital and merely to issue strongly worded proclamations. He decreed that any Peruvian citizen found to have paid extortion money to the Chileans would be considered a traitor and tried accordingly. This provided little help to the unfortunate *hacendados* who were facing the barrels of Chilean guns, and the proof of their "crime" would be immediately evident in that, if they paid, their property would not be destroyed by the invaders but would then be confiscated by the government, whereas, if they refused, they could at least save themselves the wait and watch their goods go up in smoke at once. Declaring his "taxation" to be the right of any conqueror, then burned one plantation after another and "freeing" hundreds of Chinese laborers found on them.[10] While it was true that these Chinese coolies existed in conditions very much like slavery, one wonders whether Lynch would have evidenced the same emancipatory urges had the plantation owners paid up.

After spending several days in the area of Chimbote burning crops and farm equipment, tearing up railroad tracks, and generally looting everything of interest, Lynch dispatched a force of four hundred men in a corvette to the town of Sepa to intercept a reported shipment of munitions landed from a merchantman. The raiders found the shipment to already have been landed, but pursued the wagon train inland and destroyed some 200,000 rounds of rifle ammunition and returned to Chimbote. On 22 September Lynch moved on to Paita by ship, then to Eten on the 24th, marching overland to Chiclayo. In all, he would spend some two months ravaging Peru's richest, most populous department and would destroy some 4.2 million pesos worth of equipment and merchandise. He also seized some £29,000 in cash, 11,428 peso coins, 2,500 sacks of sugar and 1,600 of rice for his trouble. That it never occurred to the Pierola administration to attack this small, isolated force, not only to protect

Peruvian territory, but also possibly to score a morale-lifting victory in this dark hour, was a tremendous embarrassment for the government.[11]

One bright spot in the military fortunes of Peru again appeared on the sea during this period. On the night of 13 September the venerable *Covadonga*, the corvette captured from Spain in 1865, had been raiding along the coast at the port of Chancay, rounding up Peruvian launches and destroying them. After pursuing one group of boats, the Chileans spotted one that had apparently been abandoned in the flight, a particularly attractive craft, and the captain ordered it brought aboard for use as his personal gig. The wily Peruvians, however, had crammed the boat with gun powder and a detonator, and the resulting explosion ripped open the side of the aged ship, sending her to the bottom with 161 out of her crew of 237.[12]

Also on the naval front, Peruvian agents in Europe (not apparently aided significantly by President Prado) had been desperately seeking to purchase new warships to rebuild the fleet. Using a Nicaraguan agent as a front, the Peruvians had been negotiating with the French for the ironclads *Solferino* and *La Gloire*, but the able Chilean minister Blest Gana discovered the plot and lodged a formal protest, and the deal collapsed. Another arrangement with corrupt Turkish officials for the British-built ironclad *Felkhz-Bolend*, which ostensibly would be going to Japan, also fell through when the Turkish Admiralty objected to the sale, of which they had apparently not been informed.[13]

In the face of the continuing dismal picture on the military front, Pierola finally accepted an American offer of mediation of the dispute on 16 September, soon followed by Bolivia. Chile agreed on 6 October. The American envoys to the region, Thomas B. Osborne in Santiago, Charles Adams in La Paz, and Isaac P. Christiancy in Lima had been working diligently for some months to bring about a meeting between the belligerents spurred on by pressure from Secretary of State Evarts. This pressure, in turn, was prompted by comments made by British Prime Minister Gladstone involving the possibility of European intervention to bring about an end to the conflict in order, presumably, to open up the region once more to unhindered commerce. Although nothing had come of this British proposal in the European capitals, primarily because Bismark had discounted it as far too costly, the suggestion of such an action had stirred American concerns about the Monroe Doctrine and the paternalistic Yankee responsibility for seeing to the harmony of the hemisphere.[14]

Whatever the motivation, the conference would be held aboard the American ship *Lackawanna* in the port of Arica, beginning on 22 October. The Chileans would be represented by Eusebio Lillo, now serving as governor of Tacna and Arica, Eulogio Altamirano, and Jose Francisco Vergara, the Peruvians by Supreme Court Justice Antonio Arenas and Capain Aurelio Garcia y Garcia from the Navy, while Mariano Baptista and Cristosomo Carrillo would represent Bolivia.[15]

Flushed with their recent victories, the Chilean delegation peremptorily laid out the conditions they demanded for a return to peace. All territory south of Camarones, which included the bulk of the nitrate lands, would be permanently ceded to Chile. The allies were to pay to Chile the sum of twenty million pesos on reparations and to return all property seized from Chilean citizens or the government, including the transport *Rimac*, still a sore point for Chilean pride. The Chileans also demanded a public abrogation of the 1873 "secret" treaty between Bolivia and Peru, and presumably also of the recently established confederation, although this might not have been taken seriously enough to have been considered worthy of mention. Chile stated that she would retain possession of Moquegua, Arica, and Tacna until all previously mentioned conditions were met, and Peru must promise not to fortify the port of Arica in the future (the present fortifications would most likely be dismantled by the Chileans before returning the place to Peruvian custody.)[16]

After the initial Chilean presentation the conference adjourned for three days to allow the delegates to digest the proceedings and to get instructions from home. In the meanwhile, Lillo engaged in the activity which seemed to have prompted his attendance at the conference in the first place, since he gave it very little chance of success, that of seeking to break the Bolivian-Peruvian alliance surreptitiously through the familiar offer of Peruvian territory being traded to Bolivia as an access to the sea. Lillo enjoyed a long friendship with Mariano Baptista, the head of the Bolivian delegation, and Baptista seems to have spoken out of school with him to some extent, complaining of the growing sentiment back home that the war had actually been fought for Peruvian territory, not Bolivian, since that was long gone, and that the "secret" treaty with Peru, far from providing any protection for Bolivia, had ultimately served as a pretext for the war where a negotiated solution might well have been worked out early on between Bolivia and Chile on their own. Baptista, who had been very vocal in his opposition to the war, was not well in tune with the true sentiments of his countrymen, and his talks with Lillo only served to give the Chileans false hopes of a bilateral settlement that would not be forthcoming.[17]

In order to encourage Bolivian flexibility, the Chilean government released some 25 Bolivian prisoners of war taken at Tacna. While this might have helped somewhat, it was not enough. Baptista favored a deal with Chile, although he argued strongly that Chile should "purchase" the Atacama, besides obviously foregoing any reparations from Bolivia. But the sticking point was that of taking a former ally's territory as part of the peace package, and this was something the leadership in La Paz, and the masses of the Bolivian people could simply not quite accept at this point.[18]

In any event, when the conference reconvened on 25 October, the allies roundly rejected the Chilean demands, as had been expected. Instead, they insisted that Chilean troops must withdraw from the occupied territories *prior* to any peace negotiations and that the border dispute should be submitted to international arbitration. To confuse things a little, Ambassador Osborne took the occasion to announce that the United States government, "does not seek the position of arbiter in this question. A strict compliance with the duties inherent to that position would involve much trouble and great labor."[19] Needless to say, without any impulse from the American representatives, the Chileans rejected the idea of arbitration, although it is highly debatable whether there might have been anything that the United States could have done to influence Chile to give up the fruits of her successful military adventure. And with that the conference ended.

As a further embarrassment to the American envoys, there was some squabbling between them over the need to send a telegram explaining the outcome of the meeting, but Osborne, citing the prohibitive cost of cables to the United States, which, interestingly, had to go by way of Paris, sent the cryptic message "Conference failed." His colleagues, were dissatisfied with this, however, and accepted an offer by the Peruvian government to pay for a more fulsome message describing the harsh Chilean terms and their rejection of arbitration. Secretary Evarts, upon hearing of Osborn's statement to the conference, issued him a rebuke, diplomatically worded to suggest that Osborn had not fully understood the wishes of his government if he thought it his duty to give the delegates the impression that the United States "would not cheerfully assume any labor and trouble incident to arbitration in the interest of peace and the service of justice." This clarification of the attitude of Washington was not, however, received by any of the participants until some three months after the conference had closed.[20]

As brief as it was, the conference had at least served the purpose of clarifying what the true Chilean war aims now were. The concept of Chile merely seeking to "recover" her territory usurped by Bolivia had obviously been overtaken by events, and the occupation of both Bolivian and Peruvian nitrate territories was no longer simply a question of denying the enemy those revenues for the duration of the conflict. Chile already considered herself the rightful victor in the war and entitled to all that the law of conquest had ever implied. Chile expected the allies to be obliged to pay every cent of what Chile's war of conquest had cost, in addition to losing the land in question. There was still the very open issue of Bolivia eventually receiving a corridor to the sea through formerly Peruvian territory, in which case the Andean republic would essentially emerge from the war in a rather better position than that in which she had entered it. But Peru was to be crippled. Chile's only feasible competitor for power along the Pacific coast of South America would be humiliated and weakened to a point that she could never pose a serious threat to Chile in the future.

With the collapse of the talks at Arica and with the population still howling for revenge for the *Loa* and the *Covadonga*, the Chilean government was obliged to turn its mind to the business of pursuing a land campaign against the Peruvian capital. The pressure for some positive news was especially intense now that the presidential election campaign was underway with Domingo Santa Maria stepping down as Minister of Interior in preparation for his role as the administration's candidate in the contest. General Baquedano estimated that some eighteen thousand troops would be required for the invasion force, with around four thousand being sufficient to garrison the occupied territories. Oddly enough, the civilian administration thought these figures much too optimistic and insisted that an initial force of twenty thousand would be required with five thousand in immediate support, plus another ten thousand for garrisons in the occupied territories and Chile itself.[21]

Needless to say, since the government was responsible for raising, arming, and training the new forces, Baquedano was not in a position to turn down the project, and plans went forward to build up the army to a total of not thirty-five thousand but eventually of forty-five thousand men. The army that was finally fielded would reach 27,042 with Baquedano for the invasion, 6,598 left in Tacna, another 828 in Iquique, 709 in Antofagasta, and 4,404 assigned to watch the Araucan frontier in the far south for a total of nearly 42,000 men.[22]

This force would be divided into three "grand" divisions, each of two brigades, commanded by Generals Jose Antonio Villagran, Emilio Sotomayor, of San Francisco fame, and Pedro Lagos. Like Escala before him, Baquedano objected strongly to a reorganization of his army which was engineered by the minister of war, now Vergara, primarily because he had hoped to name the new commanders himself, but, like Escala, his objections were largely ignored.

NOTES

1. Roberto Querejazu Calvo, *Guano, Salitre, Sangre: Historia de la Guerra del Pacífico*, La Paz: Editorial Los Amigos del Libro, 1979, p. 595.

2. Ronald Bruce St. John, *The Foreign Policy of Peru*, Boulder, CO: Lynne Reinner, 1992, p. 115.

3. Diego Barros Arana, *História de la Guerra del Pacífico 1879-1881*, Santiago de Chile: Editoral Andres Bello, 1979, p. 302.

4. Mariano Felipe Paz Soldan, *Narracion Historica de la Guerra de Chile contra Peru y Bolivia*, vol. 2, Buenos Aires: s.n., 1884, p. 218.

5. Barros, p. 307.

6. Gonzalo Bulnes, *Guerra del Pacífico*, vol. 2, Santiago de Chile: Editorial del Pacífico, 1955, p. 212.

7. Martin Congrains, *La Expedicion Lynch*, Lima: Editorial Ecoma, 1973, p. 58.

8. Barros, p. 340.

9. Congrains, p. 59.

10. Barros, p. 342.

11. Congrains, p. 88.

12. Paz, p. 256.

13. Bulnes, p. 252.

14. Herbert Millington, *American Diplomacy in the War of the Pacific*, New York: Columbia University Press, 1938, p. 66.

15. Querejazu, p. 606.

16. Valentin Abecia Baldivieso, *Las Relaciones Internacionales en la Historia de Bolivia*, vol. 2, La Paz: Editorial Los Amigos del Libro, 1979, p. 135.

17. Querejazu, p. 607.

18. Ibid., 616.

19. William Jefferson Davis, *Tacna and Arica: An Account of the Chile-Peru Boundary Dispute and the Arbitration by the United States*, New York: Archon Books, 1967, p. 114.

20. Ibid., p. 118.

21. Bulnes, p. 212.

22. Ibid., p. 288.

Chapter Ten

On to Lima

With the collapse of the Arica peace talks, it became immediately clear to the Chilean government that there would be no peace with Peru, and probably not with Bolivia either, until all vestiges of organized military force in Peru had been destroyed and the capital occupied. The Pinto administration might have taken a lesson from the Prussian experience in France barely a decade before as an indication that occupation of the enemy capital does not necessarily dictate an end to the fighting, but they can be excused for supposing that the Peruvian national commitment to the war was far less strong than the French resistance to the Germanic invasion. In any event, the seizure of Lima did not appear to be a particularly daunting task, certainly not compared to that which had faced the raw Chilean armed forces in 1879. The theoretical ability of the allies to field an army double the size of the Chilean, based on their larger populations, had proven to be a chimera, and the vaunted Peruvian fleet had been overcome at surprisingly little cost and effort. The veteran Chilean soldiers and sailors should now have no trouble simply repeating their exploits one more time against a largely demoralized, disorganized, and poorly armed enemy. That was certainly the view of Baquedano's staff as they set about planning the next phase of their campaign, the conquest of Lima.

To oppose the impending invasion, Pierola's mobilization of the male population of Peru had gathered together some twenty-six thousand men. These were loosely grouped into three armies, that of the North under General Ramon Vargas Machuca with ten thousand, the Center under Colonel Juan Nepomuceno Vargas with another ten thousand, and the South under Colonel Juan de la Torre with six thousand more. These forces contained all of Peru's surviving pre-war military units, both those who had escaped from Tacna, Leyva's 2nd Army, and garrison units from elsewhere in the country, besides at least partially trained recruits raised over the previous year. This force was notably weak in cavalry as well as in modern artillery. The Peruvians possessed a total of some three hundred guns, including some taken from their few remaining naval ships, but most of these were in fixed positions in forts on the coast, and many of this number were simple bronze muzzle-loaders cast in Peru itself and of dubious combat value.[1]

In addition, a Reserve Army under Colonel Juan Martin Echenique had been raised in Lima with some ten thousand men divided into ten divisions. This force was composed of the newest recruits and volunteers, quaintly grouped by their civilian professions. The 1st Division came from the ranks of employees of the ministry of justice (including a fair number of policemen), the 2nd from the public school teachers, the 3rd was composed of economists, the 4th of construction workers, the 5th from government-owned industry, the 6th of artisans, the 7th of journalists, the 8th of retail merchants, the 9th of decorators and hair dressers, and the 10th of railroad workers and employees from public works.[2] (We will not digress into idle speculation about the relative performance of some of these unique military formations.) The government had also mobilized some three thousand Indians from the remote Jauja Valley who paraded into Lima painted for war and carrying their deadly poisoned arrows and blow gun darts.

Although the Chilean advance had considerably reduced the territory that the Peruvians needed to defend, an unexpected and undesired benefit of the repeated allied defeats, there still remained hundreds of miles of coast line along which the Chileans could land, as Lynch's raids had demonstrated. A substantial force thus had to be kept with the Army of the South around Arequipa, but the bulk of what was left was kept concentrated by Pierola in the immediate vicinity of Lima, the only target of real significance at which the enemy might now be aiming.

Back at Arica, the Chilean command had reviewed the possible landing sites and had decided upon the conservative choice of the port of Pisco. Although the town was nearly 230 kilometers from Lima itself, it had a good protected harbor and ample water and forage to supply the army once ashore. Also, its very distance from the capital was considered an advantage in that it would allow time for the Chileans to bring the army forward in several waves, sufficient transport shipping not being available to move nearly thirty thousand men, thousands of horses and draft animals, and mountains of supplies in a single lift. Although Pierola would prove not to have the aggressive, daring character as president that he had once possessed as a conspirator and filibuster earlier in his career, the Chileans wanted to be able to land a single division, allow it time to secure the landing area, and then bring in the rest of the army and prepare for a grand advance on Lima from this point.[3]

At a council of war in Arica on 6 November 1880 the final decision was taken to move Villagran's 1st Division north and actually conduct the landing at the town of Paracas, within twenty miles of Pisco, which the Chileans expected to be stoutly defended. Villagran would march overland to Pisco and take the port with the support of the fleet and prepare the way for the rest of the army to land. To this end, Vergara had had the foresight to order built thirty-six shallow draft, flat-bottomed boats to move the infantry to shore in order to avoid the problems faced at Pisagua, trying to transfer troops in regular ships' boats under enemy fire, thus creating possibly the first purpose-built amphibious landing craft in history. These boats would be able to land three thousand men and twelve guns in a single wave, more than enough to overcome any likely resistance on the beach. One of the smaller, faster ships of the invasion fleet would remain with Vergara to bring back word of any sign of a Peruvian counterattack while the second wave was being loaded.[4]

On 14 November Villagran's division embarked at Arica with eighty-six hundred men, twenty guns, four Gatling guns, and 1,641 mules and horses aboard ten steamers and seven sailing ships, escorted by *Chacabuco* and *O'Higgins.* Jose Francisco Gana's brigade of the 2nd Division was to be brought forward as an immediate reinforcement less than two weeks later with a further thirty-five hundred men, twelve guns, and another five hundred horses. The passage was uneventful, and the fleet arrived at Paracas on 19 November. Apart from mines planted on the beach and pier, which were disarmed, the invaders encountered no resistance and occupied Pisco the next day. A small detachment of some three hundred infantry and cavalry had been in Pisco, but these scattered at the first random shots fired by *Chacabuco.* Villagran then sent Colonel Amunátegui with the 2nd Line Regiment, two hundred cavalry, and a battery on a three-day, sixty-seven kilometer march to Ica, repairing the railroad line and stringing telegraph cables as he went, a task that was also accomplished without meeting anything more than scattered sniping by the Peruvians.[5]

The Chilean plan, that was determined by a council of war on 7 December, now called for Villagran to move overland from Pisco to Chilca where the rest of the army would ultimately land. Gana's brigade would be left at Pisco to be picked up by the fleet as it brought the rest of the army north. This would involve a march of some two hundred miles, virtually to the gates of Lima over the last stretch of waterless desert terrain before the heavily irrigated fields of Peru's central valley would be encountered. There had always been friction between Baquedano and Villagran, as the latter was actually senior to the army commander in date of rank, and Villagran's lack of enthusiasm for the project was well known at Arica.

Consequently, when Baquedano and the invasion fleet arrived at Pisco on 19 December and found virtually all of the 1st Division still in the area of the port, Baquedano was furious. Villagran argued that his advance had been slowed by the necessity of scouting out and digging wells along the route of march, and by the need to send the army forward in brigade-sized detachments in order not to overload the limited water and forage supplies available. Lynch's brigade was well on the way, and a second brigade was prepared to take to the road, but had not done so yet. This explanation was totally unsatisfactory to Baquedano who, after some heated scenes with Villagran, dismissed him and placed Lynch in overall command of the 1st Division. However, having done this, Baquedano tacitly accepted Villagran's reasoning, vetoing the proposed march of the rest of the 1st Division, which would now be moved by sea with the bulk of the army, leaving Lynch's brigade to proceed on its own by land.[6]

   This development gave rise to a strange period of inactivity on the part of the
Peruvians. As we have seen, even considering the demoralized, ravaged state of
the Peruvian army, there were some twenty-five to thirty thousand men in the
area between Arequipa and Lima itself, and now, straggled out in two columns
winding through the desert *toward* the main body of the Peruvian army, was a
single Chilean brigade of two to three thousand men with little artillery and only
what ammunition and supplies it carried with it. Why did Pierola not detach
some of his forces to overwhelm this isolated force, restore the morale of his
own army and possibly cause the Chileans to abandon their plans to invade the
heartland of Peru? Perhaps a stunning defeat of Lynch's brigade might have
brought the Chileans back to the bargaining table in a more flexible frame of
mind, but nothing, in fact, was done. Of course, Pierola was aware that a much
larger Chilean force was about to descend on the coast somewhere even closer
to the capital, but that would take time to effect, and it would seem that he could
have spared enough men to gather a two or even three-to-one superiority over
Lynch in the short term, and yet he did nothing. What is more bizarre, is that
there is no mention, even in the writings of the aggressive General Caceres, who
was busy raising and training a new division at this time, that any faction within
the Peruvian military was pushing for an offensive stance.
   In any event, Lynch continued his northward march largely unhindered.
Along the way he continued his policy from his raids into northern Peru of
imposing "taxes" on haciendas and towns to support the Chilean war effort. He
also freed thousands of Chinese laborers who existed in conditions of near
slavery, and over a thousand of these joined the ranks of his army as porters,
teamsters, and ditch diggers, perhaps out of a simple desire for employment, but
perhaps also out of a desire for revenge against their former masters. These
poorly disciplined Chinese, during the rest of the campaign, would be credited
with much of the looting of captured Peruvian towns, although it is entirely
possible that this is a bit of historical fiction created to relieve the Chilean
soldiers of the responsibility of some of the more shameful aspects of the
campaign.[7]
   Meanwhile, the Peruvian army sat within its lines. Frenzied activity was
underway around the capital, digging fortifications, but these seemed more a
device for maintaining public enthusiasm for the war than serious preparations
for a military confrontation. Huge amounts were spent on the works, along with
tens of thousands of man-hours that might have been better invested in
entrenchments nearer where the initial clash with the invaders was expected to
come, some miles south of the city. The works that were dug were far too close
to the city to protect it from artillery bombardment, and were thus largely
worthless. The *Cerro de San Cristóbal* was a prime example of this, a large hill
whose summit was laboriously leveled off and studded with large caliber guns,
with terraced slopes built for rifle pits and other artillery emplacements. Later
referred to as Pierola's Citadel, its cannon would not fire a shot in defense of the
capital.[8]
   By 25 December, any chance that the Peruvians might have had for defeating
the Chilean army in detail had evaporated, either by hitting Lynch's isolated

brigade on the march or confronting the invading force as it came ashore at Chilca, barely forty-five kilometers from Lima. By that time the entire force had reunited, including Lynch's brigade from Pisco, with a total of 25,800 men with eighty guns, eight and Gatling guns. A single regiment had been left to hold Pisco, with a further 9,200 in reserve in Chile and another five thousand scattered in garrisons from Tacna and Arica down to Antofagasta. Clearly, the Chileans had won the battle of mobilization.[9]

The only noteworthy activity by the Peruvian military during the weeks since the first Chilean landings at Pisco came on the night of 27 December when the Cavalry Regiment "Rimac" under the command of Colonel Sevilla, numbering some three hundred men clashed with a brigade of Barboza's division near the town of Manzano. The affair was so confused that the word *clash* might imply more military brilliance than is actually warranted. The Peruvian troopers were either scouting the advance of Lynch's column, or were mere trying to make their way north to the main Peruvian lines before the landings at Chilca cut them off entirely. In either case, the force was not designed for offensive action, with only half of its members armed with carbines, the remainder having only lances. Either the force simply lost its way on one of the typical foggy nights along the coast, or the Chileans got word of their approach, and Baquedano had Barboza's men set up an ambush along their route of march. In either case, the force was massacred, causing only four Chilean casualties and losing about twenty killed and over one hundred captured, including Colonel Sevilla, while some 120 more escaped to rejoin the Peruvian lines at Miraflores. The action was not of overall military significance, but it can have done nothing to improve the gloomy outlook of the defenders around Lima.[10]

The only response from Pierola to this turn of events was another reorganization of the army. The newly raised militia was kept as the Reserve Army under his personal command in the capital, while the rest was now simply designated the Line Army. The Reserve Army of six thousand men was grouped now into two divisions under Colonels P. Correa y Santiago and S. Orbegoso, who, like their regimental commanders, were volunteers from Lima's upper classes but without any particular previous military experience. The Line Army was divided into four corps under Colonel Miguel Iglesias, a *hacendado* from Northern Peru and Pierola's minister of war, Colonel Seers, Bend's former chief of staff, the adept Colonel Caceres, who had been arbitrarily removed from command of the troops he had been training (who went to Iglesias), and Colonel Davila. The army at Arequipa, whose command had been removed from the inert Leyva and given to Colonel Jose de la Torre, had about six thousand unpaid, totally demoralized, and virtually unarmed men who posed no feasible threat to the Chileans at any point.[11]

The primary Peruvian defensive line was named for the town of San Juan and ran for some seventeen kilometers in the form of a backwards "J" from the town of Chorrillos south along the coastal cliffs to the Morro Solar, then east to the hacienda of Santa Teresa and then generally northeast past the town of San Juan to anchor on the foothills of the Andes. The line was built along a string of hills running inland of between fifty and two hundred meters in height, and in these positions the Peruvians had emplaced eighteen thousand men, one hundred guns ranging from a few modern European rapid-fire guns to the homemade bronze cannon cast locally, and some two dozen Gatling guns. A further three thousand men formed the garrison of the forts at Callao besides the Reserve Army, which was now grouped in the second line of defense at Miraflores on the outskirts of the capital.[12]

The San Juan (or Chorrillos) Line consisted of fairly extensive redoubts atop the hills, interconnected and surrounded by lines of trenches and rifle pits. All of these were protected by the Peruvians' favorite gadget, the land mine, both pressure-activated and the electronically detonated versions. As at Arica, the presence of these mines proved to be a minor irritant for the attackers, but fear of the unreliable devices discouraged the defenders from conducting any patrolling beyond their own works. Also by way of gadgetry, Pierola spent considerable time listening to the pitch of an American inventor, one Mr. Blackman, who claimed to be able to build an airship capable of speeds of up to an astounding twenty-five miles per hour, with which to bomb and destroy the Chilean fleet. After expending undisclosed amounts on a feasibility study, the project was quietly dropped.[13]

In the absence of any Peruvian resistance, Baquedano wasted no time in moving the bulk of his force forward to the valley of the Lurin River, only some fifteen kilometers from the main Peruvian lines, establishing a strong force there by 23 December even before his full army had landed. This raises the question of, even if Pierola could not stir himself to launch a serious attack on the Chilean army as it came ashore over a period of days, why the Peruvians did not establish their forward defenses along the banks of the Lurin itself. The forbidding nature of the coast prevented any large scale landing to the rear of this position short of Chorrillos and Callao, both of which places were well-protected with coastal artillery and sizeable garrisons, against which the Chileans had never shown any willingness to attempt an amphibious assault. The advantage to this forward defense would have been to take advantage of the river itself, not a terribly formidable stream, but still a ready-made hindrance to the movement of troops, and, more importantly, to deny this source of water to the enemy, the only water source in the forty-five kilometers separating the Chorrillos line from the Chilean beachhead at Chilca. This would have forced the invaders to fight a battle at the end of a supply line thirty kilometers long over rough desert country. In any event, as in every other case where there had appeared an opportunity for aggressive, innovative action, Pierola either failed to perceive it or chose not to run the risk.

In any event, the initiative rested with the Chileans, and it only remained for them to decide which avenue of attack to take. True to form, Vergara strongly lobbied for a sweeping flanking movement through the town of Ate, well to the northeast of San Juan, hoping to swing around the flank of the entrenched Peruvian lines. Toward that end, Barboza's brigade was sent on a reconnaissance in force around the Peruvian left on 9 January. After a sharp fight, the brigade took the town of Rinconada de Ate itself, driving the defenders off in full flight. This action convinced Vergara of the wisdom of this approach, and it also served to convince Pierola that this was precisely where the Chilean blow would fall, causing him to keep large portions of his army in reserve behind this wing throughout the coming battle.

Baquedano, however, was not so convinced. He pointed out that, to move his main force around to Ate would involve a march of forty kilometers, over very rugged terrain, and presenting his flank all the while to the entire Peruvian army.[14] This would also allow the Peruvians the option of driving directly forward toward the Chilean supply base at Chilca, possibly cutting the invaders off from the sea. In retrospect, there does not appear to have been much danger of Pierola taking such a dynamic stance, but Baquedano could hardly count on this. It should be noted that Baquedano has been criticized, mostly by the Chilean political opposition after the war, for a lack of imagination and a willingness to run up horrific casualties through blundering frontal attacks against fortified positions.[15] However, at the Battle of Moquegua, Baquedano did execute a successful double envelopment, while Chile's heaviest losses, on the basis of percentage of the forces engaged, had occurred at Tarapacá, where Vergara had planned just such a sweeping maneuver on the assumption that the enemy would simply sit there and let him do it. In the event, Barboza's reconnaissance served as an unintended diversion, thus making Baquedano's frontal attack far less costly than it might have been otherwise.

The Peruvian I Corps (more or less identical to the old Army of the North) under Iglesias, occupied the far right of the line from Morro Solar on the coast to just west of the hacienda of Santa Teresa, and its three divisions included most of the army's surviving veterans and prewar cadre, as well as being the largest corps with fifty-two hundred men. IV Corps under Caceres (the Army of the Center), held the curve of the reversed "J" around Santa Teresa north to the town of San Juan with forty-five hundred men. Davila's III Corps, a smaller force of only seven regiments, held the hills of Monterico on the far left with forty-two hundred. Suárez's small II Corps of only twenty-five hundred was held in reserve in the area of San Juan, behind Davila's Corps, protecting against a Chilean flanking attack that would never materialize.[16] Caceres, who had just arrived at his new command, unfamiliar with his men or his officers, found the men to be short on food and ammunition, and the entrenchments to be in a sorry state, with large gaps in the line, especially along the seam between his own corps and that of Iglesias, and poorly planned fields of fire that left extensive areas of dead ground through which an enemy could advance with impunity. It was thus with trepidation that Caceres learned from a captured Chilean soldier that Baquedano had moved forward and planned to attack the next morning, 13 January.[17]

Baquedano had deployed his forces in a typically straightforward manner. Lynch's 1st Division was assigned to attack the Peruvian right, aiming by chance or design exactly at the gap between the Peruvian I and IV Corps just west of the hacienda of Santa Teresa. Sotomayor's 2nd Division would simultaneously hit the Peruvian center, while Lagos' 3rd Division would swing around to attack the Peruvian left from the east, ideally driving through the line and advancing toward the coast, cutting off the escape of the rest of the Peruvian army that would be fully engaged along its front. This gave Baquedano some twenty thousand men in the assault with a further three thousand in reserve against about fourteen thousand Peruvians in the line with twenty-five hundred in reserve, although part of the main Peruvian force would idle away the battle facing the coast or in the hills to the east. Theoretically, the defenders could also call on thousands more men from the Miraflores position and Callao in the event of need.[18]

The Chileans began their march from their camp of the night of 12-13 January, some three miles from the Peruvian lines, at 0330 hours on 13 January with a view to attacking just before first light. A typical early morning *comanchaca* fog impartially affected the development of the battle. On the one hand, it caused Sotomayor's division to lose its way, which meant that, with Lagos' attack scheduled to start later in the morning, Lynch would be attacking all alone. On the other hand, the thick mist, along with the reluctance of the Peruvians to set advanced outposts among their own mines, allowed Lynch's men to march virtually up to the first trenches without being detected by the defenders.

Lynch's attack first hit the fortified hacienda of Villa, which had been incorporated as an outwork of the Peruvian line and formed the left flank of Iglesias' corps. Here the Peruvians, the best troops in their army, held out stubbornly, supported by a four-gun battery firing from the hills at Santa Teresa just behind them. Caceres happened to have been at the front when the attack broke, and he quickly took charge, bringing up units of his own corps as the fighting spread to both sides of the hacienda, and calling up a division from Suárez's reserve in support. After half an hour of stalemate, Baquedano promptly sent in a brigade under Colonel Artistides Martinez from the reserve to support Lynch's attack, and, just as these troops reached the front, Gana's brigade from Sotomayor's 2nd Division belatedly arrived and struck the left of Caceres' line, rushing forward with the bayonet only. Because the fighting was taking place just at the bend of the "J," Caceres found himself under attack from two opposing fires but continued to hold.[19]

By 0830 Iglesias, possibly disconcerted by the heavy bombardment of the right wing of his corps by the Chilean fleet, called a council of war of his officers and unilaterally decided to abandon his forward positions and to pull back to the Morro Solar. His departure unhinged the entire Peruvian line, and the Chileans poured through, rolling up the defenders' positions to the left and right, and within the hour the attackers had possession of the entire line of hills.[20]

Caceres pulled back to the Santa Teresa hacienda, hoping to rally his forces around a reserve brigade there, but the Chileans had quickly penetrated on both sides of the hacienda, and the Peruvian forces were in full flight by regiments, often with their colonels at their head. Meanwhile, Pierola had completely lost heart in the battle and had ordered both Davila's and Suárez's corps, most of which had not even been engaged, to fall back to the Miraflores line.[21]

On the far right of the Peruvian line, Lynch was advancing rapidly through the Peruvian trenches and anticipated no more problems from the demoralized enemy before him, and it was only just after 0900 hours. Consequently, he detached only three regiments to storm the Morro, a move he expected to involve no more than taking prisoner any enemy soldiers cut off there by the Chilean advance. He was mistaken, however, and the nearly four thousand heavily entrenched Peruvians cut down the attackers with a withering fire of rifles and artillery, inflicting over four hundred casualties in a matter of minutes. Lynch still did not appreciate the difficulty of the tactical situation, and he merely fed additional regiments into the attack one at a time. The Chileans clawed their way through one line of trenches after another, but there were a total of seven such lines on the Morro, and it was not until Baquedano intervened and was able to bring forward several batteries of artillery that the crest of the hill could finally be taken with well over one thousand Peruvians falling prisoner, including General Iglesias at about 1430 hours that afternoon.[22]

In all the attackers lost between seven and eight hundred men killed and over twenty-five hundred wounded, with Lynch's division alone suffering eighteen hundred of those casualties. Peruvian losses are hard to calculate, since hundreds of men took the opportunity to end their military service without benefit of paperwork, but at least two thousand were captured and another five thousand lost through either death or desertion, including virtually all of the veterans of I Corps. Add to this several hundred wounded who would have been evacuated ahead of the advancing Chileans and the 120 guns that were captured in the lines, and it becomes clear that the Peruvian army had been virtually gutted.[23]

That afternoon and evening, as the victorious army camped on the field and the exhausted, terrified survivors of the Peruvian army staggered into their new positions in the Miraflores line, another incident occurred which tarnished the glory of the day. Accounts differ as to whether any Peruvian troops attempted to defend the town of Chorrillos, located about one mile north of the Villa hacienda, but, whether they did or not, Chilean troops apparently ran rampant through the town, killing Peruvian stragglers and civilians alike, looting freely, and setting fire to most of the town. They may have been joined in this rampage by several thousand "freed" Chinese laborers, but it was clear that the Chilean commanders did little if anything to halt the rioting until it had run itself out.[24]

It could be argued that the Chileans had, on several occasions, allowed their enemies substantial time to recover from their battlefield losses, but such was not to be the case this time. On the morning of 14 January, Vergara sent General Iglesias, now a prisoner of war, to Lima with a demand for surrender for Pierola. The Chileans pointed out that, if they could crack the San Juan line in a matter of hours, they would have little difficulty with that of Miraflores and pointed out that surrender was the only way to avoid making the capital a battlefield. This argument gave rise to speculation that the burning of Chorrillos had been a calculated lesson for the benefit of the Pierola administration on what might happen to Lima if it came to a fight. Possibly stalling for time, Pierola sent Iglesias back with a message insisting that he would only treat with an envoy possessing full powers for negotiation.[25]

That afternoon, a delegation of foreign diplomats from Lima, headed by the dean of the diplomatic corps, Ambassador Pinto of El Salvador, but including the rather more influential British and French ministers as well, met with Baquedano. They provided him with a detailed map of Lima with the sectors owned and occupied by foreign neutrals clearly marked, and he assured them that their rights and the lives and property of their nationals would be protected. The diplomats, showing no doubt about the eventual outcome of the fighting, suggested that only a small Chilean garrison be allowed within the city limits to avoid possible looting.[26] Their appeal was reinforced by the presence with the delegation of British Admiral Stirling and French Admiral Du Petit, who promised to sink the entire Chilean fleet if any of the neutral embassies or compounds, in which thousands of terrified Peruvians and neutral citizens had taken refuge. Since the neutral powers had a total of about a dozen ironclads, including the Americans, Italians, and Germans, in the immediate vicinity, and could easily back up this threat, Baquedano agreed to this as well.[27]

The next morning, on the 15th, the diplomats returned to Baquedano's headquarters to determine just what his terms were for the peaceful surrender of Lima. Baquedano said that he would require the immediate surrender of Callao as a guarantee during the withdrawal of the Peruvian army beyond Lima, and he agreed to a truce until midnight on the 15th to allow the Pierola administration time to consider the offer. The diplomats were scheduled to meet with Pierola himself that afternoon at 1400 hours to deliver the terms.[28]

At this point the Peruvian forces in the Miraflores lines numbered no more than eleven thousand men. About six thousand were from Davila's and Suárez's corps who had not fought much at San Juan, about a thousand came from two regiments brought forward from the Callao garrison, and another four thousand from the Reserve Army. Seers and Davila retained command of their corps in the center and on the left respectively, and Caceres was given command of the remaining troops on the right of the line. The position they were to occupy was a mere shadow of that at San Juan, a ten-mile line running roughly east from the coast at a point just south of Miraflores to the hills at Monterrico Chico. As this was now within the belt of rich farmland that surrounds Lima, there were no significant geographic features of which the engineers could take advantage, and simple trenches were the only defense. Every so often a "redoubt," just a sandbagged artillery position, had been erected, of which there were ten in all, numbered from west to east. With the losses in men and artillery at San Juan, and with the bulk of the Chilean army still quite fresh, there was little doubt as to the outcome of the coming battle.[29]

Just after 1400 hours the representatives of the diplomatic corps, including Ambassadors Pinto and Christiancy and their British and French colleagues, Ambassadors St. John and Vorgues, arrived at Pierola's headquarters in Miraflores where the dictator had just finished his lunch. The group was about to be ushered into a meeting hall to discuss Baquedano's terms when, first one, then a great many guns fired. The rattle of rifle fire quickly spread all along the line, and the Chilean fleet began lobbing shells inland as well. The diplomats broke and ran for their train, which not all of them caught and several of them, including Mr. Christiancy, were obliged to walk the eight miles back to the capital, picking their way through refugees and stragglers from the army and occasionally dodging long range shell fire.[30]

It seems that both sides were taking advantage of the truce to move their forces up to the Miraflores line and to reposition units behind it. Allegedly, Baquedano had taken the opportunity to conduct a personal reconnaissance of the position with a cluster of staff aides and division commanders, and the sight of so many ranking enemy officers may have proven too great a temptation for a Peruvian gunner. Both sides subsequently accused the other of intentionally breaking the truce, but, in any event, the battle was now fully joined.[31]

In retrospect, it seems that it would have been unlikely for the Chileans to have picked this moment to open the battle. When the firing broke out, only Lagos' division and a couple of battalions of Urriola's brigade had come up to the line, and even Admiral Riveros had come ashore to confer with Baquedano, implying that he did not expect action in the immediate future. Caceres attempted to make the most of the discomfiture of the enemy by launching a sudden attack with all his troops against both of Lagos' flanks, supported by units from both Davila's and Suárez's corps on the extreme left of the Chilean line, nearest the sea. But Lagos' forty-eight hundred men managed to hold out, covered by fire from *Blanco Encalada, O'Higgins, Huascar,* and *Pilcomayo,* the last two former Peruvian ships now in the Chilean service, and, before long Lynch's division in the center and Sotomayor's on the right had moved up to the line, and Caceres was forced to pull back to his original position.[32]

Baquedano saw the Peruvians retreating and sent in the "Carabiñeros de Yungay" Cavalry Regiment to cut them off before they could reach the safety of their trenches. Caceres countered with a charge by the "Lanceros de Torata" and "Escolta" who managed to distract the Chileans long enough for the infantry to escape.[33]

The redoubts along the Peruvian line were each held by one of the recently raised reserve regiments under the command of an equally inexperienced and newly minted "provisional" colonel, while the line regiments filled the gaps in between them. Redoubt No. 1, which soon became the focus of the fighting on the Peruvian right, was manned by three hundred university students who valiantly held off repeated attacks by Lagos' troops.

But Baquedano again committed Martínez's reserve troops to support the stalled attack, and redoubts 1 through 3 were eventually overwhelmed. Baquedano then rushed cavalry into the gap created in the Peruvian line, and Surrey's corps to the left immediately broke and ran. Caceres had received a severe leg wound, and virtually all of his troops had run out of ammunition. As the light began to fade, the battle ended, with the surviving defenders streaming up the roads and across fields toward the capital.[34]

The Chilean losses during the four hours of fighting had been severe, over 2,100 casualties, considering that fewer than ten thousand men had actually been engaged. As usual, Peruvian losses are almost impossible to calculate, since the army essentially disintegrated, but it is safe to say that total casualties on the battlefield ran into the thousands, and the army's remaining field artillery was virtually all lost.[35]

Considerable controversy has swirled around Pierola's behavior during this period. Not only did Pierola, as commander-in-chief of the army, not bother to shift troops from his unengaged left wing to support Caceres and Iglesias on the right, but he apparently intentionally kept eleven out of the available nineteen regiments out of the battle and ordered them to abandon their lines and withdraw to Lima even before the Miraflores line had been irreparably breached.[36] Then, following the collapse of the line, instead of marshalling this force to retreat into the mountains to continue the battle, since he evidently had no intention of surrendering himself, he rejected Caceres' call for a counterattack and ordered the troops to turn in their weapons and uniforms and to return to their homes, effectively demobilizing the army. Given the state of morale at this point, it took little convincing for most of his troops to follow those instructions. No orders were given for removing or hiding any of the precious artillery or modern small arms of which there was still a considerable amount in and around the capital.[37] This would all be logical if Pierola had clearly decided to end the war, but his subsequent actions indicate that this was not his view at all.

It is known that Pierola had been suffering from insomnia for some time before the battle, and he had certainly been operating under incredible stress for months. It is also debatable just how much difference any course of action Pierola might have chosen would have made on the eventual course of events. The Chileans had a clearly dominant military position even before he took over the presidency. Although his meddling with the military commands for political reasons did nothing to improve the situation in the interim, even the most efficient handling of military affairs would likely not have altered the outcome of the campaign. Perhaps he suffered a nervous collapse as he saw the last remnants of his army streaming to the rear and could not bring himself to take the practical steps necessary for continuing the war, and yet neither could he bring himself to surrender to the invaders, so he opted for a grand gesture of defiance while effectively removing both the means and the pretext for further bloodshed.

In any event, early on the morning of 16 January the citizens of Lima awoke to find the streets of the capital thronged with ragged deserters, some still with their weapons, and wagons filled with groaning, bloody wounded from the battle. Many people, except for a few well-informed members of the government or the army itself, had believed the wildly optimistic propaganda put out by the administration and had assumed that the banging of guns the afternoon before signaled the defeat and rout of the Chilean army, not their own. Hundreds of people now mobbed the foreign consulates, seeking asylum or sought to buy their way aboard neutral warships, merchantmen, or even local fishing boats at Callao in hopes of taking passage out of the country before the Chileans would arrive. Lurid stories of the behavior of Chilean soldiers at Moquegua or Chorrillos now came starkly to mind.

Pierola had arrived in Lima at 1900 hours the night of the 15th and only spent some four hours in the capital before escaping to Canta in the interior by horse with a handful of aides. He did not bother to gather or destroy sensitive state documents or even funds from the national treasury before his flight.[38]

Looting had already begun in parts of the capital on the night of the 15th, but rioting and burning spread throughout the city on the 16th and well into the night. The municipal police had been conscripted into the army and were long gone, and any army troops still in uniform were streaming into the mountains to the east to carry on the war. It was not until the morning of 17 January that Rufino Torrico, the mayor of Lima, was able to appeal to the foreign diplomatic community to form an "urban guard" of their own nationals, mostly sailors and marines from the warships off Callao, to patrol the city and impose some kind of order, disarming deserters and rioters, killing about two hundred of them in Lima and another 150 in Callao in the process.[39]

Torrico was also the one left with the task of surrendering the capital, unconditionally in the face of Baquedano's threat to bombard the city if this were not immediately accomplished, and the first Chilean troops entered the city at 1700 hours that day. By agreement with Baquedano, supervised by the foreign admirals and diplomats, only three thousand Chilean troops would actually garrison the city, predominantly from the 1st Line Regiment that included large numbers of former members of the Santiago police force in its ranks. Earlier that day the crews of the *Atahualpa, Union,* and other Peruvian ships scuttled their vessels at Callao while the garrison blew up the forts and their guns, one after another.[40]

If the citizens of Santiago and Valparaíso had reason to celebrate the victories of Tacna and Arica at the end of the previous year, they certainly had cause to celebrate now. The last viable enemy army had not just been defeated but absolutely destroyed, the last remnants of the enemy fleet were now on the bottom of the sea. Surely the war was now well and truly over, and the victors could simply dictate the peace of their choosing at the time of their choosing. The wealth of the nitrate fields would soon replace the cost of the war in monetary terms and, while the cost in lives was certainly tragic, at the same time the glorious battles had filled the halls of honor with new heroes and martyrs to be adored for generations.

Baquedano's comments upon the fall of Lima gave a clear indication of the finality with which he viewed recent events and also of the attitude the Chileans would have in dealing with the vanquished powers. "What defeated Peru was the superiority of one race and the superiority of one history; order over disorder; one country without dictators over another that is still suffering from this terrible evil."[41]

NOTES

1. Diego Barros Arana, *Historia de la Guerra del Pacífico, 1879-1881,* Santiago de Chile: Editorial Andres Bello, 1979, p. 398.

2. Roberto Querejazu Calvo, *Guano, Salitre, Sangre: Historia de la Guerra del Pacífico,* La Paz: Editorial Los Amigos del Libro, 1979, p. 619.

3. Gonzalo Bulnes, *Guerra del Pacífico,* vol. 2, Santiago de Chile: Editorial del Pacífico, 1955, p. 302.

4. Ibid., p. 301.

5. Martin Eduardo Congrains, *La Batalla de San Juan (Chorillos)*, vol. 1, Lima: Editorial Ecoma, 1974, p. 24.

6. Bulnes, p. 316.

7. Congrains, op. cit., p. 48.

8. Mariano Felipe Paz Soldan, *Narracion Historica de la Guerra de Chile contra el Peru y Bolivia*, vol. 3, Buenos Aires: s. n., 1884, p. 18.

9. Barros, p. 411.

10. Paz Soldan, p. 12.

11. Bulnes, p. 324.

12. Congrains, op. cit., p. 115.

13. Barros, p. 417.

14. Bulnes, p. 330.

15. William F. Sater, *Chile and the War of the Pacific*, Lincoln: University of Nebraska Press, 1986, p. 185.

16. Andres Avelino Caceres, *La Guerra del '79: Sus Campañas*, Lima: Editorial Milla Batres, S.A., 1973, p. 69.

17. Ibid., p. 72.

18. Bulnes, p. 332.

19. Caceres, p. 76.

20. Congrains, op. cit., p. 135.

21. Caceres, p. 78.

22. Congrains, op. cit., p. 156.

23. Barros, p. 456.

24. Paz Soldan, p. 72.

25. Bulnes, p. 342.

26. William Jefferson Dennis, *Tacna and Arica: An Account of the Chile-Peru Boundary Dispute and of the Arbitrations by the United States*. New York: Archon Books, 1967, p. 127.

27. Querejazu, p. 624.

28. Dennis, p. 129.

29. Martin Eduardo Congrains, *La Batalla de Miraflores*, Lima: Editorial Ecoma, 1977, p. 84.

30. Dennis, p. 128.

31. Querejazu, p. 627.

32. Bulnes, p. 346.

33. Congrains, op. cit., p. 111.

34. Ibid., p. 118.

35. Bulnes, p. 347.

36. Congrains, op. cit., p. 127.

37. Caceres, p. 87.

38. Barros, p. 489.

39. Bulnes, p. 348.

40. Barros, p. 497.

41. Bulnes, p. 351.

Chapter Eleven

The Broken-backed War

After failing to convince President Pierola to continue resistance to the Chilean advance at Miraflores, General Caceres was brought back into Lima by his aides. He had lost a great deal of blood from a bullet wound in the leg and had had two horses shot out from under him and his field glasses shot out of his hand during the battle. For a man of over sixty years of age, this was something of an ordeal, and he needed time to rest and recover his strength. Caceres was encouraged by Pierola's escape to the sierra and by his public declaration that the capital of Peru was wherever the government found itself, and he vowed to join the resistance as soon as he was able.

He had originally been taken to a field hospital in downtown Lima, but word made its way through the staff that the Chileans were searching for Caceres, well known to be one of Peru's most able officers and a staunch opponent of surrender. The message was that General Baquedano wanted to greet him personally and to offer him "all class of guarantees" for his safety and freedom. Caceres then had his friends spirit him out of the hospital and he spent the following weeks moving from the house of one acquaintance to another around the city, possibly prolonging his recovery but at least keeping out of the hands of the occupying forces. By mid-April he was fit to travel and simply took a train, dressed in civilian clothes, up into the mountains where he eventually caught up with Pierola who named him political-military commander of the Department of the Center.[1]

Caceres set up his headquarters at the town of Tarma in the cordillera and reviewed his prospects. To begin with he had no troops, no arms, and no resources, but he nevertheless planned on initiating a low-scale war of attrition designed to make the occupation of Peru too costly for the Chileans to continue indefinitely. He knew that every day that they were forced to keep thousands of men mobilized and far from home would weigh heavier on them, and pressure would eventually build up among the Chilean opposition politicians to accept a decent settlement that would at least salvage some of Peru's territory and national honor. He gathered around him his entire army composed of sixteen convalescent gendarmes and the elderly Colonel Manuel Tafur and prepared for war.[2]

The Chileans, meanwhile, still confidently expected the war to be over. They eventually established a garrison of fourteen thousand men in and around the capital and the port of Callao in addition to their forces in Tacna and Arica and farther south. The administration of the occupation was set up in the Palace of Government and the University of San Marcos, one of the oldest and most prestigious universities in the Western Hemisphere, was commandeered as a barracks for their troops. It is one of the less honorable aspects of the conflict that this school and others would be stripped of their libraries and all other facilities by the occupying troops before their eventual departure.[3]

The victorious General Baquedano was hardly allowed to enjoy his success. He was immediately taken under attack by the liberal opposition in Santiago as being a member of the oligarchy who had limited military talent. They claimed that the army's victories had been won actually by the work of Sotomayor and Vergara, both of whom were staunch liberals and that it was Baquedano's blundering, unimaginative leadership that had caused the war to drag out and had resulted in far higher casualties than were truly necessary. The general returned to Santiago in mid-March 1881 and was granted a triumphal parade at the head of some of his most famous regiments, something that the populace frantically applauded and the oppositionists were too wise to attempt to prevent, but he was ultimately unable to face the constant persecution in the liberal press and withdrew from the service. Belatedly, the legislature voted him the rank, salary, and privileges of a field army commander and a prize of $100,000 for his services, although, in a particularly petty act the opposition managed to get this last element dropped and replaced by franking privileges and a free pass for travel on the state-run railroads, the same that had been awarded Admiral Riveros for his victory at Angamos.[4]

Baquedano's place as commander of the expeditionary force in Peru passed on to a series of officers, first General Saavedra, then Lagos, and finally none other than Patricio Lynch, and given his reputation from his raids in northern Peru, the move must have been met with trepidation by the Peruvians, and he did not disappoint them. One of his first official acts was to demand the payment of a "war tax" by the prominent citizens of Lima, one million silver pesos, under the threat of imprisonment of family members and/or the seizure or destruction of their property. Pierola, from the safety of his mountain fastness, unhelpfully continued to insist that anyone succumbing to the extortion of the Chilean government would be regarded as a traitor and treated accordingly without suggesting how the residents of the capital could effectively refuse the demands of the military governor.[5]

Of considerably greater moment was the decision by the Chilean government, in the absence of a Peruvian president who was willing to accept their peace terms, chose to create a new president who would do so. Consequently, on 22 February 1881, a convention of Peruvian "notables," presumably propertied citizens who were willing to accept the Chilean invitation, met outside of Lima and elected Francisco Garcia Calderon president. The fact that Santiago could not do the convention the courtesy of even allowing them to meet in their own capital did not add anything to the validity of the proceedings, but the deed was done. A congress was called to meet at Chorrillos on 15 June, and, in the meanwhile, the puppet government was established in the town of Magdalena to begin to take over some of the administrative duties of running the country as well as to begin negotiations on a formal peace treaty. Lynch even went so far as to allow the Magdalena government to raise and arm two infantry battalions of four hundred men each and two small cavalry squadrons in an attempt to give some substance to the illusion of independence and also to provide some physical protection for its members who were under constant threat of assassination by their more xenophobic countrymen.[6]

Garcia Calderon, the new provisional president who would be confirmed in the post by the rump congress that would meet in June (once a quorum of former congressmen was gathered), was faced with a thankless task. He was a forty-nine year old lawyer, a former legal advisor to the firms of Meiggs, Gibbs, and Dreyfuss, which gave him a certain familiarity with Peru's financial situation, and he accepted the post out of a conviction both that Pierola had no legal claim on the presidency and had largely abrogated his duties in any event, and that a continuation of the state of war would only impose further sacrifices on the Peruvian people without materially improving their situation. If the Chileans chose him because they thought this mild-mannered man who looked more like a comfortable hardware storeowner than a symbol of national integrity would be a malleable, complacent puppet, they were in for a surprise.[7]

Just about this time the diplomatic situation was complicated by the change in American presidents. James G. Blaine, Secretary of State for the new Garfield administration, replaced Osborne in Santiago with Judson Kilpatrick and Christiancy in Lima with Stephen A. Hurlbut, both retired Civil War generals. This was a blow to the Chileans in particular as Osborne, who was married to a Chilean woman, had been viewed as sympathetic to their cause. More importantly, Blaine outlined a new policy in June 1881 that significantly altered the benevolently neutral stance the United States had previously taken on the conflict. In rather stark wording for a diplomatic letter he stated that, "at the conclusion of a war avowedly not of conquest, but for the solution of differences which diplomacy had failed to settle, to make the acquisition of territory a *sine qua non* of peace is calculated to cast suspicion on the profession with which the war was originally declared."[8] While Blaine went on to accept the right of the Chileans to demand indemnities for the war, he insisted that territorial acquisition would only be considered justifiable if the allies proved unable to pay the required amount. While this might well have been the case, given the state of Peruvian and Bolivian finances, which was widely known, it did not appear that the Chileans ever contemplated a purely monetary settlement, and the only question was how much territory they would ultimately acquire.

This position by the United States, gave the Peruvians considerable cause for hope, if not for direct American intervention, at least for political support during the course of negotiations. Pierola had called his own congress in the city of

Ayacucho to coincide with that of Chorrillos, and this had caused the outgoing American administration to postpone recognition of the Garcia Calderon government, but Ambassador Christiancy, who had the usual broad leeway in such matters that envoys in the days before satellite communications enjoyed, finally recognized the provisional president on 26 June, just before Hurlbut's arrival at post.

The recognition by the United States was a tremendous boost for the Garcia Calderon government at Magdalena, augmented by the impression that the Americans would not recognize any peace treaty that required Peru to surrender territory to Chile, thus encouraging more and more Peruvians to flock to Garcia Calderon's banner. The only thing that remained was to eliminate Pierola as a player once and for all. To this purpose, Comandante Ambrosio Letelier had been sent at the head of his division to run the fugitive president to ground.

The expedition had departed Lima by train in mid-April to Chicla. From there the division marched into the highlands in search of Caceres, who at this time had a force of no more than one hundred men under his command. The Chilean forces were suffering from very low morale at this point, what with the rapid command changes and also with an epidemic of typhoid and small pox that had swept through their lowland camps, and it had been hoped that this outing would at least serve to give them a sense of purpose and to raise their spirits, besides getting them into a healthier climate. Such hopes were quickly dashed as the men suffered cruelly from the cold in the mountains and from altitude sickness as much of their marching was done over ten thousand feet above sea level. To make matters worse, Caceres had no difficulty avoiding the plodding Chilean columns, and Letelier seems to have spent most of his time extorting money from local *hacendados*. This practice was hardly unique for the Chilean army in enemy territory, especially since Letelier was given no supplies or quartermaster resources, implying that his superiors had expected him to live off the land, but it seems that much of the money collected found its way directly into the pockets of Letelier and his officers, not into the chests of the army, and this was unacceptable.[9]

Upon assuming command, Lynch ordered Letelier to return to the capital, but Lynch took his time in complying, claiming that his mission had not yet been accomplished. While his men roamed around the rich agricultural land of Junín Department, they managed to antagonize the Indian population to the point that the usually docile, stoic Indians rose up against the invaders who were thinly scattered over many miles. Since the Indians were largely unarmed, as the Peruvian government had no more interest in arming a people who occupied a position hardly better than that of slaves, the Chileans had little trouble beating off the attacks with their repeating rifles and rapid-fire cannon, killing hundreds, but the animosity created was exactly the opposite of what Santiago had hoped to be achieving in Peru with an enlightened military administration that would reach a quick settlement with the chastised Peruvians. When Letelier finally did reach the capital in early July, he and his officers were promptly court martialed and found to have taken "commissions" on all funds and goods "collected" for the army and were ultimately relieved of their posts.[10]

By this time, while the Chilean occupation army was suffering from frequent changes of command, epidemics, and charges of corruption, the forces of resistance in Peru were finally getting organized. Several thousand men still clustered at Arequipa where Admiral Montero had resumed command in the south, but the focus of resistance was still centered around Caceres in the center at the town of Mantucana. He had formed three "divisions," a small cavalry squadron and a couple of four-gun artillery batteries, plus another "division" with two battalions at Canta and another two at Chancay, but these forces totaled no more than two or three thousand men. They were armed in large part by weapons that had been smuggled out of Lima itself, right under the noses of Lynch's troops through a combination of the efforts of an innovative and daring network of Peruvian patriots and corrupt Chilean officials. The ranks of Caceres' regiments were swelled by deserters from the little army that Garcia Calderon had been allowed by the Chileans, men who found it difficult to serve under the constant supervision of the erstwhile enemy, and by hundreds of highlands Indians who had previously been exempted from conscription by the Peruvian government but who flocked to the banners out of a surprising sense of patriotism.[11] It is interesting to note that Chilean sources denounced the Peruvian recourse to Indian troops as a kind of servile insurrection, apparently believing that warfare should have been left between the largely European or *mestizo* classes who dominated society in both countries.[12]

By September 1881 the Garcia Calderon government, although still operating from semi-exile in Magdalena and viewed as collaborators by a large segment of the population, had achieved a certain level of legitimacy with foreign recognition and the growing war-weariness of many Peruvians. But, months after his installation by the Chileans, Garcia Calderon had yet to accept surrender terms, and the occupiers finally lost patience with him. The out-going Pinto administration in Santiago had been content to give the Peruvians time, but the newly elected President Domingo Santa Maria desperately wanted some progress on this front to help silence his many critics at home, and he finally authorized Lynch first to dissolve the Garcia Calderon government at the end of September and then, when that had no particular effect, to place the former provisional president under arrest and incarcerate him under the guns of the Chilean fleet at Callao in the hope that this icy shower of reality would prompt more flexibility in negotiations.[13]

Such was not the case, however, and Garcia Calderon defiantly named Admiral Montero his vice president and head of state in his enforced absence. Montero readily accepted the offer, taking with him support of much of the surviving army away from Pierola. Although Caceres refused to recognize the Garcia Calderon regime, he and many of his officers tacitly withdrew their recognition from Pierola, and, before the end of the year, Pierola had finally abandoned his cause and joined his predecessor in self-imposed exile in Europe. Thus, far from coercing the Garcia Calderon government into greater cooperation, the arrest only served to unite the Peruvians under one president again and to raise Garcia Calderon to the level of a national martyr.[14]

The Americans took this heavy-handed action by the Chileans as a direct affront, having succumbed to Chilean blandishments to recognize the Garcia Calderon government so recently. And Lynch did little to assuage the situation when, in late September, the Chileans "discovered" an alleged plot by Garcia Calderon to sign a treaty granting the United States a mandate over Peru, a story that was given some credence by the fact that General Hurlbut was involved with the speculators who were busily buying up Peruvian credits and nitrate futures in Europe. Lynch called on Garcia Calderon to resign, which he refused to do, seized the small treasury of paper money the provisional government had been allowed to print, and conducted a brutal search of Garcia Calderon's residence seeking incriminating documents. All of this called into serious question the Chilean claim that the provisional government had been freely elected by the Peruvian people and had not simply been installed by the conquering power.[15]

With resistance to the Chilean occupation growing daily and with opposition political leaders in Santiago howling for an end to the war and the demobilization of the army, Lynch felt pressured into eliminating the last vestiges of Peru's ability to resist militarily. Just at the start of the new year of 1882, he planned a two-pronged offensive to destroy Caceres' little army, which ranged freely in the high valleys of central Peru, after which he could deal with Montero's forces at Arequipa, which had nowhere to run, at his leisure. Lynch would lead one column of about three thousand infantry with a squadron of cavalry and two batteries of mountain howitzers directly from Lima toward Caceres' headquarters at Chosica. His chief of staff General Jose Francisco Gana would take another column of fifteen hundred men, also with his own artillery and cavalry support, on a swing to the south to take the Peruvians in the rear. If everything went according to plan, the two columns would unite at the town of Chicla around 7 January and Caceres would have been crushed between them.[16]

This was an ambitious plan that called for close coordination between widely separated forces and rapid movement at the height of the rainy season. It was a campaign completely different from anything the Chileans had experienced in the previous two years of war. No longer would lack of water be the primary consideration for the movement of troops. Here, in the highlands, water was plentiful enough and it would be the crossing of rushing streams in deep gorges that would slow the progress of advancing columns if key bridges could not be captured. Food and forage could be obtained from the local farms and haciendas, but the dense population here was wholly hostile to the invaders, and every peasant's hut contained watchers who would report on the Chilean troop movements, and every rocky outcrop could contain a swarm of guerrillas who would pop away at a distance or fall with murderous swiftness on isolated detachments. Instead of oppressive heat, the men would have to contend with bitter cold, from which nine soldiers in Lynch's column alone would die on the march. Instead of billiard table flatness, the troops would have to pick their way along narrow paths at the edge of deep cliffs and over mountains that made the crossing of the Alps look like a stroll in the park, the passes themselves sometimes rising to over fifteen thousand feet above sea level. All of the lowland Chileans would be afflicted by *soroche*, altitude sickness, which caused headaches, nausea, and insomnia, if nothing worse, and the men could not hope to carry the loads expected of them at sea level, with their lungs bursting and hearts pounding at the slightest exertion.

Lynch was obliged to send his artillery back to Lima, finding the narrow roads impassable in many places to anything other than men or horses traveling in single file. The two columns finally met at Chicla, a week later than planned, and Caceres and his thoroughly acclimatized troops, now numbering about twenty-five hundred men, had little trouble in moving out of their way, being fully informed of Lynch's campaign plans as early as mid-December.[17]

Not that Caceres had things very easy on his side of the hill. A typhoid epidemic was sweeping through his ranks, and the only way he had of obtaining money or food was to wait until the Chileans had extorted a town or hacienda to gather cattle or grain for their army and then send a flying column to ambush the supply convoy, thus stealing what the Chileans had already stolen. The writ of the provisional government did not run very far in the mountains and, while the bulk of the population sympathized with the resistance, there was little in the way of voluntary contributions to Caceres' war chest, and he did not want to risk alienating his only possible base of support by commandeering necessary resources the way the Chileans did.

Caceres also had to face dissention in his own ranks. Just prior to Lynch's offensive, his force had numbered nearly five thousand men, but desertion and sickness had cut that force in half. Then, in the midst of his efforts to sidestep the converging Chilean columns, he was obliged to face a mutiny by the "Cazadores del Peru" Cavalry Regiment, who had previously been Pierola's personal escort. The uprising was put down by the intervention of Caceres' old "Zepita" Regiment, of which few of the original members still survived, and after a few executions, calm returned to the ranks. In another incident, one Captain Lara, commanding a scratch force of guerrillas at the town of Sisicaya had apparently lost his nerve and allowed a Chilean column to pass through the ambush his men had set up. The men subsequently murdered him and hurled his body into a gorge, but Caceres apparently was willing to tolerate this kind of rough and ready military justice and let the matter drop.[18]

At this point Lynch was in favor of abandoning the pursuit, but pressure from the Santa Maria administration forced him to continue. Lynch returned to Lima, leaving Gana in command of a new column of twenty-three hundred men, well equipped with artillery and with cavalry for patrolling purposes. Through the rest of January, Gana followed Caceres over the mountains into Junín Department, losing men to the cold and altitude sickness, and raising funds and supplies for the operation as he went. On 1 February command passed to Colonel del Canto who split his force into two columns to follow both banks of the Rio Grande up to Concepción with Caceres staying ten to fifteen miles ahead of him.[19]

Caceres' force had now dropped to only eleven hundred infantry, about ninety artillerymen, and barely forty cavalry, and these were in a constant state of fatigue, with many more men straggling along with his column but totally worthless in combat due to illness. Still, as he managed to get his men across the rain-swollen Pucara River, he decided to take advantage of the favorable ground and make a stand on 5 February both to get del Canto to keep a more respectful distance and to give his sick and wounded a chance to get more of a head start.

Del Canto had moved up by a forced night march, hoping to cut off Caceres' rear guard at the river. Even when he realized that the Peruvians had already made the crossing, he forged ahead, running directly into a counterattack by Caceres himself and supported by fire from the rest of the Peruvian force on the heights beyond the river. With a two-to-one superiority in numbers and even more in artillery, it is likely that del Canto could have forced the crossing despite the good defensive terrain, but he broke off the battle after an hour or so after each side had lost several dozen killed and wounded, besides some 40 Peruvian wounded the Chileans had swept up on the near side of the river. Del Canto then withdrew, possibly because the Chilean command did not want to bring the Peruvians to battle unless they had overwhelming strength, not wanting to rack up any more casualties than absolutely necessary, especially now that it appeared that Caceres was not at all loathe to accept battle himself.[20]

Although Caceres' troops may have been elated at what amounted to a minor victory, at least in that they avoided extermination, their Calvary was not over. The march continued toward Ayacucho, but the column was struck by a terrible storm of rain and sleet while on a narrow mountain path alongside a deep ravine. No fewer that 400 men perished from the cold, from sickness, or from simply being washed over the precipice to their deaths along with many valuable mules and one of the army's few artillery pieces. When the column staggered into the town of Julcamarca two weeks later, barely four hundred men were left in the ranks, and no more than half of these were fit for service.[21] What the Chileans had failed to accomplish in battle, Mother Nature had done easily with the elements.

One of the reasons that Caceres had stopped to fight del Canto at the Pucara River crossing was that he was daily expecting the arrival of a Colonel Panizo with seventeen hundred men from Ayacucho. It was not until Caceres approached the city himself that he learned that Panizo had declared himself beyond the authority of the provisional government, probably anticipating that a new president would step forward, either installed by the Chileans or by force of arms among the Peruvians, and he likely hoped to sell his services to the highest bidder. When Caceres and his bedraggled troops finally neared Ayacucho, instead of reinforcements, they found Panizo's little army deployed for battle blocking their way.

Outnumbered at least four-to-one, and barely able to drag themselves forward, Caceres' men nonetheless formed up and rushed the defenders with the bayonet. Apparently Panizo's troops had little spirit for fighting against one of the few surviving heroes of the Peruvian war effort, and after a brief exchange of gunfire, they surrendered en masse, their commander fleeing on horseback. Virtually all of Panizo's men subsequently joined Caceres' ranks, and he was thus able to spend the next three months in the safety of Ayacucho, resting his men and training new recruits.[22]

By early July, Caceres was satisfied enough with the progress of his force, which had now grown to about three thousand men including local militia, that he planned an offensive of his own with the goal of trapping del Canto in the valley of the River Mantaro. His plan called for three separate columns to converge on the Chilean garrison. One force under Colonel Gastó would swing through the uplands east of the Mantaro to seize the town of Concepción in del Canto's rear. A second force under chief of staff Colonel Manuel Tafur would move to the west and take the town of Oroya with its key bridge, cutting off del Canto's route of escape, and Caceres would take the bulk of his forces himself to attack the Chileans frontally at Pucara. The different forces started out on 29 June to allow time for Tafur and Gastó, who had much farther to travel, to get into position in time for a joint attack on 9 July.[23]

Not anticipating anything more than the continual harassment his forces had been experiencing from scattered guerrilla forces for weeks, del Canto had scattered his men in small garrisons throughout the valley, to facilitate both foraging and collecting "taxes" in the form of cattle or money and to attempt to avoid the epidemics of typhoid and small pox that were ravaging the occupation forces elsewhere. Caceres had little trouble pushing back the outpost at Pucara, only an isolated company, and even the main body of del Canto's force was obliged to evacuate the town of Huancayo, pulling back in the direction of Concepción.[24]

At the same moment, however, Gastó's column fell on the little garrison of that town, one company of seventy-seven men from the regiment "Chacabuco" under Lieutenant Ignacio Carrera Pinto. Despite various warnings of an impending attack, Carrera had left his men divided into several separate detachments housed in several buildings around the town. In the early afternoon the Peruvians opened a heavy fire from the surrounding hills, forcing the defenders to take shelter in the few stone buildings in the town. The attackers then systematically tore down the walls of the compounds and houses, in order to close with the defenders without exposing themselves to Chilean fire in the streets. At some point there was apparently a call to surrender which was contemptuously rejected. The house-to-house fighting thus went on all night long, and when del Canto's column finally arrived at about 1000 hours on 10 July, all that they found were dead bodies, which the Chileans later claimed had been brutally mutilated.[25]

Tafur had failed to take the bridge at Oroya, and del Canto was able to evacuate the Junín Department without further incident, but it had been a telling defeat for the Chileans. In all they had lost 154 killed in combat, another 277 dead from disease, and over one hundred deserters, a total loss of over 20 percent of del Canto's entire force. At the same time, although the Peruvian losses had almost certainly been much higher, word of this victory gave heart to the resistance that now spread throughout the highlands of central Peru.[26]

The impact of this setback on the Chileans was out of all proportion to the numbers of troops involved. Reminiscent of the last stand of the French Foreign

Legion at Cameron in Mexico or of Custer's 7th Cavalry at the Little Big Horn, the defeat at Concepción brought home to the Chilean people the cost of this continuing war, a war that was supposed to have already been over. At the same time, the massacre, in which Chilean sources claimed the Peruvians had employed over two thousand men, including savage Indians, and the alleged killing of the wounded and the mutilation of the corpses, enraged public opinion and spurred calls for a more aggressive prosecution of the war. This decision was all the easier to reach since the composition of the Chilean army had long since changed. The gentlemen volunteers from the better classes of Chilean society had lost their interest in seeking glory on the battlefield, and the ranks were now filled with the "dregs of society," conscripted farm laborers and the sweepings of the prisons of Santiago and Valparaíso. Thus, the "butcher's bill" that came home each month from Lima may have caused a due amount of grief in the families of the men involved, but they were not longer the families that mattered.[27]

On the other hand, the war was costing Chile some $2.5 million per year, and in return the Chileans felt that they were providing their neighbors with the "best government they had ever had."[28] Presumably, this was offset by the more than 500,000 pesos that Chile was receiving from the sale of guano and nitrates per month and the various "taxes" that Lynch was collecting in the occupied territories, but there was still a growing impatience among the Chileans for the start of the era of plenty that the possession of the nitrate-rich region was supposed to provide. And still there was no peace.

The diplomatic front had hardly made any additional progress due to the assassination of U.S. President Garfield and his replacement by Chester A. Arthur in January 1882. The change of administration also brought in a new secretary of state, Frederick Frelinghuysen who had very different opinions about what the American role in the conflict should be. Just before the assassination, William Trescott, an experienced diplomatic troubleshooter, had been sent as a special envoy to see if any break could be made in the logjam in the peace process. Meanwhile, new American ambassadors had been named to both Lima, where the United States still recognized the Garcia Calderon government, and to Santiago, James R. Partridge and Charles A. Logan respectively. This further disrupted the ongoing contacts with the belligerents, but the purpose of the personnel change was to eliminate the baggage of Hurlbut's alleged involvement with European speculators in Peruvian credits and Kilpatrick's alleged favoritism for Chile due to his having married a Chilean woman as had his predecessor. (Chile's reputation for beautiful women is apparently justified.)

After talks in Lima, with both Lynch and Garcia Calderon, Trescott moved on to Santiago to meet with the new Santa Maria administration, but he was chagrined to find out upon his arrival that U.S. policy had altered radically even while he was at sea. Under Secretary of State Blaine, the U.S. position had been strongly against any peace involving the forcible transfer of territory except in voluntary payment of indemnities, and the Peruvians had taken great heart in this policy. This was to have been put into effect at a hemispheric peace conference to be held in Washington sometime in 1882.[29]

When Trescott disembarked at Valparaíso, however, he was suddenly confronted with the news that the new instructions for his mission applied, that, instead of actively engineering a peace conference, the United States would only use its "pacifying influence" to help the belligerents arrive at a solution to the conflict on their own. The fact that these instructions had been relayed to Trescott by Chilean Foreign Minister Balmaceda was a source of considerable embarrassment for the American delegation. Apparently, Balmaceda's envoy in Washington had translated and cabled a version of the new diplomatic policy directly from open press reports, while the State Department had decided to save the cost of the telegram by sending Trescott's new directions by post. It seems that rumors of the involvement of former Secretary of State Blaine with the French financial firm of Credit Industriale, which held a great block of Peruvian credits secured with nitrate exports, had suddenly become public, and the new Arthur administration wanted to avoid any appearance of misconduct, thus choosing to bow out of active sponsorship of a peace program.[30]

Under the circumstances, Trescott felt obliged to sign the Viña del Mar Protocol which essentially ruled out any direct American intervention in the conflict but noted that the United States proffered its good offices to the belligerents. The document laid out once more Chile's demands which included cession of all territory south of Camarones and the Chilean intention of holding Tacna and Arica for ten years as guarantee against the payment of an indemnity of twenty million pesos by Peru, with ownership to become permanent if Peru failed to comply. Trescott canceled plans to continue on for talks in Buenos Aires and Rio de Janeiro and returned to Peru to present his credentials and the Chilean position to Vice President Montero, Garcia Calderon having already been taken to even closer confinement in Chile itself, traveling by mule to the town of Huaraz to do so. The younger Blaine, meanwhile, made a separate trip to La Paz to perform the same service in Bolivia, although neither mission obtained any significant results. In fact, the only permanent development coming out of this period was the sudden death of both Ambassadors Hurlbut and Kilpatrick from illness just before they were to have formally turned over their posts. [31]

Without a diplomatic breakthrough, the debate in Santiago raged between those who wanted to press the war to a successful conclusion once and for all and those, including President Santa Maria, who favored simply evacuating Lima and establishing possession of everything south of the Sama River until the Peruvians could sort out their own political house and come to a reasonable agreement. This debate was cut short, however, when, General Miguel Iglesias, formerly minister of war under Pierola and currently commander of the Army of the North under Montero, despite the fact that he had been released as a prisoner of war after the Battle of Chorrillos/San Juan by the Chileans on his parole, suddenly leaped onto center stage. On 1 April 1882 Iglesias issued a manifesto calling for peace with Chile on any terms available since victory for the allies was clearly an impossibility.

Iglesias followed this up in early August with a more formal document, later called the "*Grito de Montan*" (the "Call of Montan," apparently modeled on the famous "*Grito*" of Mexican independence).

They speak of a question of honor that impedes a peace agreement that would cede a piece of land. In order not to let it go, something that represents a mere handful of gold,. . . we permit the banner of the enemy fly over our highest towers . . . that they sack and burn our homes, that they profane our temples, that they insult our mothers, wives, and daughters. To maintain that false honor, the Chilean whip lashes our helpless brothers; for that false honor, widows and orphans of those who fell on the field of battle are impoverished, at the mercy of the enemy, to whom they extend the hand of a beggar.[32]

The anti-Chilean invective aside, this was exactly the message that the occupying forces wanted the Peruvian people to hear, and Lynch welcomed the convention of representatives of the seven departments of northern Peru that Iglesias called at Cajamarca and which duly elected him "Regenerating President" in December of 1882.[33] As he had done with Garcia Calderon, Lynch granted Iglesias a monthly stipend of thirty thousand pesos, later raised to ninety thousand for the expenses of his administration and also supplied him with 150 rifles and ammunition for a small gendarmerie. Although the towns in the area actually occupied by what had been Iglesias' Army of the North had denounced Montero as had a few other locales under Chilean occupation, Lynch knew full well that the only way to establish the Iglesias regime as the bona fide government of Peru would be to eliminate the last vestiges of armed resistance once and for all.[34]

Toward this end, Lynch planned a three-pronged advance into the interior of the country to pin and destroy Caceres and his little army. One division under Colonel Leon Garcia with some two thousand men, would head north to Nievería and Punabamba, thence to the town of Canto and on to Chicla. In the south, del Canto would take fifteen hundred men up the valley of the Lurin toward Chicla, while Colonel Urriola would take the main force of three thousand men straight up the valley of the Rimac. Ideally, any one of these columns should prove a match for Caceres, and it would be virtually impossible for him to avoid all of them. If any two of them could manage to catch the slippery Peruvian between them, he would be crushed. The march started on 6 April 1883, with Garcia's column starting first as it had the longest distance to travel to the rendezvous at Chicla.[35]

At this point Caceres had some one thousand to fifteen hundred regulars, a small cavalry force, and perhaps two batteries of guns, most of them museum pieces. However, throughout central Peru he had set up a system of local militias not unlike the Minute Men of the American Revolution. Wherever the Chileans attempted to march through the interior, they would be shadowed by guerrilla bands on foot or horse, their movements reported, and stragglers or foraging parties cut off and ambushed. And, when Caceres' main body was obliged to offer battle, he could count on augmenting his force with hundreds of local volunteers who would turn out to defend their homes and villages, poorly armed, if at all, but usually enthusiastic, and at least Caceres did not have to supply them with food and uniforms on the prodigious marches his little army was constantly undertaking as they kept one step ahead of their pursuers.

By the 24th of April all three Chilean columns were on the march, and Caceres was obliged to pull back to Tarma in an effort to avoid the closing jaws of the trap by the start of May. It was soon clear to the Peruvians that this was a serious offensive as the Chileans were breaking with their tradition of generally brushing aside or ignoring the harassment of the numerous guerrilla bands they encountered along their way. Now, Lynch and his subordinates took the time to root out and destroy any armed forces they encountered, killing hundreds and not bothering to take prisoners. By 5 May all three Chilean columns had reunited at Chicla and immediately drove on toward the key bridge at Oroya, defended by troops under General Pedro Silva. Avoiding a frontal attack across the narrow stone bridge, Lynch sent a detachment across the river farther downstream that was able to flank Silva, and the Chileans took the town unopposed.[36]

In the face of the Chilean advance, Caceres called a council of war at Tarma on 20 May, the day Oroya fell. He asked his senior officers' opinions on the desirability of making a stand against Lynch in territory with which their troops were at least familiar, even though they would be outnumbered. His chief of staff, the fiery Colonel Manuel Tafur, despite his being over seventy years old, called for battle, but most of the other commanders, Colonels Secada, Borgono, Carrion and others all advised against it, citing the lack of ammunition and a severe shortage of cavalry, which would put the army in grave danger should the Chileans manage to break their lines and start a pursuit. Caceres reluctantly agreed with the majority and determined to retreat to the north, abandoning the Junín Department and voluntarily placing himself under the command of General Jesus Elias, the new commander of the Army of the North, named by Montero to replace the turncoat Iglesias, since the move would place him in Elias' jurisdiction. The small but proud army gathered itself and set out on 21 May 1883 in a heavy rain.

With recent recruiting and the drawing in of the small garrisons that had been scattered around Junín Department, Caceres now had twenty-three hundred men, eight guns of various origins, and a single small cavalry squadron. This was now organized into four divisions, each about the size of a pre-war regiment. The 1st was commanded by Caceres' brother Manuel, the 2nd by Colonel Juan Gastó, the 3rd by Colonel Tafur's brother Maximo, and the 4th by Navy Captain German Astete. The combined Chilean force pursuing them under del Canto and Gastó, since Lynch had returned to his duties in Lima, numbered about three thousand men, but these possessed an overwhelming qualitative superiority in both small arms and artillery and a clear advantage in cavalry, besides the intangible quality of markedly better morale than the consistently defeated and hunted Peruvians.[37]

Caceres' retreat continued into mid-June through bitter cold weather, the worst part of the winter, when he arrived on the plains of Huaraz, three hundred miles to the northwest of Tarma. There he linked up with the bulk of the Army of the North, some nine hundred men, but these barely made good the wastage of his own forces on the march. More and more during this period one notes Caceres, in his own memoirs, referring to his forces as the "resistance," more like the French *maquis* fighting the Germans in World War II than a fully constituted, regular army.

The Huaraz Valley, carved by the northward flowing Santa River, is hemmed in by the Cordillera Negra to the west and the Cordillera Blanca to the east, with small towns hugging the river valley up and down its length. Caceres learned that the pursuing Chileans were now under the command of Colonel Arriaga, and not far behind, so he quickly gathered his men and crossed the Cordillera Blanca, its passes reaching fifteen thousand feet, in a blinding snowstorm, arriving at the town of Pomabamba on 25 June where he joined with about one thousand men under Colonel Isaac Recabarren, a welcome reinforcement. Unfortunately, the Chileans did not give up so easily, and word arrived that Arriaga had also crossed the mountains, forcing Caceres to continue on to the north.[38]

Late on 4 July, Peruvian guerrillas turned over to Caceres a captured Chilean courier, and a doctor with the army was able to decipher the crudely encoded message. This indicated that a Chilean force under Comandante Herminio González was at the town of Santiago de Chuco with a force of only eight hundred men and five guns, only one long day's march away. Caceres, always eager for a chance to strike at the enemy, and even more eager to get his hands on some modern rifles and artillery, planned to move his whole army to the attack, hopefully before another Chilean column under Colonel Gorostiaga could come up.

The departure was planned for dawn on 6 July, giving his men at least time to rest a little and prepare a rare hot meal, as well as to gather more food for the journey. However, the need to punish some deserters from Recabarren's division, by summary execution, delayed the start of the march, and the column was further slowed by the need to pass single file over an incredibly narrow mountain road, which also obliged the men to disassemble the guns and load them on pack mules for the passage. When the little army finally did come within view of Santiago de Chuco, Recabarren, whose division was in the vanguard, apparently lost his nerve and refused Caceres' order to launch an immediate attack from the line of march, forcing Caceres to wait for Secada to bring up the main body. In any event, it turned out that Gonzalez had moved on to Huamachuco, some ten miles farther north, which obviated the chance of an immediate assault.[39]

That evening, some civilians who claimed to have been detained by Chilean patrols reported to Caceres that Gorostiaga had come up by forced marches with a further five hundred men and would join with Gonzalez in the next day or so. Caceres immediately called a council of war and announced to his commanders that he planned to hit Gonzalez before the juncture could take place. During the night march, Caceres' forces lost nearly six hundred deserters, nearly all from among Recabarren's northerners, leaving him with a total force of barely eighteen hundred, still enough to deal with Gonzalez alone, but probably not if Gorostiaga joined him. Caceres was aware that more Chilean troops would be arriving shortly, and he had noticed that virtually no new volunteers had joined the army since he entered the territory of the Army of the North, contrary to the practice back in Junín Department where local militia would show up to fight whenever action promised near their homes.[40]

The town of Huamachuco, with a population at the time of about eight thousand, sits in a small valley, about four kilometers by two, and was an important crossroads for shipments coming from the gold mines in the northern mountains. The town is flanked on the west and south by the Huamachuco River, with high mountains beyond it, and with a long, narrow ridge, the Morro Santa Barbara starting at the eastern edge of town and paralleling the river for about one mile to the east. A broad plain covers the northern side of town and stretches out to the east before running into another wall of mountains. The northern side of this plain, the *Llano de Purrubamba*, is framed by a high tableland called the Cerro Sazon, topped with a crown of Inca ruins and with a belt of marshy ground at its base. It was atop Cerro Sazon that Gonzalez had dug his troops in, abandoning the town as indefensible amid its surrounding hills.[41]

By the time the Peruvians sent their first scouts into the town, it was already too late. Gorostiaga had come up on 7 July, and the combined Chilean force now numbered nearly sixteen hundred men and eight guns, which were well-entrenched atop their hill and amid the massive stone blocks of the Inca ruins. It was vital for them to hold this position, as Arriagada had been tricked by Caceres' intentional misdirection into believing that the Peruvians were doubling back to the south, and he eventually returned to Lima on 5 August, having lost over seven hundred of his original thirty-three hundred men between desertion, sickness, or death from fatigue and cold, a 20 percent loss without a single battle casualty. Caceres thus did not have to worry about his own rear, but Gorostiaga knew that, barely one hundred miles farther north lay the town of Cajamarca, where Iglesias had set up his puppet government, and this was very likely the goal of Caceres' campaign, to oust the pretender and derail the promising Chilean efforts at getting some kind of negotiated peace signed. The Chileans knew that the relative quiescence of the north was due to the presence of the Iglesias government, and its destruction would likely spread the flames of insurrection throughout the whole country.[42]

When Caceres arrived at Huamachuco early on 8 July, his men discovered Chilean documents that indicated that he might be facing as many as two thousand men, compared to his eighteen hundred and eleven guns, but had also learned that a Colonel Puga was in the neighborhood with several hundred more Peruvian militia and would be in a position to fall on the Chilean rear by the next day. Throughout the day on the 9th, therefore, the two armies faced each other across the plain, the Chileans on Cerro Sazon, and the Peruvians in the town and on the Santa Barbara ridge. That morning the Peruvians scored a minor victory by capturing a mule train spotted bringing supplies up to the Chileans, and that afternoon a force of two hundred militia from Santiago de Chuco arrived to improve the odds slightly. On the other hand, many of the residents of Huamachuco were Iglesias loyalists, and they generally denied Caceres any support.[43]

Caceres had planned to launch his attack on the 10th, with Recabarren's unreliable troops demonstrating frontally while Secada's division from the old Army of the Center would swing around the Chilean left for the decisive stroke. However, Recabarren fell ill, and Caceres did not dare replace him with one of his own officers as the troops from the Army of the North strongly distrusted the veterans from central Peru, and this could prompt their mass defection to Iglesias. Since the odds were too close to take this risk, Caceres decided to postpone the attack until the 11th, thus also giving Puga more time to get into position behind the Chileans, and he ordered his men to stand down.[44]

That was the plan, but things worked out differently, as they often do in war. Just after dawn on the 10th, Gorostiaga sent forward two companies of skirmishers to conduct a reconnaissance of the Peruvian right across the plain. However, instead of simply approaching to within rifle range of the Peruvian lines and observing their dispositions, the commander of the small force got carried away and became hotly engaged with some of Tafur's troops. Gorostiaga then sent in a troop of cavalry to cover the withdrawal, and Caceres in turn, hoping to bag a sizeable number of the enemy outside of their entrenchments, ordered Gastó's division to execute an enveloping maneuver. In response, the entire Chilean line moved forward, down the slopes of the Cerro and out across the plain, and Caceres had no choice but to throw in Astete's and Recabarren's troops as well.[45]

By 0900 hours, both of the contending forces were engaged in heavy fighting stretching from the houses on the edge of Huamachuco all the way across the plain to the east. By 1100 hours, the Peruvian regiments were fast running out of ammunition, and the Chileans, sensing the decrease in the volume of fire, fixed bayonets and charged once more, shattering the Peruvian line. Caceres threw in his last reserve, the division commanded by his own brother, but these troops also broke. He attempted to form a line along the Santa Barbara ridge, but his army was in full flight, and a furious attempt to stop the Chileans by leading a charge of his own small cavalry escort hardly even slowed the attackers down, while it nearly resulted in his own capture, his troopers all being cut down around him. Needless to say, Colonel Puga's force, if it ever really existed, never showed up on the battlefield.[46]

The Chilean losses for the day numbered no more than 60 killed and perhaps 80 wounded. The Peruvian losses were never officially tabulated, but the army had ceased to exist. Tafur, Astete, and Gastó were all killed, and Recabarren wounded, and many of the Peruvian wounded were shot out of hand by the victorious Chileans.[47]

Caceres escaped from the battlefield alone, his horse wounded in several places. He eventually hooked up with Colonel Borgono and a handful of junior officers. A few days later the little party came suddenly upon a troop of Chilean cavalry in a misty mountain pass, and Caceres was about to surrender when he learned that they were deserters, and both parties went their separate ways in peace. Caceres would spend the next several months evading roving Chilean cavalry patrols and attempting to reconstitute an army based on one hundred men under Dávila near Ayacucho, but, even though a few survivors of Huamachuco eventually drifted into his camp, he would never have more than a thousand men under arms at once.[48]

After the disintegration of Caceres' army, things unraveled very quickly for the remaining independent Peruvian forces. More and more towns declared their recognition of the Iglesias government and, apart from scattered guerrilla bands, like the one Caceres was attempting to organize into an army around Ayacucho, only Montero's army at Arequipa remained in the field. These constituted about two to three thousand regulars and perhaps double that number of militia. Santa Maria selected Colonel Jose M. Velásquez to lead a two-pronged expedition to eliminate this center of resistance. One division of twenty-two hundred men under Colonel Vicente Ruiz would move overland from Tacna while a second of three thousand under del Canto would be brought by sea from Callao to Pacocha, and the two columns would join at Moquegua for a final march on Arequipa.[49]

Ruiz's troops got under way in early September and, by the 14th, had occupied Moquegua without meeting any resistance. By 1 October del Canto's division had also reached Moquegua without incident, and the march began on Arequipa, which the army neared on 22 October. Montero gamely deployed his forces before the city, with a substantial numerical superiority over the five thousand or so Chileans, but with a marked inferiority in artillery and in weaponry in general. However, there was not destined to be a Battle of Arequipa. The population of the city, weary after four long years of war and well aware that they represented the last vestige of "free Peru," mutinied against a continuation of the war, and the bulk of Montero's troops joined them. He was thus obliged to surrender both city and army on 29 October.[50]

The laying down of arms of the last significant Peruvian army was something of an anticlimax. The Iglesias government had been engaged in what would amount to final peace negotiations with Chile for some time. Throughout March, April, and May of 1883 Iglesias' envoy Jose Antonio Lavalle had been conducting a series of meetings with his Chilean counterpart Jovino Novoa in Chorrillos and Anacin, and the Peruvians had finally agreed to an end to the fighting, to the permanent loss of Tarapacá, and to a Chilean occupation of Tacna and Arica for a period of ten years at the end of which time a plebiscite would be held in the territory to determine the will of the inhabitants as to which country they wished to belong. The winner in the plebiscite would then pay the loser the sum of ten million pesos by way of indemnity. In exchange, Chile was to extend formal recognition to Iglesias as legitimate head of state, and Chilean troops were to evacuate Lima after an occupation of nearly three years, which was accomplished on 23 October, with the final Chilean withdrawal from Peruvian territory (other than Tacna and Arica) taking place the following August. The treaty was finally signed on 20 October, just prior to Montero's surrender, and ratified by the legislatures of both countries within the next few months, thus becoming the Treaty of Anacin.[51]

The signing of this agreement brought a howl of protest from La Paz, since Iglesias had not bothered to inform, much less include, Bolivia in the negotiations, in violation of the 1873 treaty of alliance. Of course, La Paz did not have formal diplomatic relations with Iglesias, still recognizing the Garcia Calderon/Montero government, so this may be a moot point. More importantly, Bolivia had been engaging in on-going negotiations of her own with Chile throughout this period, an exercise in diplomacy that defied the rules of logic. The main Chilean position at these talks had consistently been to offer Bolivia a corridor to the sea and a port taken from formerly Peruvian territory, an offer that had been on the table since before the fighting had commenced. The Campero administration had just as consistently rejected this offer as dishonorable, although Foreign Minister Mariano Baptista was very much in favor of it. It should be noted that, at none of these talks did the Bolivians insist on Peruvian representation, so their protests after the Treaty of Anacin ring a little hollow. More importantly, while rejecting Chilean peace offers, Bolivia made no effort to reconstitute its field army after the Battle of Tacna or to support the Peruvian resistance to Chile in any way other than allowing small shipments of arms and munitions to cross its territory from Europe via Argentina.[52]

The Bolivian government was hopelessly divided between hawks, mostly Liberals led by President Campero and Fernando E. Guachalla, and doves, Conservatives led by Vice President Aniceto Arce, Foreign Minister Baptista, and mining baron Gregorio Pacheco. But, with the removal of Peru from the war, there seemed little option left other than to accept Chilean terms and, on 7 December 1883, Belisario Boeto and Belisario Salinas were sent to Santiago to make the best deal possible. It must have been with some effort that Chilean Foreign Minister Aldunate restrained himself from laughing at the new Bolivian willingness to accept the gracious Chilean offer of Arica as a Bolivian port, now that the war was over with Peru and there was no longer any particular incentive for Chile to seek to woo Bolivia away from the Peruvian alliance. Aldunate limited himself to pointing out that Peru had fought on for two extra years, *alone*, precisely in an effort to hold on to Tacna and Arica, and it would not be acceptable to either the Chilean or the Peruvian public that Bolivia should now be given part of this territory as a present, and that, in any case, this would be a violation of the Treaty of Anacin. Aldunate also rejected the idea of a Bolivian corridor to the sea anywhere south of the Chilean-Peruvian border, as this would physically sever one piece of the Chilean fatherland from another.[53]

Ultimately, the best that the Bolivians could obtain was a truce, which was signed at Valparaíso on 4 April 1884. Under its terms Bolivia did not formally recognize a permanent transfer of her coastal province to Chile but accepted continued Chilean administration of the territory until a final peace accord could be arranged. In the meanwhile, Bolivia could import goods through the ports of Arica and Antofagasta and set up a customs house there at which import duties would be divided with 75 percent going to Bolivia and 25 percent to Chile. All property seized by the Bolivian government from Chilean citizens was to be restored, along with any profits gained from it during the war, and an indemnity paid for any damages. As an aside, the agreement also allowed for Chilean goods to enter Bolivia duty free, and the same for Bolivian goods to Chile, although this clause obviously favored industrially advanced Chile far more than Bolivia. And thus, with a whimper, the war ended.[54]

NOTES

1. Andres Avelino Caceres, *Memórias del Mariscal Andres A. Caceres,* vol. 3, Lima: Editorial Milla Batres, 1986, p. 45.

2. Ibid., p. 68.

3. Mariano Felipe Paz Soldan, *Narracion Histórica de la Guerra de Chile contra Peru y Bolivia,* vol. 3, Buenos Aires: s.n., 1884, p. 115.

4. William F. Sater, *Chile and the War of the Pacific,* Lincoln: University of Nebraska Press, 1986, p. 54.

5. Roberto Querejazu Calvo, *Guano, Salitre, Sangre: História de la Guerra del Pacífico,* La Paz: Editorial Los Amigos del Libro, 1979, p. 635.

6. Gonzalo Bulnes, *Guerra del Pacífico,* vol. 3, Santiago de Chile: Editorial del Pacifico, 1955, p. 11.

7. Querejazu, p. 637.

8. William Jefferson Dennis, *Tacna and Arica: An Account of the Chile-Peru Boundary Dispute and of the Arbitrations by the United States,* New York: Archon Books, 1967, p. 144.

9. Bulnes, p. 21.

10. Ibid., p. 25.

11. Caceres, p. 110.

12. Bulnes, p. 81.

13. Valentin Abecia Baldivieso, *Las Relaciones Internacionales en la História de Bolivia,* vol. 2, La Paz: Editorial Los Amigos del Libro, 1979, p. 154.

14. Querejazu, p. 644.

15. Dennis, p. 159.

16. Bulnes, op. cit., p. 142.

17. Ibid., p. 145.

18. Caceres, p. 135.

19. Bulnes, p. 146.

20. Ibid., p. 150.

21. Caceres, p. 148.

22. Ibid., p. 152.

23. Ibid., p. 178.

24. Bulnes, p. 157.

25. Caceres, p. 179.

26. Bulnes, p. 166.

27. Sater, p. 215.

28. *The Chilean Times,* Valparaíso, 2 September 1882.

29. Robert N. Burr, *By Reason or Force: Chile and the Balance of Power in South America, 1830-1905,* Berkeley: University of California Press, 1967, p. 159.

30. Gordon Ireland, *Boundaries, Possessions and Conflicts in South America,* New York: Octagon Books, 1971, p. 57.

31. Ronald Bruce St. John, *The Foreign Policy of Peru,* Boulder, CO: Lynne Rienner, 1992, p. 120.

32. Querejazu, p. 672.

33. Frederick B. Pike, *The History of Modern Peru,* New York: Praeger, 1982, p. 150.

34. Querejazu, p. 674.

35. Caceres, p. 190.

36. Ibid., p. 194.

37. Eduardo Mendoza Melendez, *Historia de la Campaña de la Brena,* Lima: Editorial Milla Batres, 1981, p. 310.

38. Jacinto Lopez. *História de la Guerra de Guano y el Salitre.* Lima: Editorial Universo, 1980, p. 159.

39. Caceres, p. 217.

40. Mendoza, p. 335.

41. Caceres, p. 221.

42. Bulnes, p. 250.

43. Caceres, p. 225. Note that Chilean sources place Caceres' strength as high as 3,800, but this is almost certainly an exaggeration, Bulnes, p. 255.

44. Caceres, p. 228.

45. Lopez, p. 162.

46. Caceres, p. 230.

47. Bulnes, p. 258.

48. Caceres, p. 246.

49. Lopez, p. 164.

50. Bulnes, p. 295.

51. Abecia, p. 159.

52. Querejazu, p. 677.

53. Abecia, p. 163.

54. Burr, p. 165.

Chapter Twelve

Loose Ends

With the acceptance by the more-or-less recognized government of Peru of the Treaty of Anacin, followed by the collapse of the last of the resistance forces in the interior of the country, and the subsequent truce between Bolivia and Chile, the war was finally over for all practical purposes. However, it would take many more years before the last of the peace conditions would be satisfied, the last protocols signed, and an official state of peace returned to the region. To an extent, this was a largely academic exercise. Chile had what it wanted, and its army could at last be brought home and demobilized, allowing the orphan government of Peru to drift back into the looted and vacant public buildings in Lima to attempt to put the country back together.

But the nineteenth century was nearly over, and with it the era when the cavalier transfer of territory from one nation to another by right of conquest was ending with it. It was becoming increasingly necessary for nations to have "legal" justification for their actions. It would not be until Woodrow Wilson's famous "fourteen points" became a watchword for international relations, at least in theory, that this trend would really take root, but a movement in that direction began in the closing years of the nineteenth century. Thus opened some of the most convoluted peace talks that would ever clutter the pages of diplomatic history.

The most volatile situation existed in Peru after the Chilean withdrawal. It would be wrong to classify Iglesias simply as some kind of Quisling willing to do the Chileans' bidding. He had fought with some energy, if not with much success, in the later stages of the conventional war, and he had lost a son at Chorrillos. Perhaps this personal sacrifice, besides his strong oligarchic background as a *hacendado*, prompted him to see the continuation of the war actually as a cowardly course of action, one in which the leaders of the country who had embroiled the nation in a war they could not win were willing to allow their people to suffer endlessly rather than face the unwelcome consequences of their own decisions. Arguably, considering the absolute defeat of all Peruvian military forces and the enemy occupation of not only the disputed territory but the nation's capital and heartland as well, the Treaty of Anacin was not such a bad deal for Peru, as it at least fell short of what the most jingoistic Chilean politicians were demanding, complete cession of Tacna and Arica as a shield for Chile's newly acquired nitrate lands. And there were many Peruvians who agreed with Iglesias, willing to have the war over at any price so that the nation could get on with its life.

But there were also many Peruvians who did not agree, who saw the acceptance of Chilean terms as a treacherous stab in the back by the politicians of the army. In a way, the Treaty of Anacin gave these hard-liners new spirit as the Chilean withdrawal now left Iglesias alone to face his domestic opponents.

Naturally, the leader of this movement was none other than Caceres, who, on 16 July 1884, declared himself to be the legitimate president of Peru, having been named second vice president by Montero before the fall of Arequipa, since both Garcia Calderon and Montero had now been forcibly removed from office by the invaders. A number of towns, particularly in Junín Department where he had fought for so long, declared for him, and the stage was set for a full-scale civil war.[1]

An early attempt by Caceres to take Lima by storm ended in failure. With only some two thousand men to face Iglesias' more than six thousand, Caceres relied on daring and the possibility that many of the loyalist troops would either sit out the battle or come over to his side. In the event however, on 27 August 1884, units of Caceres' little army did manage to seize the cathedral while others assaulted the Palace of Government, but the army did not yet desert Iglesias, and Caceres was driven out of the city and all the way to Ayacucho.[2]

Caceres spent the following months organizing a new "Army of the Constitution," although he never did manage to gather more than about two thousand men at one time. Iglesias attempted negotiations with the recalcitrant Caceres numerous times, but without success, and, in September of 1885, he finally sent two armies into the field to bring the rebels to heel. Following the practice of Lynch in his frustrating campaigns, Iglesias sent one army straight to the valley of the Mantaro River where Caceres was recruiting, while a second one moved by rail to Chicla from which it would march on Oroya to cut off Caceres' retreat. Either one of the columns easily outnumbered and outgunned Caceres's force by more than two-to-one, and a quick end was anticipated.

Unfortunately for Iglesias, retreat had never occurred to Caceres, and he instead sidestepped the approaching divisions and conducted a harrowing series of forced marches through snow-covered mountain passes at sixteeen thousand feet in terrible storms, coming out at Chicla on 27 November, well behind the loyalist forces and with a direct rail line to Lima open before him. In a panic Iglesias attempted to call back his armies, but too late. The Army of the Constitution stormed the capital on 30 November, finally capturing the Palace of Government and forcing Iglesias to surrender in order to avoid further bloodshed.[3]

Shortly thereafter the Council of Ministers recognized Caceres as president and the legislature confirmed this in May 1886, with Caceres's formal inauguration taking place on 5 June. In an effort to heal the wounds of the war, Caceres graciously rehabilitated Iglesias, returning to him the rank and privileges of a full general.[4]

But Peru had been altered irrevocably by some seven years of war and civil war. The economy of the nation was in a total shambles after years of blockade and the ravages of the invading army up and down the length and breadth of the land. Not only were the rich nitrate lands lost, but years of neglect and outright destruction of the rest of the nation's infrastructure would take decades to repair, and few foreign creditors would be willing to touch Peruvian bonds for years to come. The former landed oligarchy had been devastated by the war, and now a new class of leaders would emerge whose wealth and power derived from positions of influence in the government, just about the only going concern left in the country. The military had been humiliated in one battle after another, and the attitude of the institution was that they had been hamstrung by the politicians who had not provided them with the wherewithal to fight the war and yet had herded them into the conflict through their inept handling of foreign policy. This would give rise to an attitude favoring military intervention in politics that would continue well into the next century. It could be argued that the discovery of the guano and nitrate deposits and their commercial value, the discovery that had seemed a blessing from heaven in the mid-1800s, had turned out to be a curse after all.

Relations with the former ally Bolivia were resumed under Caceres. War hero Eliodoro Camacho was sent to Lima in October 1886 with the primary goal of getting Peru to cancel Bolivia's war debt, La Paz obviously hoping to benefit from the close relationship of Camacho with his former comrade-in-arms. Since Peru had ended up arming virtually all of the troops that Bolivia contributed to the war effort, this was a substantial sum, but Caceres and the Peruvian legislature, perhaps eager just to put a stop to the whole disastrous adventure, agreed. In an act of colossal ineptitude, however, Bolivian Foreign Minister Cristósomo Carrillo in La Paz, presumably aware of why the Bolivian delegation had gone to Lima in the first place, unilaterally negotiated an agreement with the Chilean ambassador reducing the debt to one million pesos, instead of eliminating it entirely, and then compounded the blunder by having the National Assembly hurriedly ratify the agreement. Camacho was then obliged, hat in hand, to go back to Lima to get the Peruvians to disregard Carrillo's treaty.[5]

In Bolivia, the military had been so completely discredited by the disaster of the war that the country would enter into a relatively long period (for Bolivia) of civilian rule, although true political stability and a respect for democratic institutions would not even begin to emerge until the end of the twentieth century. On a more negative note, the loss of Bolivia's sea coast would give rise to a sense of *revanchism*, not against Chile, since the Bolivians had no hope of being able to confront the conquerors militarily, but against the only neighbor to whom Bolivia had not already lost territory, little Paraguay. A wholly unrealistic dream of gaining access to the Atlantic, via the navigable portion of the Paraguay River led to an aggressive policy in the Chaco, an area almost as inhospitable as the Atacama, that would lead to another disastrous war half a century later.[6]

In Chile the end of the war had not brought the universal happiness that everyone had hoped for. As thorough as the military victory had been, there were still numerous critics who insisted that it could have been done better, faster, and cheaper. Such criticism had led to the resignation of Baquedano, and the overall impression that the public was left with was that it had been men like Sotomayor and Vergara who had really engineered the victory while the professional military officers like Lynch and Baquedano or Escala and Arteaga before them, had bumbled along and generally gotten in the way. This led to a sullen return to the barracks by the military in Chile, although the animosity between the civilians and the military would erupt in violence on more than one occasion in the coming decades.[7]

While Chile may have had economic troubles prior to the start of the war, some rational, fairly modern steps to rectify the situation had been proposed, including a modest income tax, although tax evasion was widespread. With the conquest of the Atacama, and later of Tarapacá, everyone looked to the windfall of this rich export to save the country and to pay for the war into the bargain. A tax was immediately put on nitrate exports of forty *centavos* per quintal (compared to the ten cent Bolivian municipal tax over which the war was allegedly being fought), and this was later raised to 1.50 pesos per quintal. The popular cry was never to have a war on behalf of Gibbs & Edwards, one of the British firms heavily involved in nitrate mining. Since this tax was essentially falling on the European consumers, it was immensely popular in Chile, and more than a little addictive to the politicians.

During the course of the war, the government began to finance its operations by printing paper money, first in limited quantities, then in the millions of dollars worth. This was considered better for the economy than loans as it would stimulate, rather than retard commercial activity. However, this attitude gave rise to unlimited public spending, including telephone systems for Santiago and Valparaíso and electric street lighting, and the country literally shut down for several days at a time to celebrate Independence Day or any significant victory in the war, over and above the continuing vast cost of running the war, which the legislature was chagrined in 1882 to find out had cost the government thirty-four million pesos more to wage than had been officially authorized.[8]

In any event, by the end of the Santa Maria administration, half the revenues from the export of guano and nitrates from the occupied territories had been used to pay off 240 million pesos owed to Peruvian bondholders in Europe. This left a like amount available, supposedly, for the free use of the Chilean government, not a development that was designed to encourage frugality and fiscal responsibility. In fact, in the twenty years from the conquest of the nitrate regions to the end of the century, the gross value of the nitrate exports from Atacama and Tarapaca were close to three billion pesos.[9]

Santa Maria's successor in 1886, his last Minister of Interior, Jose Maria Balmaceda, carried on with the lavish spending programs, including a new ironclad for the navy in case Chile should have to fight to retain Tacna and Arica, and made no effort to modernize the revenue structure of the state, still avoiding the possibility of income tax or even looking seriously at broadening the economic base beyond the golden goose of the nitrate mining industry.[10] But it was largely the high-handedness of the Balmaceda administration in the spending of this largess, and the widespread corruption that was alleged to be involved, that prompted a brief and violent civil war in 1891, pitting Balmaceda and the army on one side against the legislature and the navy, centered on the figure of Jorge Montt, on the other. After several months of maneuvering and fighting, Balmaceda was defeated and ultimately committed suicide inside the Argentine Embassy where he had taken refuge.

In any event, after a full generation of dependence on the nitrate regions for as much as half of the government's revenues, which was only increased by the heavy demand for explosives during the First World War, the bottom suddenly dropped out of the market when a scientist, Franz Halen, developed a means for synthesizing ammonia, and the delicately structured Chilean economic house of cards came crashing down. It would take decades to develop other sources of export earnings, long neglected by the government, and it might be argued that, for Chile as well as for Peru and Bolivia, the discovery of the nitrates and their value was more of a curse than a blessing.

While the three belligerents were individually stumbling on toward their respective futures, they did brush together periodically, at least enough to finally bring a formal end to the War of the Pacific, but almost as an afterthought. The first of these encounters would be between Chile and Peru starting in 1893 when the ten-year period in Tacna and Arica ran out and a plebiscite was called for by the provisions of the Treaty of Anacin. The problems that resulted probably came as no real shock to the participants. They all knew that, even before the war, much of the labor and capital involved in developing this stretch of coast had come from Chile, although this was less true in Tacna and Arica than farther south in Tarapacá. Still there had always been a substantial Chilean minority in the area. It was also hardly surprising that the administrating power, i.e., Chile, would use its position of authority both to bring in new immigrants who would be sure to vote in its favor and to attempt to prevent the return of many Peruvians who had departed at the time of the conquest, or even to attempt to expel Peruvians still living there. Formal protests in this vein were levied by the Peruvians both before and after the 1893 deadline, with accusations that Peruvian schools had been closed, priests expelled, and returning refugees prevented from crossing the border.[11]

Since no meaningful agreement had been reached on what criterion would be used to determine a resident's eligibility to vote in the plebiscite or for establishing some sort of oversight commission to supervise the voting, 1893 came and went with no action being taken. Five years later, in 1898, it briefly appeared that something might happen, with both the Peruvian legislature and the Chilean Foreign Ministry approving plans for a plebiscite with arbitration of the conditions for the vote provided by the Queen Regent of Spain. This, in turn, had been prompted by a brief war scare between Argentina and Chile, which made it politic for Santiago to seek as quiet a northern frontier as possible, but, when tensions with Buenos Aires calmed, so did the fervor for an arrangement with Peru, and the Chilean Senate ultimately rejected the protocol.[12]

The only diplomatic decision that was taken prior to the end of the nineteenth century was an agreement that included Bolivia in the plebiscite agreement for Tacna and Arica. Under these provisions, the voters in the region would be given three possible choices for future sovereign power, Chile, Peru, or Bolivia. If Bolivia were to win the vote, she would pay Chile five million pesos, a knockdown bargain from the ten million Peru or Chile would have to pay each other. This, however, was strictly a courtesy, a salve to Bolivia's prestige for essentially having been ignored in the negotiations since the end of the fighting. None of the parties considered it a serious possibility that the residents of the region would select Bolivia as the Bolivian population even in the Atacama, prior to the war, had been a very small minority indeed.[13]

The next milestone on the road toward a permanent peace was reached between Bolivia and Chile some years later, in 1904. The newly elected Bolivian President Ismael Montes had made it a pillar of his campaign to settle the boundary dispute with Chile once and for all. Bolivia had just come through a low-intensity conflict with Brazil over the rubber-producing Acre region of the Amazon Basin, with an outcome hardly favorable to Bolivia, and this had served to underline the necessity of both ending the technical state of war with Chile and of regularizing Bolivia's access to the sea, at least for the free importation of goods. Consequently, in October of 1904, the two countries agreed on a peace treaty that essentially embodied the terms of the truce of 1884 with minor modifications.

The 1904 Treaty called for the reestablishment of diplomatic relations, broken since 1879, as a first step. Bolivia would formally recognize Chilean ownership of the Atacama in exchange for a payment of £300,000 plus the payment or forgiving by Chile of an additional £6 million in debts arising from the war or owed by Bolivia to Chilean citizens for the seizure of property during the war. Bolivian goods could be brought in duty-free at all Chilean ports, notably Arica and Antofagasta, and Bolivia would have the right to establish customs houses in those ports. Lastly, Chile would undertake to construct a railroad linking the port of Arica with La Paz. This rail line would be a massive engineering feat. It was finally begun in 1909 and completed in 1913. It ran for some 452 kilometers, and the highest point in its climb over the crests of the Andes was at 4,256 meters above sea level.[14]

Needless to say, the terms of the agreement were bitterly debated in the Bolivian legislature. Opponents referred to the treaty as the "Polonization of Bolivia," and a precursor to the ultimate demise and division of the nation among its neighbors. They pointed out that Bolivia would be utterly dependent upon Chile for the passage of her imports in the future and would thus never again enjoy an independent foreign policy, since, regardless of the wording of the treaty, Chile would have it in her power to cut Bolivia off from the world whenever the occasion suited her interests. Montes and his supporters, however, argued that this was the situation that existed now, with the only difference being that Bolivia did not have even the tenuous protection of Chile's agreement in international law to guarantee Bolivian access to the world market. Bolivia simply did not have the military power to redress the situation on that level and, a full generation after the war, it was highly unlikely that Chile would do so out of a sense of goodwill. The treaty was duly ratified, and one corner of the tragic triangle was permanently erased.[15]

Talks between Chile and Peru continued off and on through the end of the nineteenth century and the first decade of the twentieth without major progress, although British intervention with Chile had resulted in a notable reduction in the indemnities that Peru was obliged to pay for the war. Besides the details of voting requirements for the plebiscite, also under debate was the territory to be included, since Chile occupied the district of Tarata, which Peru argued had never belonged to either Tacna or Arica and should simply be returned to Peruvian control without being risked in the vote, a point the Chileans consistently refused to accept. No international attention was gained during the First World War, although hopes in both Peru and Bolivia had been raised by the atmosphere of Woodrow Wilson's famous Fourteen Points, and it would not be until the administration of U.S. President Warren G. Harding that both Peru and Chile accepted an invitation to come to Washington for substantive talks aimed at setting the rules, and a date, for the plebiscite.

While no final agreement was reached at the talks, held in the Pan American Union Building in Washington, D.C., from May through July 1922, Secretary of State Hughes did produce a protocol that ultimately formed the basis of the final peace treaty. Both parties agreed that the only outstanding issue remained that related to the fate of Tacna and Arica and that this would be resolved through arbitration by the President of the United States, without right of appeal. Harding accepted the invitation to preside in early 1923, but it would remain for his successor, Calvin Coolidge, to hand down his opinion and award in March 1925. This called for a plebiscite to include males of twenty-one years or older who were literate or who owned real property and who were either born in Tacna-Arica or Peruvian or Chilean citizens who had lived there for two years continuously prior to July 1922 and through the date of voter registration. The committee of observation would be presided over by General John J. Pershing of the United States, Agustin Edwards from Chile, and Manuel de Freyre y Santander from Peru. It should be noted that the protocol dismissed without comment Bolivia's inclusion in the vote.[16]

Ultimately, this opinion and award went in favor of Chile in that it called for the plebiscite to be held, which was what the Chileans had been hoping for. Peru had been arguing for an elimination of the plebiscite completely on the basis of more than ten years having already passed since the signing of the Treaty of Anacin, but President Coolidge determined that the treaty stated that the vote would be taken "after" the lapse of ten years, and not necessarily immediately thereafter, reasoning that the parties to the treaty wanted *at least* ten years to pass to allow the passions of the war to cool but not being so precise as to set a specific time limit. It was conceded that Chile had engaged in some acts the intentions of which were designed to influence the voting, such as subsidizing Chilean settlers to move into the region or expelling Peruvians, but this had not been done on such as scale as to invalidate the concept of a plebiscite. On the other hand, the commission ruled in favor of Peru in that the disputed territory of Tarata should be returned to Peru and not included in the plebiscite due to an error in establishing the boundary of Tacna province. Also, the qualifications established for voting in the plebiscite were generally favorable to Peru.[17]

By October 1925 the Pershing commission had issued a report decrying various Chilean practices aimed at limiting the effectiveness of the commission, such as restricting travel by American officers on the commission and the continued expulsion of Peruvians from the disputed territories. Ultimately, however, the Chileans acceded to the commission's requests, reducing the number of soldiers and police in the region to the level prior to July 1922 and even removing a number of Chilean commission officials whose activities had caused protests by the Americans. Finally, after some additional wrangling, 1 February 1926 was set as the date for the plebiscite.[18]

However, nothing happened this easily in the Tacna-Arica dispute. Interference by the Chilean authorities continued despite efforts by Santiago to meet commission demands. Moreover, rioting became widespread between returning Peruvians who had been expelled by the Chileans and pro-Chilean mobs, sometimes supported by the police, with considerable loss of life on both sides. The Peruvians finally requested an indefinite postponement of voter registration and the plebiscite itself, and the Americans agreed, determining that the conditions for holding a fair and open plebiscite did not exist in the territory in June 1926.[19]

The Peruvians viewed this event as a major moral victory. The language used by the American commissioners left no doubt that the blame for the failure of the peace efforts lay with the Chileans. More importantly, Secretary of State Kellogg argued publicly that Chile, by making impossible the taking of the plebiscite, had invalidated her rights to the territory, which should revert to Peruvian control. While pleasing to the Peruvians, this statement was not pursued in fact by any of the parties and it was generally disregarded.

It would take an additional three years for a final settlement to be reached, by now under the auspices of President Herbert Hoover. After decades of futile negotiations, it was an elegantly Solomonic decision. Tacna would revert to Peru, Arica to Chile, with no plebiscite involved. Chile would pay Peru six million pesos, and all other debts between the two countries arising from the dispute would be cancelled. There were other minor considerations, such as allowing children of Peruvians in Arica or Chileans in Tacna to retain the nationality of their parents until their majority at which time they could choose between the two, and Chile promised to erect at the Morro of Arica a monument to the peace between the two nations. One final provision, kept from the public at the time, prohibited the cession of any part of the territory in question to a third party without the consent of both signatories. This ruled out either Peru or Chile granting Bolivia a corridor to the sea and has remained a point of bitter frustration for Bolivia to this day. But, at last, the document was ratified on 28 July 1929, and the province of Tacna passed officially back to Peruvian control on 28 August of that year.[20]

Thus, more than half a century after it began, the War of the Pacific formally ended. As wars go, it was not overly brutal or costly. The battle deaths numbered in the thousands for each of the belligerents, notably higher for Peru and Chile than for Bolivia, with at least as many more men dying from disease or being permanently incapacitated during the four years of active campaigning. The economic costs were greater, with Peru and Bolivia descending into economic ruin and Chile, drunk with sudden unearned wealth coming close to following them not long after. Peru lost valuable territory, but Bolivia would never again feel the brush of waves on her shores and would be relegated to the ranks of the Third World *avant la lettre.*

The world got a frighteningly close look at the firepower of modern breech-loading rifles and artillery, the importance of entrenchments, and the virtual invulnerability of the modern ironclad. It also got a lesson in the rapidity with which military technology would become obsolescent in the modern age, with the revolutionary French Chassepot rifle of the Franco-Prussian War seeming a virtual museum piece in 1880, and the Peruvian ironclads built in the 1860s proving almost defenseless against their Chilean counterparts built less than a decade later. Gone were the days when the design of a gun, musket, or a ship changed hardly at all in the course of a century. The European powers were about to embark on an arms race that would nearly bankrupt them all, a pursuit of all that was newer, stronger, faster, and heavier than anything that had gone before, which would ultimately contribute to the holocaust that was the First World War.

Bolivia learned that, at least in the nineteenth century, it was not sufficient to have legal title to a territory if a country did not have the initiative to occupy and make use of the land. Chile originally held a position that would have resonated with Americans during that period, being the aggressive, energetic neighbor that was, in fact, developing a deserted region, but her successive advances to grab all of the valuable territory in the vicinity and then more besides to serve as a buffer for her conquests, devalued her claims of "reoccupation" and made it look something very much like unbridled greed. Peru found that the lesser of two evils might ultimately turn out to be not that much less evil after all. From a position in which Peru had no good choices, she ended up in one in which she had no choices at all. For the rest of us, we can see that a similarity of ethnic, historical, and political background does not always serve to guarantee against conflict when there are parochial interests to be served. Compared to the nations of Europe, the history of Latin America since independence has been one of virtually undisturbed peace. In terms of the numbers of men engaged, the War of the Pacific was barely a ripple on the surface of the sea of history. Yet, for the men involved and the nations they represented, this was a total war, and it does their memories a disservice not at least to attempt to draw some lessons for our own time from their suffering and sacrifices.

NOTES

1. Fredrick B. Pike, *The History of Modern Peru,* New York: Praeger Publishers, 1982, p. 152.

2. Andres A. Caceres, *Memórias del Mariscal Andres A. Caceres,* vol. 3, Lima: Editorial Milla Batres, S. A., 1973, p. 225.

3. Ibid., p. 248.

4. Ronald Bruce St. John, *The Foreign Policy of Peru,* Boulder, CO: Lynne Rienner, 1992, p. 125.

5. Roberto Querejazu Calvo, *Guano, Salitre, Sangre: História de la Guerra del Pacífico,* La Paz: Editorial Los Amigos del Libro, 1979, p. 708.

6. Bruce Farcau, *The Chaco War,* New York: Praeger, 1992, p. 15.

7. William F. Sater, *Chile and the War of the Pacific,* Lincoln: University of Nebraska Press, 1986, p. 215.

8. Ibid., p. 192.

9. Querejazu, p. 728.

10. William Jefferson Dennis, *Tacna and Arica: An Account of the Chile-Peru Boundary Dispute and the United States Arbitrations,* New York: Archon Books, 1967, p. 195.

11. Ibid., p. 199.

12. Gordon Ireland, *Boundaries, Possession, and Conflicts in South America,* New York: Octagon Books, 1971, p. 165.

13. Querejazu, p. 731.

14. Valentin Abecia Baldivieso, *Las Relaciones Internacionales en la História de Bolivia,* vol. 2, La Paz: Editorial Los Amigos del Libro, 1979, p. 352.

15. Ibid., p. 363.

16. Ireland, p. 169.

17. Dennis, p. 222.

18. Ireland, p. 170.

19. Dennis, p. 259.

20. Ireland, p. 174.

Selected Bibliography

BOOKS

Abecia, Valentin Baldivieso. *Las Relaciones Internacionales en la Historia de Bolivia.* 2 vols. La Paz: Editorial Los Amigos del Libro, 1979.

Ahumada Moreno, Pascual. *Guerra del Pacífico.* Santiago de Chile: Editorial del Pacífico, 1884-1892.

Amayo Zevallos, Enrique. *La Politica Britanica en la Guerra del Pacífico.* Lima: Editorial Horizonte, 1988.

Arguedas, Alcides. *Los Caudillos Barbaros.* La Paz: Gisbert & Cía., S.A., 1975.

Armaza, Miguel. *La Verdad Sobre la Campaña de San Francisco.* La Paz: Imprenta de La Union, 1897.

Bader, Thomas McLeod. *A Willingness to War: A Portrait of the Republic of Chile during the Years Preceding the War of the Pacific.* Ann Arbor, MI: Xerox University Microfilm, 1967.

Baptista Gumucio, Mariano. *Historia Grafica de la Guerra del Pacífico.* La Paz: Ultima Hora, 1978.

Barros Arana, Diego. *Historia de la Guerra del Pacífico 1879-1881.* Santiago de Chile: Editorial Andres Bello, 1979.

Basadre, Jorge. *Reflexiones en Torno a la Guerra de 1879.* Lima: F. Campodonico, 1979.

Baxter, James Phinney. *The Introduction of the Ironclad Warship.* New York: Anchor Books, 1968.

Bazo, Cesar A. *La Guerra del Pacífico.* Lima: Litografia e Imprenta Badiola y Berrio, 1905.

Benavides Santos, Arturo. *Historia Compendado de la Guerra del Pacífico.* Buenos Aires: Editorial Francisco de Aguirre, 1972.

Birbuet Espana, Miguel. *Recuerdos de la Campaña del 1879.* La Paz: Editorial Isla, 1986.

Blanlet Holley, Anselmo. *Historia de la Paz entre Chile y el Peru, 1879-1884.* Santiago de Chile: Balcillo y Cia., 1919.

Blest Gana, A. *Narrative of the Events which Led to the Declaration of War by Chile against Bolivia and Peru.* London: Waterlow & Sons, Ltd., 1879.

Bowman, Isaiah. *Desert Trails of Atacama.* New York: American Geographical Society, 1924.

Bulnes, Gonzalo. *Guerra del Pacífico,* 3 vols. Santiago de Chile: Editorial del Pacífico, 1955.

-----. *Resumen de la Guerra del Pacífico.* Santiago de Chile: Editorial del Pacífico, 1976.

Burr, Robert N. *By Reason or Force: Chile and the Balance of Power in South America, 1830-1905.* Berkeley: University of California Press, 1975.

Cabrera, Ladislao. *La Guerra de Chile.* La Paz: Imprenta de la Tribuna, 1896.

Caceres, Andres Avelino. *Memorias del Mariscal Andres A. Caceres.* 3 vols. Lima: Editorial Milla Batres, 1986.

-----. *La Guerra del '79: Sus Campañas.* Lima: Editorial Milla Batres, S. A., 1973.

Campero, Narciso. *Diario de la Campaña de la Quinta Division del Ejercito Boliviano.* Sucre: Tipografía de la Libertad, 1882.

Campo, Jose Rodolfo del. *Campana Naval 1879.* Lima: Instituto de Estudios Historicos-Maritimos del Peru, 1976.

Campuzano, Severino. *Documentos Relativos a la Organizacion y Campaña de la Quinta Division, 1879.* La Paz: Imprenta de La Razon, 1884.

Cardenas Sanchez, Ines L. *Biografia y Campanas del Gran Mariscal del Peru: Andres A. Caceres.* Lima: Libreria Importadora, 1979.

Carigno, Tomasso. *Historia de la Guerra de America entre Chile, Peru y Bolivia.* 2 vols., Arequipa: Tipgrafia Muniz, 1905.

Carmona Yañez, Jorge. *Notas al Margen de una Historia de Chile.* Santiago de Chile: Imprenta Universitaria, 1953.

Carrasco, Rufino. *Manifesto Relativo a las Distintas Comiciones que Ha Desempeñado durante la Guerra del Pacífico.* Sucre: Tipografia del Progreso, 1884.

Castro Vasquez, Aquilino. *Los Guerrilleros de Chupaca en la Guerra con Chile.* Lima: Editorial Universo, 1982.

Cayo Cordoba, Percy, ed. *En Torno de la Guerra del Pacífico.* Lima: Pontificia Universidad Católica del Peru, 1983.

Chesnau, Roper, ed. *Convey's All the World's Fighting Ships 1860-1905.* New York: Mayflower Books, 1979.

Civati Berrasconi, Eduardo H. *Guerra del Pacífico 1879-1883.* Buenos Aires: s.n., 1946.

Claros, Manuel P. *Diario de un Excombatiente de la Guerra del Pacífico.* La Paz: Imprenta de la Nacion, 1962.

Collier, Simon, and William F. Sater. *A History of Chile, 1808-1994.* New York: Cambridge University Press, 1997.

Congrains Martin, Eduardo. *Batalla de Tacna.* Lima: Editorial Ecoma, 1972.

-----. *Batalla de Arica,* 2 vols. Lima: Editorial Ecoma, 1973.

-----. *Demistificacion de Pierola.* Lima: Editorial Ecoma, 1973.

-----. *La Expedicion Lynch.* Lima: Editorial Ecoma, 1973.

-----. *Tarapacá.* Lima: Editorial Ecoma, 1973.

-----. *La Batalla de San Juan (Chorillos).* 2 vols. Lima: Editorial Ecoma, 1974.

-----. *Miguel Grau, "el Leon del Pacífico."* Lima: Editorial Ecoma, 1974.

-----. *Primeros Enfrentamientos: Pisagua, San Francisco,* Lima: Editorial Ecoma, 1975.

-----. *La Batalla de Miraflores.* Lima: Editorial Ecoma, 1977.

Costa, Arturo de la Torre. *Diarios y Memorias de la Guerra del Pacífico.* 2 vols. La Paz: Biblioteca Paceña, 1980.

Dalence, Zenon. *Informe Historico del Servicio Prestado por el Cuerpo de Ambulancias del Ejercito Boliviano.* La Paz: Imprenta de la Tribuna, 1881.

Delgado, Luis Humberto. *Guerra entre el Peru y Chile, 1879.* Lima: Ariel Editores, 1965.

Dellepiane, Carlos. *Historia Militar del Peru.* Buenos Aires: Círculo Militar, 1941.

Dennis, William Jefferson. *Tacna and Arica: An Account of the Chile-Peru Boundary Dispute and of the Arbitrations by the United States.* New York: Archon Books, 1967.

Di Cis, Miguel Angel. *Chile contra Bolivia: La Guerra de los Diez Centavos.* Buenos Aires: Editorial Moharra, 1979.

Duarte, Luis M. *Exposicion a los Hombres de Bien.* Cajamarca, 1884.

Ekdahl, Wilhelm. *Historia Militar de la Guerra del Pacífico entre Chile, Peru y Bolivia.* Santiago de Chile: Imprenta Universo, 1917.

Escala Escobar, Manuel. *El General Erasmo Escala.* San Felipe, Chile: Editorial Jeronimo de Vivar, 1972.

Fernandez Larrain, Sergio. *Santa Cruz y Torreblanca: Dos Heroes de las Campanas de Tarapaca y Tacna.* Santiago: Editorial Mar del Sur, 1979.

Garcia Salazar, Arturo. *Resumen de Historia Diplomatica del Peru, 1820-1884.* Lima: Editorial Los Andes, s.n., 1928.

Garland, Alejandro. *South American Conflicts and the U.S.* Lima: Imprenta Newton y Cia., 1900.

Gonzalez Salinas, Edmundo. *La Politica contra la Estrategia en la Guerra del Pacífico, 1879-1883.* Santiago de Chile: s.n., 1981.

Grau, Miguel. *Diario Abordo del Huascar.* Buenos Aires: Editorial Francisco de Aguirre, S.A., 1880.

Guerrero, Julio C. *La Guerra de las Ocasiones Perdidas, 1879-1883.* Lima: Editorial Milla Batres, 1975.

Gutierrez, Alberto. *La Guerra del 1879.* La Paz: Ediciones Populares Camarlinghi, 1976.

Guzman, Trinidad. *Apuntes para la Historia: La Division Rios en la Campaña, Battalla, y Retirada de Tarapaca.* Cochabamba: Imprenta de El Heraldo, 1882.

Guzman Palomino, Luis. *Campaña de la Breña: Coleccion de Documentos Ineditos, 1881-1884.* Lima: Consejo Nacional de Ciencias y Technologia, 1990.

Howard, Michael. *The Franco-Prussian War.* New York: Collier Books, 1969.

Ireland, Gordon. *Boundaries, Possessions and Conflicts in South America.* New York: Octagon Books, 1971.

Irigoyen, Manuel. *Contra-manifestacion que el Gobierno del Peru Dirige a los Estados Amigos con Motivo de la Guerra que le ha Declarado Chile.* Lima: Impresora del Estado, 1879.

Jackson, Leland Herschel. *Naval Aspects of the War of the Pacific, 1879-1883.* n.p., 1963.

Klein, Herbert S. *Bolivia: The Evolution of a Multi-Ethnic Society.* New York: Oxford University Press, 1982.

Langlois, Luis. *Influencia del Poder Naval en la Historia de Chile, desde 1810 a 1910.* Valparaíso: Imprenta de la Armada, 1911.

Larenas Q., Victor Hugo. *Patricio Lynch, Almirante, General, Gobernante, y Diplomatico.* Santiago de Chile: Editorial Universitaria, 1981.

Lecano Villavisencio, Fernando. *La Guerra con Chile en sus Documentos.* Lima: Editorial Rikchay Peru, 1979.

Leiva Vivas, Rafael. *Posicion de Centroamerica en la Guerra del Pacífico.* Tegucigalpa: Universidad Nacional Autonoma de Honduras, 1989.

Le Leon, Eugene. *Souvenirs d'une Mission a l'Armee Chilienne.* Buenos Aires: Editorial Francisco de Aguirre, 1969.

Lizardo, Andrés Taborga. *Apuntes de la Campaña de 50 Días de las Fuerzas Bolivianas en Calaman, con Motivo de la Invasion Chilena.* Sucre: Tipografía de la Libertad, 1879.

Lopez Martinez, Hector. *Guerra con Chile: Episodios y Peronajes.* Lima: Editorial Minerva, 1989.

-----. *Pierola y la Defensa de Lima.* Lima: Editorial Ansonia Talleres Graficos, S.A., 1981.

Lopez, Jacinto. *Historia de la Guerra del Guano y el Salitre.* Lima: Editorial Universo, S.A., 1980.

Luna Vegas, Emilio. *Caceres, Genio Militar.* Lima: Libreria Editorial Minerva-Miraflores, 1978.

Lynch, Patricio, D. *Memoria que el Contra-almirante D. Patricio Lynch, General en Jefe del Ejercito de Operaciones en el Norte del Peru Presenta al Supremo Gobierno de Chile.* 3 vols. Lima: Imprenta Calle 7 de Junin, 1882-1884.

Lyon, David Stears. *Steel and Torpedoes: The Warship in the Nineteenth Century.* London: His Majesty's Stationery Office, 1980.

Macintyre, Donald, and Basil W. Bathe. *Man-of-War: A History of the Combat Vessel.* New York: McGraw-Hill Book Company, 1969.

Manrique, Nelson. *Campesinado y Nacion: Las Guerrillas Indigenas en la Guerra con Chile.* Lima: Centro de Investigaciones y Capacitacion, Editora Ital Peru, 1981.

-----. *La Guerra del Pacifico y la Crisis de la Fraccion Terrateniente de la Sierra del Peru, 1879-1888.* La Molina: Taller de Estudios Andinos, Universidad Nacional Agraria, 1980.

Markham, Clement R. *The War Between Peru and Chile 1879-1882.* London: S. Low Marston & Co., 1927.

Marshall, Ian. *Armored Ships.* Charlottesville, VA: Howell Press, 1993.

Mendoza Melendez, Eduardo. *Historia de la Campaña de la Brena.* Lima: Editorial Milla Batres, 1981.

Mercado, Miguel M. *Guerra del Pacifico: Nuevos Esclarecimientos, Causas de la Retirada de Camarones, Asesinato de Daza.* La Paz: s.n., 1956.

-----. *Historia Internacional de Bolivia.* La Paz: Editorial Don Bosco, 1972.

Merrill, Andrea T., ed. *Chile: A Country Study.* Washington, D.C.: American University Press, 1982.

Meson, Theodorio Bailey Myers. *Guerra en el Pacifico del Sur.* Buenos Aires: Editorial Francisco de Aguirre, 1971.

Millington, Herbert. *American Diplomacy and the War of the Pacific.* New York: Columbia University Press, 1938.

Molina, Modesto. *Hojas del Proceso: Apuntes para un Libro de Historia.* Arica: Imprenta del Boletin de la Guerra, 1880.

Morales, Waltraud Queiser. *Bolivia: Land of Struggle.* Boulder, CO: Westview Press, 1992.

Moreno, Gabriel Rene. *Daza y las Bases Chilenas de 1879.* La Paz: Editorial Universo, 1938.

Oblitas, Edgar Fernández. *Historia Secreta de la Guerra del Pacífico.* Sucre: Editorial Tupac Katari, 1983.

Ochoa, Juan Vicente. *Diario de la Campana del Ejercito Boliviano en la Guerra del Pacifico.* Sucre: Tipografia y Libreria Economica, 1899.

O'Connor d'Arlach, Tomás. *Dichos y Hechos del General Melgarejo.* La Paz: Ediciones Isla, 1975.

Ortega, Eudoxio H. *Francisco Bolognesi: El Titan del Morro.* Lima: Biblioteca Hombres del Peru, 1963.

Ortega, Luis. *Los Empresarios, la Politica, y los Origenes de la Guerra del Pacifico*. Santiago de Chile: Programa FLACSO, 1984.

Palma, Ricardo. *Cronicas de la Guerra con Chile 1881-1883*. Lima: Mosca Azul Editores, 1984.

Paz Soldan, Mariano Felipe. *Narracion Histórica de la Guerra de Chile contra el Peru y Bolivia*. 2 vols., Buenos Aires: s.n., 1884.

Peri Fagerstrome, Rene. *Los Batallones Bulnes y Valparaiso en la Guerra del Pacifico*. Santiago: n.p., 1980.

Peru. Ministerio de Relaciones Exteriores: "Memorandum sobre el Plan del Gobierno de Chile para Consumir su Conquista en el Pacifico." Buenos Aires: Impresora de la Nacion, 1882.

Phillips, Richard Snyder. *Bolivia in the War of the Pacific*. (Microfiche), n.p., 1973.

Pike, Fredrick B. *The History of Modern Peru*. New York: Praeger Publishers, 1982.

Pinochet de la Barra, Oscar. *Testimonios y Recuerdos de la Guerra del Pacifico*. Santiago de Chile: Editorial del Pacífico, 1978.

Pinochet Ugarte, Augusto. *Guerra del Pacifico: Campaña de Tarapaca*. Santiago de Chile: Editorial Andres Bello, 1980.

Querejazu, Roberto Calvo. *Guano, Salitre, Sangre: Historia de la Guerra del Pacifico*. La Paz: Editorial Los Amigos del Libro, 1979.

-----. *Aclaraciones Historicas sobre la Guerra del Pacifico*. La Paz: Libreria Editorial Juventud, 1995.

Reategui, Wilson. *La Guerra del Pacifco*. Lima: Universidad Nacional Mayor de San Marcos, 1979.

Riquelme, Daniel. *Bajo la Tienda*. Santiago de Chile: Editorial del Pacifico, 1966.

-----. *Cuentos de Guerra*. Santiago de Chile: Imprenta Universitaria, 1931.

Riveros, Galvarino. *Angamos*. Santiago de Chile: J. Nuñez, 1882.

Roberts Barragan, Hugo. *Gran Traicion en la Guerra del Pacifico: Dolorosa Version Historica y Relacion Veridico de los Hechos*. La Paz: n.p., 1979.

Rocales, Justo Abel. *Mi Campaña al Peru 1879-1881*. Concepcion: Editorial de la Universidad de Concepcion, 1984.

Rodriguez Sepulveda, Juan Agustin. *Patricio Lynch, Vicealmirante y General en Jefe: Sintesis de la Guerra del Pacifico*. Santiago de Chile: Editorial Nascimiento, 1967.

Rosales Justo, Abel. *Mi Campana en el Peru 1879-1881*. Concepcion de Chile: Editorial de la Universidad de Concepcion, 1984.

Roso, Alejandro. *Dos Episodios Ignorados de la Guerra del Pacifico*. Potosí: Imprenta de Artes y Oficios, 1931.

Ruiz-Tagle Orrego, Emilio. *Bolivia y Chile: El Conflicto del Pacifico*. Santiago: Editorial Andres Bello, 1982.

Ruz Trujillo, Fernando. *Rafael Sotomayor: El Organizador de la Victoria*. Santiago de Chile: Editorial Andres Bello, 1980.

St. John, Ronald Bruce. *The Foreign Policy of Peru*. Boulder, CO: Lynne Rienner, 1992.

Sanchez, Simon I., *Resistencia de la Brena*. Lima: Municipio Distrital de San Juan de Lurrizondo, 1979.

Sandler, Stanley. *The Emergence of the Modern Capital Ship*. Dover: University of Delaware Press, 1979.

Santa Maria, Ignacio. *La Guerra del Pacifico*. Santiago de Chile: Imprenta Universitaria, 1919.

Santiago Sanz, Luis. *Zeballos: El Tratado de 1881 Guerra del Pacifico*. Buenos Aires: Editorial Plemar, 1985.

Sater, William F. *Chile and the War of the Pacific*. Lincoln: University of Nebraska Press, 1986.

Scheina, Robert L. *Latin America: A Naval History 1810-1987*. Annapolis, MD: Naval Institute Press, 1987.

Solar del, Alberto. *Diario de Campaña: Recuerdos Intimos de la Guerra del Pacífico 1879-1884*. Buenos Aires: Editorial Francisco de Aguirre, 1967.

Taborga, Miguel. *Correspondencia Cambiada con el Sr. Elidoro Camacho sobre la Traicion de Camarones*. Sucre: Tipografia del Cruzado, 1889.

Teran Erquicia, Vicente. *La Muerte del Tirano: Asesinato del General Melgarejo en Lima*. La Paz: Producciones CIMA, 1982.

Thorndike, Guillermo. *La Batalla de Lima*. Lima: Promoinvest Compania de Inversiones, 1979.

-----. *El Viaje de Prado*. Lima: Libreria Pacifico, 1977.

Toro Davila, Agustin. *Sintesis Historico Militar de Chile*. 2 vols. Santiago de Chile: Fondo Editorial Educacion Moderna, 1969.

Turpo Choquehuanca, Fortunato. *Caudillos y Culpables: Historia Politica en la Guerra del Pacífico*. Arequipa: Ediciones Aswan Qari, 1982.

Ugarte Chamorro, Guillermo. *Diario de la Campana Naval Escrito Abordo del Huascar*. Lima: Oficina de Asuntos Culturales de la Corporacion Financiero de Desarrollo, 1984.

Ugarte, Ricardo. *Efermides de la Guerra del Pacífico*. La Paz: Imprenta de la Tribuna, 1882.

-----. *La Primera Pajina en la Guerra del Pacífico*. La Paz: Imprenta de la Tribuna, 1880.

Ulloa y Sotomayor, Alberto. *Don Nicolas de Pierola, una Epoca de la Historia del Peru*. Lima: Imprenta Editorial Minerva, 1981.

U.S. 47th Congress. First Session, S. Exec., Doc. 79.

U.S. 48th Congress. House of Representatives Miscellaneous Document 30, 2nd Session.

U.S. Department of State. *The War in South America and Attempts to Bring about a Peace*. Washington, D.C.: Government Printing Office, 1882.

Uriburu, Jose Evaristo. *Guerra del Pacífico*. Buenos Aires: Compania Sud-americana de Billetes de Banco, 1899.

Valdizan Gamio, Jose. *Historia Naval del Peru,* vol. 4. Lima: Direccion General de Intereses Marítimos, 1987.

Valega, Jose M. *Causas y Motivos de la Guerra del Pacífico*. Lima: Imprenta Moderna, 1917.

Varas, Antonio. *Correspondencia de Don Antonio Varas sobre la Guerra del Pacífico, 1879*. Santiago de Chile: Imprenta Universitaria, 1918.

Vargas Hurtado, Gerardo. *La Batalla de Arica: Coleccion Documental de la Historia del Peru*. Lima: Comision Nacional, 1980.

Vargas Ugarte, Ruben. *Guerra con Chile: La Campana del Sur*. Lima: Editorial Milla Batres, 1987.

Varigny, Charles Victor Grosnier de. *La Guerra del Pacífico*. Buenos Aires: Editorial Francisco de Aguirre, 1971.

Vicuña Mackenna, Benjamin. *Episodios Marítimos*. Santiago: Impresora Libertad, 1880.

-----. *Historia de la Campaña de Tarapacá*. 2 vols. Santiago de Chile: Imprenta y Litografia de Pedro Cadot, 1880.

Villanueva, Victor. *Ejército Peruano: Del Caudillo Anárquico al Militarismo Reformista*. Lima: Libreria Editorial Juan Mejia Baca, 1973.

Viscarra, Eufronio. *Estudio Historico de la Guerra del Pacífico*. Cochabamba: Impresora de "El Progreso," 1889.

Weems, John Edward. *To Conquer a Peace: The War between the United States and Mexico*. New York: Doubleday, 1974.

Wilson, Joe F. *The United States, Chile, and Peru in the Tacna and Arica Plebiscite.* Washington, D.C.: University Press of America, 1979.

PERIODICALS

El Comercio. La Paz, Bolivia
El Comercio. Lima, Peru.
El Comercio. Valparaíso, Chile.
El Independiente. Santiago de Chile.
El Mercurio. Valparaiso, Chile.
El Nacional. Lima, Peru.
La Crónica. Santiago de Chile.
La Patria. Lima, Peru.
La Patria. Valparaiso, Chile.

Index

About the Author

BRUCE W. FARCAU is a twenty-year veteran of the Foreign Service with numerous assignments in Latin America and Europe. He has published extensively on Latin American Military History and Politics.